PROPHETS ABROAD

The Reception of
Continental Holy Women in
Late-Medieval England

Scholars have long been aware of the impact of the lives and works of Continental holy women on English spirituality; female mystics such as Margery Kempe were inspired by their predecessors abroad, whose visionary experiences and spiritual reflections were recorded and widely read. The essays in this volume investigate the influence of Hildegard of Bingen, Marguerite Porete, Mechtild of Hackeborn, Bridget of Sweden and Catherine of Siena through examination of manuscripts, spiritual guides, devotional collections, and the translation, illumination, adaptation and alteration of their works for an English audience. Other essays take a new look at Continental influences on Margery Kempe and the neglected figure of Elizabeth Barton. Overall, the volume offers new evidence of the ways in which Continental sensibility and spiritual reflection were altered for English devotional practice and spirituality.

Dr ROSALYNN VOADEN is a Research Fellow at St Anne's College, Oxford.

British Library MS Cotton Claudius B.I., fol. 34r, detail: the *Liber Celestis* of St Bridget of Sweden. *By permission of The British Library*

PROPHETS ABROAD

The Reception of
Continental Holy Women in
Late-Medieval England

EDITED BY Rosalynn Voaden

D. S. BREWER

First published 1996
D. S. Brewer, Cambridge

ISBN 0 85991 425 9

D. S. Brewer is an imprint of Boydell & Brewer Ltd
PO Box 9, Woodbridge, Suffolk IP12 3DF, UK
and of Boydell & Brewer Inc.
PO Box 41026, Rochester, NY 14604–4126, USA

British Library Cataloguing in Publication Data
Prophets abroad : the reception of continental holy women
in late-medieval England
1. Christian women – Europe – History   2. Spirituality
– Europe – History – Middle Ages, 600–1500   3. Spirituality
– England – History – Middle Ages, 600–1500
I. Voaden, Rosalynn
274.5'0922
ISBN 0859914259

Library of Congress Cataloging-in-Publication Data
Prophets abroad : the reception of Continental holy women in late
-medieval England / edited by Rosalynn Voaden.
        p.   cm.
Includes bibliographical references.
ISBN 0–85991–425–9 (alk. paper)
1. Women mystics – Europe.   2. Christian women saints –
Europe.   3. Women in Christianity.   4. England – Church history
– Medieval period, 1066–1485.   5. Mysticism – History – Middle
Ages, 600–1500.   6. Mysticism – England – History.   7. Spiritual
life – Christianity.
I. Voaden, Rosalynn, 1949–   .
BV5077.E54P76   1996
270.5'082 – dc20   96–20394

This publication is printed on acid-free paper

Printed in Great Britain by
Boydell & Brewer Ltd, Woodbridge, Suffolk

CONTENTS

Acknowledgements   vii

Introduction   *by Rosalynn Voaden*   ix

KATHRYN KERBY-FULTON

     Hildegard and the Male Reader: a Study in Insular Reception   1

NICHOLAS WATSON

     Melting into God the English Way: Deification in the Middle   19
     English Version of Marguerite Porete's *Mirouer des simples*
     âmes anienties

ROSALYNN VOADEN

     The Company She Keeps: Mechtild of Hackeborn in   51
     Late-Medieval Devotional Compilations

ROGER ELLIS

     The Visionary and the Canon Lawyers: Papal and Other   71
     Revisions to the *Regula Salvatoris* of St Bridget of Sweden

JOAN ISOBEL FRIEDMAN

     MS Cotton Claudius B.I.: a Middle English Edition of St Bridget   91
     of Sweden's *Liber Celestis*

JANETTE DILLON

     Holy Women and their Confessors or Confessors and their Holy   115
     Women? Margery Kempe and Continental Tradition

DENISE L. DESPRES

     Ecstatic Reading and Missionary Mysticism: *The Orcherd of*   141
     Syon

DIANE WATT

     The Prophet at Home: Elizabeth Barton and the Influence of   161
     Bridget of Sweden and Catherine of Siena

IAN JOHNSON

     Auctricitas? Holy Women and their Middle English Texts   177

ACKNOWLEDGEMENTS

While editing this volume, I have at times felt like a medieval holy woman: my study a cell, my penance to insert three hundred inverted commas, my demons the postman who never even rang once and the blank-faced computer I wrestled with daily. But my sustenance has been the lively, thought-provoking essays which make up this book, and the patience and cooperation of the contributors. And my good angels were surely Alastair Minnis of the Centre for Medieval Studies at York, and Caroline Palmer, editor at Boydell and Brewer.

Sustenance of a more material nature, for which I am most grateful, was provided by the Social Sciences and Humanities Research Council of Canada and by St Anne's College, Oxford.

Rosalynn Voaden
Oxford, 1995

INTRODUCTION

Last year, in one of those huge American record stores where the sound of cash registers almost drowns out the blaring music, I was astonished to see a large number of identical posters, of true rock star proportions, featuring a vaguely medieval, vaguely nun-like figure. *Visions*, these posters proclaimed, in immense letters, *The Music of Hildegard of Bingen.*

In a period when Hildegard can make the Top Ten, when Bridget of Sweden appears in calendars and adorns address books, and when the faithful can enjoy 'Meditations with Mechtild of Magdeburg', the time seems remote when these names were little known, and their works even less so. The present feminist movement has, over the last two decades, stimulated both academic and popular interest in the history and culture of late-medieval women. It is now even something of a cliché in academic circles to comment on the blossoming of female spirituality which emerged in the thirteenth and fourteenth centuries. But familiarity makes this blossoming no less noteworthy than it was when, in 1940, Hope Emily Allen identified a 'remarkable . . . feminist movement' of Continental piety, and argued, briefly, for its effect on the devotional practices and expression of late medieval England.[1] She promised further investigation of the influence of Continental holy women; unfortunately, she died before the work was accomplished. I hope that this collection of essays will help to remedy the loss.

One of the potential problems of a volume such as this, which assembles essays on a number of historical figures by a variety of scholars all with differing methodologies, interests and approaches, is that of cohesion. As editor, I was delighted that a number of common threads emerged, and that it is possible to make some generalizations about the ways in which the works of Continental women visionaries contributed to English piety and devotional praxis. Perhaps the most evident and obvious thread, one which unites all the essays, is that of acculturation. These works were not simply *adopted*, they were *adapted* to suit the needs of the native tradition. Another thread which links several essays is the issue – or sometimes non-issue – of gender and authority. A third thread is the examination of the response of a native tradition, in which the religious solitary was perceived as the acme of holiness, to Continental writings extolling the virtues of communal life and shared ecstasy.

Mystical utterances have always provoked unease amongst the

---

[1] Sanford Brown Meech, ed., *The Book of Margery Kempe* (Oxford: EETS, 1940), lix.

ecclesiastical hierarchy, and never more so than when those who speak are women. A prophet may be without honour in her own land – but perhaps one of the reasons for a more respectful reception abroad is that translation provides an opportunity for judicious emendation, which can defuse the potentially destabilizing effect of such works. In her wide-ranging, perceptive essay Denise Despres describes this 'devotional paternalism' in connection with *The Orcherd of Syon*, the Middle English translation of *Il Dialogo* of Catherine of Siena written for the nuns of Syon Abbey. She asserts that the aim of the translation is not to produce a mysticism imitative of Catherine's, that is, ecstatic and communal, but to 'provide nuns with small portions of doctrinal food for contemplation and meditation'. Denise Despres uses the illustrations of Catherine of Siena in the Carew-Poyntz Hours to support her argument. Here the visionary is portrayed as a solitary figure, in mystical communion with God, but not with man – or woman. In other words, Catherine is depicted as a holy woman representative of the tradition which received her rather than that from which she came.

Reinforcing Denise Despres's argument as to the value of manuscript illuminations as indicators of the reception of a Continental work is Joan Friedman's essay on the illuminations in the Cotton Claudius B.I. manuscript of the *Liber Celestis* of Bridget of Sweden. This is the only extant illuminated manuscript of the English translation of Bridget's revelations; one of the illuminations serves as a frontispiece to this volume. Given the popularity of Bridget's revelations, and the iconographic impact of some of her visions, notably that of the Nativity, it is instructive to discover that the translation was accompanied by English illuminations. In a study which is itself illuminating, Joan Friedman compares the illuminations in Cotton Claudius with a number of contemporary Continental illuminated copies of the *Liber Celestis*. She concludes that the iconography in Cotton Claudius shows little influence of Continental models, and can, in fact, be identified as distinctively English. This, combined with the sumptuousness of the illuminations themselves, can be seen as testimony to the high esteem in which Bridget was held in late-medieval England.

The English reception of Bridget of Sweden also informs Roger Ellis's meticulously argued essay. Taking an innovative approach to the concept of reception, he traces the differences between the original, divinely inspired *Regula Salvatoris* of Bridget of Sweden and the Rule as it was approved by Urban V in 1370. He maintains that Urban's revisers, in their efforts to reinforce and perpetuate safer, traditional patterns of devotion, diluted the potential of the earlier Rule to offer nuns a more enriching spiritual life. He also suggests that the Syon Additions, legislation specifically created for the administration of the Order at Syon Abbey, provided for a lower level of religious observance than the original Rule intended.

Continental models of devotion not only affected individual spiritual expression in England, but also relationships between the clergy and the faithful. Janette Dillon's essay is a comprehensive and incisive survey of the affiliation between Continental holy women and their confessors in the late Middle Ages. She identifies reciprocal fear and love as the basis of this relationship, and demonstrates that the confessor was the vital factor in establishing a woman's holiness. She argues that it was the mutual bonds of affection, obedience and control which made possible the writing of the revelations which 'testified to both the sanctity of the women and the holy calling of her confessor'.

Janette Dillon considers Margery Kempe's relationships with her confessors in the light of the Continental tradition, and suggests that in this case it did not travel well. The unsatisfactory, turbulent, and often adversarial nature of these associations indicates that her confessors failed fully to understand their role *vis-à-vis* a holy woman. Specifically, her confessors neither controlled Margery's 'disobedience' nor construed it as a sign of sanctity; the scribe reproduced this negative construction in the text. Consequently, Margery failed – and continues to fail – to achieve recognition for her holiness. Except, like all true prophets, she was always accorded more respect abroad, by foreigners, than she was in her own country and by her compatriots.

While ambivalence about Margery Kempe as a visionary was undoubtedly linked to her gender, Kathryn Kerby-Fulton argues that in the Insular reception of Hildegard of Bingen gender was rarely an issue. She most usefully examines rubrication, annotation, selection and ownership in a number of English manuscripts of Hildegard's works, and of the *Pentachronon* of Gebeno of Eberbach, an abridged compilation of extracts from her voluminous works. Working imaginatively from this hitherto little-known evidence, Kathryn Kerby-Fulton demonstrates conclusively that in late-medieval England, an England vitally concerned with the power of the papacy, the issue of clerical disendowment, fraternal controversy and the growth of Wycliffite heresy, it was Hildegard's extensive writing on ecclesiastical politics which excited the greatest interest. This meant that in England her work did not circulate as 'women's writing', and her late-medieval audience was primarily male. Any hostility to Hildegard's thought arose not because of her sex, but because of the particular 'interpretive community' to which her readers belonged.

If gender was only a minor issue in the English reception of Hildegard, it was not an issue at all in the case of Marguerite Porete. Her book, *Le Mirouer des simples âmes*, was officially condemned as heretical in 1310 and burned, as was its author. However, it continued to circulate under anonymous authorship, presumed male. The Middle English translation, *The Mirror of Simple Souls*, and its glosses by M.N., is the subject of Nicholas Watson's densely argued, carefully reasoned essay. He examines the modern as well as the medieval reception of *The Mirror*, pointing out how, in the former, there is a tendency for 'the present to repeat the past by working within the same categories as caused the condemnation of Porete's thought in the first place'. He concludes however, that, while far from being the model of carefully orthodox presentation which some modern scholars have discerned, neither is the Middle English translation of *Le Mirouer* merely evidence of the reception of the work into a parochial, naïve environment unaware of its heretical affiliations and unattuned to its heretical implications. While Nicholas Watson admits that the development of religious writing in England at the end of the fourteenth century was unsystematic and localized, compared to that on the Continent, he argues for a native tradition of passionate interest in what he calls the rhetoric of ecstasy. Out of this tradition, he suggests, evolved M.N.'s fascinated response to *Le Mirouer des simples âmes*.

Of course, translation was not the only, or even the principal, way in which the works of Continental visionaries were adapted for English readers. Many of the more familiar holy women found their way into English households through devotional compilations which contained 'improving' extracts from their writings, or prayers attached to their names. This is certainly the case with Mechtild of Hackeborn, as I demonstrate in my own contribution to this volume. While Mechtild's book of revelations, the *Liber specialis gratiae* was translated into English as *The Booke of Gostlye Grace*, she seems to have been most widely known through her inclusion in devotional anthologies. I suggest that the positive reception of a Continental holy woman could indeed be influenced by the company she kept; that is, by her association in such works with other writers whose reputations had been established and whose popularity was assured. Devotional compilations were often assembled by, or directed at, groups with specific devotional affiliations. Accordingly, the extracts tended to enhance and reinforce existing patterns of spirituality rather than challenge them. Sometimes, after going through the mill of translation, abridgement, adaptation, and rewriting, the original 'mete of hye contemplacyoun' was more like a thin gruel, bearing little resemblance to its source. This, it seems to me, often happened to work attributed to Mechtild.

Although the works of Continental holy women were adapted through translation and abridgement for English consumption, this is not to minimize their effect on native devotion. Certainly, Margery Kempe, and her scribe, looked to the example of Continental women to justify her own spiritual experiences and behaviour. So, too, there is evidence that Elizabeth Barton, the 'Holy Maid of Kent' was influenced by Bridget of Sweden and Catherine of Siena. Elizabeth Barton was executed in 1534 for treason, a charge incurred by her continual prophesying against the divorce of Henry VIII. Diane Watt, in a discriminating and stimulating study of this frequently neglected English holy woman and martyr, discerns parallels between reports of Elizabeth Barton's temptations and miracles and those experienced by Bridget and Catherine. However, she argues that it is as a political prophet, operating in the public arena and attempting to manipulate both churchmen and statesmen, that Barton departs from the more common patterns of English female religious rebellion and most clearly reflects the influence of the two Continental women.

Hildegard of Bingen, Mechtild of Hackeborn, Catherine of Siena, Bridget of Sweden, Margery Kempe: familiar names in late-medieval England, familiar names once again. Was there – indeed, is there – a canon of Middle English works by holy women? In his provocative essay, Ian Johnson argues that the existence of such a canon constituted a space within the patriarchal culture which at once permitted and limited the authority of holy women. He examines with imaginative perception the various ways in which holy women, dead and alive, native and foreign, were licensed to speak and accepted as *auctrices*, constructed as legitimate purveyors of divine knowledge according to reigning orthodoxy, and yet limited in autonomy and agency.

The essays in this volume demonstrate both the truth of Hope Emily Allen's claim of 'a remarkable . . . feminist movement' and the enormous effect which the writings of Continental holy women had on the spiritual expression and devotional practice of medieval England. Without these works, there would have been little religious writing by women available, and few models for devout women to emulate. The present day impact made by Hildegard and her holy sisters when they crossed the Atlantic to storm the bastions of pop music, New Age culture, and academia is but a whimper compared with the profound reverberations which resulted when they crossed the English Channel more than half a millennium ago.

Hildegard and the Male Reader:
a Study in Insular Reception

KATHRYN KERBY-FULTON

When one thinks of the influence of Hildegard of Bingen, images of serenely and intellectually developed women's communities come to mind: images of textual communities[1] – textual daughter-houses, if you will – like those initially fostered by actual correspondence with Hildegard (such as the community at Schönau led by her protégé, Elizabeth, or the Cistercian nunnery of St-Thomas-an-der-Kyll, to which Hildegard addressed some of her most profound thoughts on the need for *discretio*).[2] Or, in the period after her death, one thinks of remarkable literary coteries of visionaries like the one at Helfta, among whom the reading of Hildegard is simply assumed by historians of women's spirituality; or of the tantalizing hints of her influence at the inception of the Beguine movement in Belgium, during the development there of what McDonnell called the 'full tide of articulate mysticism" in the thirteenth century.[3] Sadly,

---

[1] For the term 'textual communities' see note 34 below.

[2] On Hildegard's relationship with Elisabeth of Schönau see: K. Kerby-Fulton and Dyan Elliott, 'Self-Image and the Visionary Role – Two Letters by Elisabeth of Schönau and Hildegard of Bingen', *On Pilgrimage: The Best of Vox Benedictina 1984–1993*, ed. Margot King, special issue of *Vox Benedictina*, vol. 11 (1994), 535–548, reprinted from *VB* 2/3 (1985), 204–223; Barbara Newman, *Sister of Wisdom* (Berkeley: University of California Press, 1987), 36–41; Anne Clark, *Elizabeth of Schönau* (Philadelphia: University of Pennsylvania Press, 1992), 4–5, 14–15, 21–25, 34–36; Adelgundis Führkötter, *Hildegard von Bingen Briefwechsel* (Salzburg, 1965). On her advice to the nuns of St Thomas-an-der-Kyll, see Hiltrud Rissel, 'Hildegard von Bingen und Elisabeth St Thomas an der Kyll', *Citeaux* 41 (1990), 5–43 (correcting Dronke's earlier theory of the addressee of one of her letters, *Women Writers of the Middle Ages* (Cambridge: CUP, 1984), 186–187).

[3] Hildegard's influence on the Helfta visionaries in fact remains to be established, but provisionally see Caroline Walker Bynum, *Jesus as Mother: Studies in the Spirituality of the High Middle Ages* (Berkeley: University of California Press, 1982), especially 177 and 245; and, less reliably, Lucy Menzies, *The Revelations of Mechthild of Magdeburg* (London: Longman, 1953), xxvii (Mechthild's denunciation of clerical abuse is in fact, as Menzies suggests, quite Hildegardian in tone); on her influence in Belgium, see Ernest W. McDonnell, *The Beguines and Beghards in Medieval Culture* (New York: Octagon, 1969), 281–298 (291 for quotation cited above).

tempting as it is to extrapolate from these instances, the ruthless statistical realities of manuscript dissemination paint a narrower picture of what her actual influence may have been. Although the study of Hildegard's influence is still largely uncharted territory,[4] the facts thus far acquired are inconsiderately unhelpful to the modern historian of women's spirituality. Late medieval library lists of books belonging to convents and orders with an obvious interest in women's visions rarely contain a copy of Hildegard's works.[5] Moreover, the list of extant manuscripts of her genuine works is relatively short. The appendix of Schrader's and Führkötter's monumental study establishing the canon of Hildegard will serve as a convenient guide: of her three mammoth visionary works, there are ten full manuscripts of *Scivias*,[6] five of the *Liber Vitae Meritorum*, and four of the *Liber Divinorum Operum* (to which should be added British Library Add. 15418, making five). Her letters, the other major source of her visionary thought, fared a little better (in fact, it was McDonnell's impression that it was her correspondence that sustained her later medieval reputation): Schrader and Führkötter list sixteen manuscripts (and Van Acker a further three);[7] however, some of those contain only a few of the over 390 extant letters she wrote. On the face of it, these are not impressive statistics of manuscript survival, especially in comparison with Elizabeth of Schönau, whose works survive in some 145 manuscripts. It appears, as Anne Clark has recently said, that the 'modern preference for Hildegard stands in contrast to the apparent medieval preference for Elizabeth's works, witnessed by the substantially greater number of manuscripts transmitting them' (5).

Although, as I hope to show, these simple statistical comparisons are rather misleading, there can be no doubt that even when we turn to internal evidence, Hildegard's influence in the visionary and mystical spheres of the later Middle Ages is disappointingly oblique. Her dignified,

---

[4] On Hildegard's influence (in addition to the studies cited above, and those by Kerby-Fulton in notes 15 and 19 below) see Marianna Schrader, 'Hildegarde de Bingen', *Dictionnaire de Spiritualité*, vol. VII, cols. 505–21; F. Jurgensmeier, 'St Hildegard "Prophetissa Teutonica" ', *Hildegard von Bingen, 1179–1979* (Mainz: Selbstverlag der Gesellschaft für Mittelrheinische Kirchengeschichte, 1979), 273–93. Barbara Newman's Introduction to Mother Columba Hart's and Jane Bishop's translation of *Scivias* (New York: Paulist, 1990), 46–7, briefly survey's Hildegard's influence as well. Barbara Newman and I are planning a collection of essays which would cover the range of her influence in medieval and renaissance Europe.

[5] See for instance the lists of extant books from nunnery and Charterhouse libraries in N.R. Ker, *Medieval Libraries of Great Britain* (London: Royal Historical Society, 1964).

[6] See A. Führkötter and A. Carlevaris, *Hildegardis Scivias*, Corpus Christianorum, CM, XLIII and XLIII A (Turnhout: Brepols, 1978) for descriptions, and for a list of the seven further manuscripts containing extracts from *Scivias* (independent of those found in Gebeno's compilation, on which see below notes 14 and 22).

[7] These, of course, are again independent of those in Gebeno's compilation; see below, notes 14 and 22, and L. Van Acker, ed., *Hildegardis Epistolarium*, Corpus Christianorum, CM, XCI (Turnhout: Brepols, 1991).

emotionally detached style of visionary experience had few imitators beyond the twelfth century. As Ute Stargardt has said:

> The mysticism of such women as Hildegard of Bingen and the instruction of such eminent teachers as Meister Eckhart, Tauler, and Suso promised the development of a speculative feminine mysticism in the Dominican houses comparable to that of Julian of Norwich in England. But this potential was never realized . . . [As] Joseph Quint observes . . . 'One looks in vain for something like a speculative system in . . . mystics [like Mechthild of Magdeburg and Hadewijch]. The center of their mysticism, its driving concern, is not Eckhart's unlimited desire for understanding, but the love of Bernard for the heavenly bridegroom'.[8]

These comments are arresting for many reasons, not least of which is the conjunction of Hildegard's and Julian's names. Although speculative mysticism is not exactly the term I would have chosen to describe Hildegard's visionary experience, both women display a strikingly similar serenity and intellectual detachment. But if Julian was in any way influenced by Hildegard, even indirectly, how did it happen, when the evidence suggests that even where Hildegard's influence is thought to be most profound, in Germany and the Low Countries, it is somewhat elusive?

Mariana Schrader tried to explain Hildegard's apparent lack of influence by noting that she was one of the last representatives of pre-scholastic spirituality, that interest in her work dropped off rapidly after her death partly as a result of this, and partly because Hildegard was not, 'à proprement parler', a mystic, like Bernard of Clairvaux, her exact contemporary; rather, as a prophetess, her major works were all in a prophetic genre, which succumbed to '[l]a domination des courants scolastique et mystique' (519). It is true that mysticism, even in Hildegard's lifetime, was poised to take an entirely different direction, and that after the twelfth century the split between mysticism and prophecy became even more distinct.[9] The difference is neatly expressed by Bernard himself in the second of his *Sermons* on the Song of Songs, in which he imagines the 'perfectus' of Old Testament times, tired of the dense, clouded words of Moses, Isaiah and Jeremiah, and longing instead for '[i]pse potius speciosus forma prae filiis hominum, ipse me osculetur osculo oris suis' [(rather let) him who is the most handsome of the sons of men, let him kiss

---

[8] Ute Stargardt, 'The Beguines of Belgium, the Dominican Nuns of Germany, and Margery Kempe', *The Popular Literature of Medieval England*, ed. T. Heffernan, (Knoxville: University of Tennessee Press, 1985), 291; citing Josef Quint, 'Mystik', *Reallexikon der deutschen Literaturgeschichte*, ed. Werner Kohschmidt and Wolfgang Mohr, 2nd ed. (Berlin: de Gruyter, 1962), 2:549.

[9] Even in England twelfth-century mysticism was affectively inclined; see Peter Dinzelbacher, 'The Beginnings of Mysticism Experienced in Twelfth-Century England', *The Medieval Mystical Tradition in England*, Exeter Symposium IV, ed. Marion Glasscoe (Cambridge: D.S. Brewer, 1987), 111–131.

me with the kiss of his mouth].[10] One cannot imagine anything so diametrically opposed to Hildegard's own spirituality; her language is laced with the words of the Old Testament prophets whom Bernard finds so impersonal. In stark contrast even to her contemporary Elizabeth, Hildegard's visionary experience never approaches anything personal, never mind the erotic dimension at which Bernard hints.[11] Psychologically speaking, Hildegard's mysticism was not on the side of history.

However, when she died in 1179 there was an aspect of the medieval future to which some part of her writings would always be relevant, and this was an unusual one for a woman writer: the polemics of interclerical controversy. Hildegard was read, copied and cited most frequently where issues of clerical abuse of power were discussed, where tensions arose between new religious orders and old ones, where heresy was a threat to the clerical establishment and, of course, where a mounting sense of crisis brought on apocalyptic expectations. This is where her most obvious, long term influence lay, not just with male authors and thinkers, but even with female visionary writers – it is only when Mechthild of Magdeburg, or Bridget of Sweden[12] discuss issues like these that Hildegard's stamp is easiest to discern. She did in fact discuss these issues in her letters to women during her lifetime, most notably in her correspondence with Elizabeth on the rising Cathar threat.[13] However, because it was men, not women, who dealt most heavily in ecclesiastical politics, Hildegard's late medieval audience appears – surprisingly to modern assumptions – to have been primarily male.

The reasons for this are complex, but the most straightforward one is codicological, and has entirely to do with the pragmatics of transmission. Unlike, for instance, the popular *Liber viarum dei* of Elizabeth of Schönau, all of Hildegard's major works are voluminous. Only Gebeno of Eberbach, in the days when her general reputation was still high, had the foresight to do an abridged compilation of extracts which would prove more user-friendly in the libraries and scriptoria of medieval monastaries.

---

[10] Bernard of Clairvaux, *Sermones super cantica canticorum*, ed. J. Leclercq *et al.* in *S. Bernardi Opera* I (Rome: Editiones Cistercienses, 1957), 9; for translation see *Sermons on the Song of Songs*, Killian Walsh (Kalamazoo: Cistercian Institute, 1981) I, 8–9. This passage is also discussed in Anne Clark Bartlett, 'Miraculous Literacy and Textual Communities in Hildegard of Bingen's Scivias', *Mystics Quarterly* 18 (1992), 45.

[11] See the description of her experience in the letter to Guibert of Gembloux, edited by Peter Dronke, *Women Writers*, 250–256.

[12] For Hildegard's influence on Bridget, see Tortsch's fifteenth-century compilation of her prophetic visions, the *Onus mundi*, ed. Ulrich Montag, *Das Werk der heiligen Birgitta von Sweden in oberdeutscher Uberleiferung* (Munich, 1968). Tortsch is explicit about Bridget's relationship with Hildegard even if Bridget was not. On Hildegard's influence on Mechtild's denunciations of clerical abuse, see Menzies, xix.

[13] Raoul Manselli, 'Amicizia spirituale ed azione pastorale nella Germania del sec. XII: Ildegarde di Bingen, Elisabetta ed Ecberto di Schonau contro l'eresia catara', *Studi e materiali di storia delli religioni* 38 (1967), 302–313.

However, Gebeno was interested primarily in clerical reform, the rise of heresy and apocalyptic thought, and this is the Hildegard he gave the later Middle Ages; his compilation, done in 1220 and called the *Pentachronon* (a reference to Hildegard's prophecies of the five remaining ages of history), survives in manuscripts 'innombrables'[14] in European libraries. Thus, it was largely through Gebeno's compilation that her prophetic visions continued to exert an influence on medieval thought in the centuries after her death, although it is never counted among the statistics of survival of her genuine works, as we have seen, and this despite the fact that Gebeno was not imaginative enough to add much of his own to the extracts he collected. These prophecies, her most controversial writings, became the inspiration for a discernable genre of visionary reformist prophecy especially in Northern Europe, where readers, translators, and writers responded eagerly to her ecclesiastical apocalypticism.[15]

The English transmission of Hildegard's works is especially interesting, not just because one of its major poets, William Langland, knew the genre, but also because of the general Insular penchant for (and delight in) interclerical controversy, which provided a climate in which her ecclesiastical apocalypticism could be readily assimilated to a variety of polemics. As the evidence of a number of extant Insular manuscripts and citations indicates, Hildegard had an intelligent, and respectably diverse, following in England and Ireland, initially among monastic thinkers interested in history and apocalypticism, and then, with the development of antifraternalism and finally Lollardy, among those who were caught up in clerical controversy.[16] This British attraction to the polemical Hildegard can be explained in various ways: for instance, her prediction that the institutional power of the papacy would pass away, and that Rome would be reduced to the status of an ordinary bishopric no doubt endeared her to the notoriously antipapal English. But her prophecies (both genuine and pseudonymous) seem also to have been especially consulted with respect to two peculiarly English preoccupations of the late-fourteenth century: the issue of clerical disendowment and the growth of the Wycliffite heresy.[17] Furthermore, both of these issues were related to another British obsession:

---

[14] Schrader, 519. There is no full printed edition of Gebeno's *Pentachronon*, but I have cited the partial edition in J.B. Pitra, ed., *Analecta sacra*, vol. viii (Montecassino, 1882), 483–488.

[15] On the Northern European apocalyptic tradition (as distinct from the Joachite one which originated in Italy), see Kerby-Fulton, *Reformist Apocalypticism and Piers Plowman* (Cambridge: CUP, 1990), 76–77.

[16] See Kerby-Fulton, *Reformist Apocalypticism*; and Kerby-Fulton and E.R. Daniel, 'English Joachimism, 1300–1500: The Columbinus Prophecy', *Il profetismo gioachimita tra Quattrocento e Cinquecento*, Atti del III Congresso Internazionale, ed. Gian Luca Potesta (San Giovanni in Fiore: Centro Internazionale di Studi Gioachimiti, 1989), 313–350.

[17] On disendowment issues see Kerby-Fulton, *Reformist Apocalypticism*, 37–44, 173–177; and Steven Justice, *Writing and Rebellion: England in 1381* (Berkeley: University of California Press, 1994), 105–106, 236–240.

the fraternal controversies which gripped Insular writers like Pecham, Fitzralph and Wyclif, and in which Hildegardian prophecies played a key role. Among writers like these both her prophecies and, once in a while, her gender attracted comment.

We do not know how Hildegard's works first came to circulate in Britain, but what we know of the introduction of Elizabeth's writings is instructive, especially on the question of how women's visions were regarded in twelfth-century monastic circles. An English Cistercian, Roger of Ford, who was visiting a Cistercian house in France sometime between 1169 and 1178, sent home to his abbot a copy of Elizabeth's *Liber viarum dei*, with the comment: 'Et quidem nescio quid de hoc opere in vestra regione censebitur; hoc autem scio quod in his nostris partibus *non solum ab indoctis*, sed ab ipsis episcopis et abbatibus *nostris* certatim et scribitur et legitur et auditur.' [Indeed I do not know how this work will be appreciated where you are, but I do know that in these parts it is eagerly copied and read and heard *not only by the unlearned* but by bishops (themselves) and *our* abbots].[18] This indicates that the initial audience for women's writing was presumed to be the unlearned ('indoctis'), but since Elizabeth's *Liber* is in Latin, the word must be qualified: it apparently refers to those religious with only a working command of Latin. Roger stresses, however, that 'bishops and *our* abbots' (i.e. Cistercian ones) are reading the work; no doubt an instance of what McGuire has called the 'dawning Cistercian fascination with the content of female visions'.[19] What is instructive is that, in contrast, I can find little evidence that English monastic readers approached Hildegard's works as '*female* visions'. This is because, first of all, Gebeno's compilation does not make an issue of gender (Gebeno himself persistently compares Hildegard to St John), and, secondly, because both in manuscripts and medieval library catalogues Hildegard's works were more likely to be associated with prophetic and polemical literature by men than with female visions. Another revealing point in this case of Elizabeth's is that the whole English manuscript tradition (five extant copies) descends from Roger's copy.[20] This is in contrast to the complexity of the English transmission of Hildegard's works, which includes, to my knowledge at present: three full manuscripts of her major visionary works; six copies of Gebeno's compilation; six of extracts; eleven of pseudonymous works; seven citations in medieval library catalogues; and over a dozen citations by medieval

---

[18] Cited in Clark, *Elizabeth*, 25 and note 91; I have modified her translation.

[19] Clark, *Elizabeth*, 49; we might note here that Hildegard's visions are not in the anthology of visionary writing made by Peter of London c.1200 (Lambeth Palace 51), but that Elizabeth's are; this suggests that Hildegard's works were already not circulating as visions. It was the inception of the mendicant orders which brought Hildegard's work into prominence again in the mid-thirteenth century. See Kerby-Fulton, 'Hildegard of Bingen and Antimendicant Propaganda', *Traditio* 43 (1987), 386–399.

[20] Clark, *Elizabeth*, 159, note 92.

English authors. British audiences, then, unlike their European counterparts, seem to have preferred Hildegard to Elizabeth.[21]

This paper will survey a few of the most interesting features of the Insular reception of Hildegard's ideas, and, using the evidence of manuscript selection, rubrication, annotation, and ownership of her works, it will try to suggest something about who was reading her controversial, even daring, ecclesiastical apocalypticism in the clerical turbulence of late medieval England and Ireland. I will not be able to give more than a few instances of Insular readings of Hildegard, nor do more than touch upon the difficult and elusive question of how Hildegard's visionary style was read by her English audience. But I can say that from the evidence of annotation in manuscripts like Bodleian Library Digby 32 of Gebeno's *Pentachronon,* it appears that some Insular readers, at least, were interested in her visionary iconography as well as her apocalypticism. Moreover, some scribes and annotators were interested in defining the visionary-prophetic genre in which she wrote, and many more in the question of the papal authorization of her visions. This makes sense, of course, because, her visionary apocalypticism and her distinctive visionary spirituality were inseparable, and Gebeno's compilation transmitted – could not help but transmit – both. The choice of extracts for copying and the choice of passages for annotating betray a number of anxieties in her British readers, among which are anxieties about the coming of Antichrist, the imminence of clerical chastisement, the rise of heresy, and the validation of visionary experience. Most interesting, however (because it upsets some modern assumptions), is the way in which a reception study reveals how her primarily male audience responded to her as a feminine authority figure.

Although the evidence is not yet all in, there is enough to support the following generalizations: (1) while certain pieces were frequently extracted, and certain passages usually excite notice, medieval readers of Hildegard responded diversely to her work – there is no such thing as '*the* medieval reader', at least not of Hildegard; (2) only among readers outside the monastic world, and even there only rarely, is her gender an issue – it is when her works cross boundaries into other reading communities (notably, among university or university-trained readers) that questions arise; (3) open hostility to her work only appears in polemical situations where Hildegard is being quoted by the enemy camp; (4) in the late-fourteenth/early-fifteenth century, in a church troubled by heresy, schism, the growth of 'enthusiasm', and the clamour of women mystics for recognition – when works like the *Chastising of God's Children* were being written in England – Hildegard's writings took on a new interest for English clergy,

---

[21] For a parallel phenomenon of British fascination with Joachite prophecy on ecclesiastical abuse, see Kerby-Fulton and Daniel, 'Columbinus'.

both orthodox and heterodox, and were even used in one instance against the Lollard encouragement of women.[22]

To find comments on Hildegard's gender (other than simple references to her status as abbess (*magistra*), or virgin (*virgo*)), one pretty much has to go outside the monastic context of her English transmission. I am aware so far of only one early instance, and that is in Merton College MS 160, a complete copy of Hildegard's *Scivias* made at the beginning of the thirteenth century. The circumstances of its acquisition are now unknown, but it was in the College before 1360, and was certainly read by, if not actually made for, a university setting (likely Merton itself)[23] – making it unusual among extant manuscripts containing Hildegardiana, most of which were produced and read in monastic settings at this date. The colophon at the end of the manuscript (fol. 127v) reads 'Finit tercia Pars libri Hildegardis Scivias, id est simplicis uidentis; dicitur simplicis uidentis propter sexum infirmiorem, quod nunc dicitur propheta, olim dicebatur uidens. Scivias est uisio ueracium.' [Here ends the third part of the book of Hildegard, *Scivias*, that is, 'of simple seeing'; it is called of simple seeing on account of the weaker sex; what now is called a prophet, once was called a seer. *Scivias* is a true vision (*visio*).][24] Although his consciousness of Hildegard's gender has inspired a less than flattering interpretation of the title (*Scivias* actually means 'Know the Ways'), the scribe appears to have grasped the essence of the genre in which she is writing (and prefers the concept of 'vision' to what he apparently sees as the newfangled notion of modern 'prophecy'). Most importantly, he asserts the veracity of *Scivias* – indeed to copy a work of its length without such a conviction would be torture – even though he implies that the visionary mode of revelation, though time-honoured, is a concession to the weaker sex. Now this attitude is less likely among monastics, where visions were more common and often respected,[25] which suggests that this copy of *Scivias* has crossed

---

[22] This seems in part to have been due to her emphasis on *discretio*, which the English transmission of the *Pentachronon* emphasizes. The textual differences between Insular and Continental versions of the *Pentachronon* are complex and cannot be addressed here; provisionally, one could compare the selection and ordering of the extracts in Paris, Bibliothèque Nationale MS 3322 and London, British Library Arundel 337. On textual matters see (provisionally) Kerby-Fulton, *Reformist Apocalypticism*, 28–31 and notes 15–17.

[23] The manuscript is of English provenance and the attention to *ordinatio* (see below) could suggest a scholastic setting. See F.M Powicke, *Medieval Books of Merton College* (Oxford: OUP, 1931), no. 1212, section IV, 236.

[24] My transcription differs slightly from the one printed in Führkötter and Carlevaris, xlix, from which the 'est' in the last sentence was inadvertently left out; their 'propheta' could also be expanded 'prophetia', but their reading perhaps suits the sense of the passage better. Barbara Newman has helpfully suggested that the scribe's 'simplicis videntis' must have been prompted by the reference to Hildegard as 'simplicis hominis' at the opening of *Scivias*, 3.

[25] C.J. Holdsworth, 'Visions and Visionaries in the Middle Ages', *History* 48 (1963), 141–153.

into a different kind of reading community – either a more intellectually pretentious monastic house or a scholastic one (like Merton itself).[26] Certainly the rubrication of the manuscript suggests someone with the obsession for *ordinatio* found most often in a scholastic context. Chapter summaries were initially provided in lists at the head of each of the three large sections, with numbers for easy cross-referencing, but someone quickly found even this inadequate; this person then re-wrote them as rubricated summaries crammed unhappily into the narrow margins between the columns. He added this indignant note to the bottom margin at the end of the first list of summaries for Book I (fol. 1v): 'Qui hunc librum transcribere voluerit rubricas in suis locis, id est, in capitulorum exordio diligenter conscribat, nam in hoc libro breviandi causa omissa fuerunt. Notandum etiam quasdam . . .' [Whoever wishes to transcribe this book should copy the rubrics diligently in their own places, that is, at the beginning of each chapter, but in this book they were omitted for the sake of brevity. Besides, it should be noted that these . . .] – unfortunately (or perhaps fortunately) the rest of the diatribe has been lost through cropping.[27]

Evidently those involved in the production and use of Merton 160 took *Scivias* seriously, which is interesting in light of the much cherished modern view that Hildegard's works were spurned by scholastics. Certainly aspects of her work did appear quaint or simple to such readers, but they were not dismissed.[28] We see a very similar attitude in a scholastic correspondent of Hildegard's during her lifetime, a certain Master of Theology at Paris, who accepts that her learning came through divine inspiration, compliments her on her great reputation in Paris, and asks her to settle a question raised by Gilbert de la Poirrée: 'whether God is both paternity and divinity?'.[29] Hildegard responds in her usual manner, attributing everything she knows on the subject (which, by the way, includes a good deal of the methodology of disputational theology) to the voice of the Living Light. As Anne Clark Bartlett has said of this letter, and of Hildegard's authorial stance as 'paupercula feminea forma' [poor little womanly creature], it has a decidedly polemical message for readers 'instructing and exhorting both theologians and exegetes alike in the meditative disciplines of monastic reading, inviting their participation in the monastic

---

[26] See Bartlett's discussion of the Villers monastic community which begged Hildegard for solutions to thirty-eight theological questions: 'Ernest McDonnell has discussed the Villers community's "open hostility to scholastic philosophy", and has argued that their library holdings and the works composed in the house's scriptorium "reveal a pious, but not especially learned, community" ' (154); and her article in *Viator* 23 (1992), 153–66.

[27] Führkötter and Carlevaris give no provenance (xlviii), but the orthography and hands look English.

[28] E. Colledge makes a similar point about the erudite and worldly in Bridget's initial audience in 'Epistola solitarii ad reges: Alphonse of Pecha as Organizer of Birgittine and Urbanist Propaganda', *Mediaeval Studies* 43 (1956), 19–49.

[29] Bartlett, *Elizabeth*, 45; (see *PL*, vol. 197, col. 351).

textual community in which she participated and the visionary community of which she was the undisputed leader' (46). Bartlett stresses that Hildegard's visionary experiences, at least as they are recorded, are clearly structured within the monastic system of *lectio,* the system of reading aloud and hearing what Leclercq called the 'voice of the pages' in his classic archaeology of monastic reading practices (50). I would agree with Bartlett's assessment, and simply add that this technique, coupled with her firm denial of *exstasis* or any trance-like experience such as Elizabeth of Schönau claimed, made her visionary works approachable to those within the monastic tradition, male or female, and even to some outside it.[30]

However, no reader external to monasticism was ever as comfortable with Hildergard's visionary mode as those within it. As Brian Stock has suggested, one of the things that distinguishes the monastery as a textual community is its way of reading: 'the monastic reader engaged his mind and his senses, he rehearsed, revivified, and ultimately relived the experience which created the mystical state'.[31] That monastic readers were more amenable to her visionary mode of conveying knowledge is everywhere evident in their responses, but perhaps never more so than in Gebeno's own prologue, which came to be so much a part of the fabric of the transmission of Hildegard that English scribes who plundered the *Pentachronon* for extracts also plundered Gebeno's prologue for rubrics and annotations. Among the most highlighted and re-copied comments in his prologue are the following: first prize for most marginal annotation in Insular manuscripts goes to his statement that '[l]ibros S. Hildegardis plerique fastidiunt et abhorrent, pro eo quod obscure et inusitato stylo loquitur' [many disdain and abhor the books of Hildegard because she speaks[32] in an obscure or unusual style]. Such readers, he goes on to say, do not understand that this obscurity is 'argumentum verae prophetiae' [proof of true prophecy] (485). He later calls her style a witness of 'veri digiti Dei' [the true finger of God] (485), which would actually appear to be a metaphor alluding to the use of the *declamatio* gesture in medieval religious art to indicate visually the presence of an authoritative speaking voice.[33]

But Gebeno does not simply rely on metaphors to convey his sense of Hildegard's authority. In the prologue to Book III Gebeno explicitly sets Hildegard among the great religious figures of his times, providing in

---

[30] See Kerby-Fulton and Elliott.

[31] Brian Stock, *The Implications of Literacy* (Princeton: PUP, 1983), 409.

[32] Reflecting the older form of authorship by dictation; see Paul Saenger, 'Silent Reading: Its Impact on Late Medieval Script and Society', *Viator* 13 (1982), 367–414.

[33] Michael Camille, 'Seeing and Reading: Some Visual Implications of Medieval Literacy', *Art History* 8 (1985), 22–45. Barbara Newman has helpfully mentioned that Hildegard uses the 'finger of God' motif in the *Symphonia*, and that it was probably originally derived from the 'Veni Creator'; it should be noted, however, that the visual image goes back to classical times, as Camille shows.

passing an interesting list of monastic heroes: Bernard of Clairvaux, Hugh and Richard of St. Victor, and *'in Anglia*, St Thomas, bishop and martyr, and in the same land, the venerable Abbot of Rievaulx; *in Calabria,* Abbot Joachim' (488). Most important from the standpoint of medieval readers, however, was a passage in Gebeno's dedicatory letter to his patrons in which he pulls out his trump card – the fact that, as he says, the books of St. Hildegard were received and authorized ('canonizati') by Pope Eugenius at the Council of Trier, in the presence of as many French as German bishops, and of St. Bernard of Clairvaux (484). Of course, the detail that it was only the first parts of *Scivias* which were examined he quietly drops, and by the later Middle Ages the reference to Eugenius's approval is appropriated in rubrics to introduce any extract, letter or even pseudonymous piece which any scribe wished to copy. Moreover, Gebeno begins the dedicatory letter with a casually magisterial survey of Hildegard's reputation:

> Sancta virgo Hildegardis, fundatrix et magistra monasterii sancti Ruperti . . . quantae sanctitatis, quantique meriti fuerit apud Deum et apud homines, charitatem vestram latere non credo. Sed si forsitan ignoratis, legite libellum vitae ejus; legite diversas epistolas magnatum terrae ad eam transmissas, trium videlicet apostolicorum Eugenii, Anastasii et Adriani, Conradi quoque regis, Frederici imperatoris, patriarchae Hierosolymitani, archiepiescopiorum, episcoporum, abbatum, praepostitorum: et tunc in veritate dicere poteritis: Magnificavit eam Dominus in conspectu regum.

> [I believe that it has not escaped the generosity of your regard that the holy virgin Hildegard, founder and abbess of the monastary of St Rupert . . . [was possessed] of so much holiness and merit with God and with men. But if perhaps you are unaware, read the book of her life, read the diverse letters of great ones of the earth sent to her, namely, [those] of three popes, Eugenius, Anastasius and Adrian, of King Conrad, of Emperor Frederick, of the Patriarch of Jerusalem, of archbishops, bishops, abbots, and church officials, and then in truth you will be able to say 'the Lord has magnified her in the sight of kings']. (483)

This is quite a send off. But perhaps the best evidence that Hildegard's works were the centre of a textual community, for Gebeno and for many others, lies in the awe with which he regarded her texts, and his sensitivity about his own work as a compiler.[34] In his prologue to Book II he directly addresses the nuns of Rupertsberg:

---

[34] I am using textual community here in the sense that Stock does when he speaks of groups whose 'organizational principles . . . were clearly based on texts, which played a predominant role in the internal and external relationships of the members', particularly involving an individual who 'mastered' the interpretation of the text and then used that in 'reforming a group's thought and action' (90). It is appropriate that Stock's study is of monastic, reformist or dissenting groups in exactly the period in which Hildegard wrote.

Nuper quum essem apud vos, et libellum illum in manibus haberemus, et de ipso colloqueremur, quem de quinque futuris temporibus ex libris sanctae matris vestrae compilavi, una ex vobis verba illa S. Hildegardis, quae loquitur in fine Divinorum Operum, videlicet: 'Nullus hominum [tam audax sit, ut verbis hujus scripturae aliquid augendo apponat, vel minuendo auferat, ne de libro vitae] . . . deleatur', me ex obliquo, ut puto, reprehendens.

[Lately when I was with you, and we held that book in our hands, and we also spoke together of that [book, i.e., the *Pentachronon*] which I have compiled concerning the five future times from the books of your holy mother, one among you voiced the words of St. Hildegard from the end of the *Liber Divinorum Operum,* namely, 'let no person be so bold as to add something to the words of this writing, or remove anything from it, lest he be deleted . . . from the Book of Life', reproving me indirectly, as I think.]

(487)

He then goes on to defend his work as compiler[35] by analogy to one who glosses the Book of Revelation, and who selects in order to apply and expound; he finishes by setting the seal of approval on his activity by quoting Hildegard's blessing from *Scivias* on any who would reproduce her prophecy 'in vias planas' [in clear ways] (487). If this is not a textual community I don't know what is, and it must be added that Gebeno's reverence for her text is mirrored in the common scribal practice in *Pentachronon* manuscripts of rubricating, underlining or otherwise distinguishing Hildegard's own words from the commentary by Gebeno and by others.

Clearly even many monastic readers found her awe-inspiring and obscure. In a note in the front of a large fifteenth-century manuscript of her letters, now in the British Library (Add. 15102), John Tritenheim, Abbot of Spanheim warns the reader 'In omnibus autem opusculis suis beata hildegardis mistice valde et obscure procedit: vnde nisi a religiosis et devotis vix eius scripta intelliguntur' [In all her (short) works the blessed Hildegard proceeds very mystically and obscurely; whence her writings are scarcely understandable unless by the religious and devout] (fol. 1v). But the coming of the mendicant orders in the thirteenth century was to steer audience response away from the issues of mystical obscurity or visionary style which exercised earlier scribes and editors, and toward Hildegard's polemical views on the dangers of novelty in the religious life (Hildegard herself, a staunch Benedictine, had lived during the heyday of the founding of new orders, and had much to say in defence of monastic tradition).[36] Most importantly, however, readers seized upon her

---

[35] On the role of medieval compilers (which could involve extensive editorial activity – thus Gebeno's sensitivity), see Alastair Minnis, *Medieval Theory of Authorship*, 2nd ed. (Philadelphia: UPP, 1984).

[36] See Kerby-Fulton, 'A Return to the "First Dawn of Justice": Hildegard's Visions of

predictions of the rise of a new heretical group ('populus errans'), the worst in a long series of forerunners of Antichrist, who would be hypocritically devoted to abstinence and poverty, but whom she distinguished from the Cathar heretics of her own day. Hildegard had written this prediciton in a scorching letter on clerical laxity to the clergy of Cologne, where, as I have shown elsewhere, the prophecy was a matter for local terror decades afterwards; even the first Dominican friars to arrive in the city were taken as the long-feared *populus errans*.[37] It was however Gebeno who drew international attention to what would otherwise have remained a marginal theme in her prophecy. Although Gebeno says initially that his motive for making the compilation was 'ad confutandos . . . pseudo-prophetas' [to confute . . . the pseudoprophets] (484) who were making a sensation with cheap news about the birth of Antichrist, it soon becomes apparent that he is longwindedly obsessed by the growing threat of the Cathar heretics – so much so that Cardinal Pitra, the *Pentachronon*'s only modern editor, at one point threw up his hands and, inserting editorial ellipsis points, wrote impatiently in his stiff nineteenth-century Latin 'Inde per sex columnas excurrit in Catharos' [here follow six more columns in which he inveighs against the Cathars] (487). In her letter to the clergy of Cologne, Hildegard had prophesied that these heretics would win over the nobility and secular princes, and convince them to despoil the religious of their endowments and temporalities. While in 1220 Gebeno had read the Cologne letter as prophesying a renewed Cathar threat, it was shortly to become the cherished property of the antimendicant propagandists, who gleefully took it up as a prophecy of the friars. In England it became the most popularly extracted, annotated and cross-referenced piece from Hildegard's works; in fact, one of the first professional Latin poets of England, Henry of Avranches, even versified it, treating Hildegard's text with an unimaginative reverence which would even have satisfied the disgruntled nun who had objected to Gebeno's compilation. Even though the poem says nothing of the friars, because of course the Cologne letter itself does not, Matthew Paris, the scribe of Cambridge University Library Dd.11.78 in which Henry's poem survives, supplied the rubric 'Prophecia Sancte Hildegardis de novis fratribus' [Prophecy of St Hildegard on the New Friars].[38] Now, Henry himself was not given to antifraternal sentiments; in fact, he wrote a life of St Francis. But even Matthew's trick (if indeed it was his) of supplying a falacious rubric seems tame compared to other tactics of the antimendicant propagandists as the centuries wore on.

Clerical Reform and the Eremitical Life', *American Benedictine Review* 40.4 (1989), 383–407.
37 See Kerby-Fulton, *Traditio.*
38 I would like to thank Professor George Rigg for communicating this to me. See his 'Medieval Latin Poetic Anthologies' (V): Matthew Paris' 'Anthology of Henry of Avranches' (Cambridge University Library MS Dd.11.78), *Mediaeval Studies* 49 (1987), 352–90.

Some of the charges Hildegard had laid against the coming heretics in her original prophecy could be easily applied by later writers to the friars: false piety and austerity, the seduction of women, and in England in particular, the charge of collusion with secular princes to take away ecclesiastical temporalities – in 1371 two friars had laid just such a proposition before Parliament.[39] But Hildegard had inconsiderately neglected to foresee other charges which would have been useful to the thirteenth-century propagandists, notably charges of falacious begging or appropriation of the more lucrative duties of pastoral care, so her text had to be 'improved'. One English (Corpus Christi College, Cambridge 404) and one Irish (Trinity College, Dublin 516) manuscript contain as yet unnoticed pseudonymous reworkings of the Cologne letter which slyly use the opening words and a few key phrases from the original, but have the virtue of being much shorter and nastier.[40]

Even more outrageous, and massively more popular, is the fully pseudonymous 'Insurgent gentes', which, as I have suggested elsewhere, was probably originally concocted in the circle of William of St Amour at Paris. It is extant in countless manuscripts across Europe, of which there are eight English and one Irish, and a good dozen citations in Insular writers, some even in Middle English texts. It is ruthlessly antimendicant, and makes no attempt to imitate Hildegard's imagery or style.[41] The fact that Hildegard had died before the inception of the mendicant orders, which might be thought to provoke healthy scepticism in some, was now eagerly trumpeted in rubrics introducing 'Insurgent' as verification of her prophetic gift. Interestingly, 'Insurgent' never appears in an English manuscript with the genuine letter to the clergy of Cologne – any non-partisan reader who placed the two prophecies side by side could hardly have been fooled, as perhaps the makers of antimendicant anthologies were only too aware.[42] The pseudonymous text is narrowly (and shoddily) calculated for specific purposes and it contains none of the broader concerns of Hildegard's Cologne letter: imminent chastisement of all clergy, the subsequent new dawn of justice, nor any of the exotic imagery and fluid allegory that characterizes her style. Most pointedly it contains none of Hildegard's appeals for reform: antimendicant propagandists were not looking for the reform of the friars, they were working for their annihilation.

Did any medieval reader pick up on the fact that 'Insurgent' was a forgery? The eminent thirteenth-century English Franciscan, John of Pecham, seems to have realized something was amiss. As a friar, he had

---

[39] See V.H. Galbraith, 'Articles Laid before the Parliament of 1371', *EHR* 34 (1919), 579–582.

[40] The texts are very similar: Corpus Christi College, Cambridge, 404, fol. 38v and Trinity College Dublin, 516, fol. 43.

[41] See Kerby-Fulton, *Traditio*.

[42] For a fuller discussion and comparison of the styles of the genuine and pseudonymous pieces, see Kerby-Fulton, *Traditio*.

no reason to be well-disposed to Hildegard, who, by Pecham's time, had become a kind of adopted saint of the antimendicant camp, and as a scholastic theologian, he was less likely to be comfortable with an appeal to visionary authority. So perhaps it is not surprising that he wrote a virulent attack on Hildegard – indeed the only such one written by an Englishman of which I am aware. In Pecham's *Tractatus paupertis,* written against William of St. Amour and his party around 1270, he notices (with respect to the enemy's charge that the friars are the pseudo-apostles) that: '[a]d hoc allegant prophetias cuiusdam prophetisse teutonice nomine Hildegardis, que nonnulla mala dicit de quibusdam religiosis' [to this purpose they allege the prophecies of a certain Teutonic prophetess by the name of Hildegard, who says some evil things concerning certain religious].[43] This is a coolheaded and largely accurate summing up of what Hildegard did indeed say – which was not much (the Cologne prophecy is quite vague in its description of the coming pious heretics). Pecham seems to have also known 'Insurgent', because his next remark appears to allude to one of the rubrics to 'Insurgent' mentioned above: he contrasts Augustine's citation of the Sibyl with antimendicant citations of Hildegard in a manner which suggests that he did not believe Hildegard to have predated the Mendicant orders, whereas he knew the Sibyl to have predated Augustine – which makes her prophecy genuine, Hildegard's (by implication) a fake.[44] His application here (or nearly) of the kinds of techniques of historical criticism one usually associates with Italian humanists is intriguing – but clearly he had no way of checking Hildegard's actual date of death. It is especially intriguing in view of the fact that he had already resorted to gender discrimination in his efforts to rule Hildegard out of court ('Prophetias Hildegardis non multum pondero, sed magis eos arguo qui mulieris doctrinam in ecclesias introducunt, quam apostolus docere in ecclesia non permittit [I do not consider the prophecies of Hildegard to have much importance, but I would censure more strongly those who introduce into the Church the doctrines of women, whom the apostle (Paul) does not permit to teach in church] (76)), but clearly he was not content to let the matter rest there. The propagandists had obviously tried to head off just this criticism by referring to both Bernard's and Pope Eugenius's approval of Hildegard, to which Pecham retorts that he can find nothing in Bernard to authorize this particular prediction of hers; he goes on to charge that if Bernard did collect and study Hildegard's texts, he may have done so in order to refute them, just as he did the errors of Abelard.[45] To the suggestion that Pope Eugenius had authorized her works

---

[43] C.L. Kingsford *et al.*, *Fratris Johannis Pecham, Tractatus Tres de Paupertate* (Aberdeen: Typis Academicis, 1910), 64.

[44] Kingsford, *Pecham*, 76.

[45] *Ad quod dicunt quidam Bernardum prophetias Hildegardis collegisse, si verum est huiusmodi prophetie auctoritam non ostendit: collegit enim Bernardus quedam at repro-*

he has a simple reply: 'plane est mendacium'; the apostolic throne, he says, does not confirm such things of its own accord, and there are many errors to be found in her writings. Of course he does not bother to give any details of these, and the remark may simply be intended as a slur. On the other hand, it may suggest that some of Hildegard's prophetic writings would have got her into trouble had she lived in the next century; apocalyptic denunciation of ecclesiastical abuse did become much more sensitive and dangerous in the thirteenth century, regardless of the gender of the prophet. With rising impatience he caps his counterargument with the remark 'Credo autem donec aliud mihi innotescat, prophetiam Hildegardis ex dyaboli astutia processisse' [Moreover, until I come to know otherwise, I do believe the prophecy of Hildegard to have proceeded from the cunning of the devil] (76).

Pecham's response is interesting because we can observe that, despite his lapse into antifeminism (and what I have quoted is about the extent of it), he quite justifiably smelled a rat, and came closer than any medieval author I know of to detecting the pseudonymity of (apparently) 'Insurgent'. That Pecham's bitterness and rigidity on the point of women teaching arises from the polemical situation in which he found himself can hardly be doubted, but more striking is the fact that he also shares with many other university trained men a distrust of revelatory knowledge. In another tract, 'Contra Kilwardby', Pecham warned against too much credence in the prophecies of both Joachim of Fiore and Hildegard on the grounds that it can be difficult to tell true revelations from apocryphal ('apocryphas') ones when the medium is dreams ('sompnia').[46] This argues for no very close knowledge of either prophet (*neither* of whom used the medium of dreams), but it serves to demonstrate that his dislike of Hildegard was not entirely gender based, or even polemically based. Rather, it suggests a confrontation between the sensibilities of two different interpretive communities: the monastic (with its tolerance of visions and mystical experience), represented by Hildegard and Joachim, and the scholastic (with its preference for intellectual analysis). As Eric Colledge observed long ago about Alphonse of Pecha's defence of the *Revelations* of St Bridget,[47] the problem for Alphonse was the contrast between his traditional monastic receptivity to visionary writing and the scepticism of his opponents, 'doctors in both laws, no doubt' of the type that would dismiss revelations as a source of knowledge generally.

In fact, in determining medieval attitudes toward vision and prophecy,

---

bandum, sicut errores Abelardi, quedam ad experiendum, sicut forsan huiusmodi mulieris verba. Et quod dicunt papam Eugenium ea confirmasse, plane est mendacium, quia sedes apostolica non sole dubia confirmare, maxime cum hec in aliis temeritatis sue scriptitationibus suis noscatur plura erronea reliquesse (76).

[46] Kingsford, *Pecham*, 122; Pecham claims here nonetheless to know 'quid scripserit contra aliquos Hildegarde quid Joachim divinaverit'.

[47] Colledge, '*Epistola*', 49.

neither gender nor even party politics seems to have been as crucial a factor as intellectual training and the (often to us) invisible boundaries it established between clerical communities. This is well illustrated by the case of Wyclif, who had every reason to welcome the use of Hildegard's name as a weapon of antifraternal propaganda (and some of his followers did just that).[48] But Wyclif held a similar attitude toward the credibility of visions as Pecham had. Wyclif, who was also of course a university man, counselled against trusting in the sayings of 'Merlin and Hildegard',[49] a comparison which, once again, makes one wonder how much he could have bothered to read of Hildegard's writings (which are utterly unlike what Shakespeare called the 'skimble-skamble stuff' of 'the dreamer Merlin and his prophecies').[50] For Wyclif true prophecy was interpretation, of the Bible that is. Here again gender is not the issue, the nature of revelation is. Wyclif's response to Hildegard may have been based upon the fact that one of the most noticed and excerpted of her prophecies from the late-fourteenth century onwards in England is an extract in which she had condemned the novelty of new religious orders.[51] The 'novelties' of the Wycliffites, for instance, aroused the ire of the late-fourteenth-century annotator of Bodleian Library MS Digby 32, who wrote beside this passage from Hildegard: 'Ecce quam plane loquitur hic de lollardi' [Behold how plainly she speaks here of the lollards] (fol. 70). This copy of the *Pentachronon* – in defiance of all I've said about scholastic intellectual communities – appears to have been an Oxford Dominican friar's *vade mecum* book. It is littered with anti-Lollard annotations: for instance, where Hildegard asks rhetorically why the old ways of the Church fathers are no longer good enough for some, the annotator enthusiastically responds 'Optimum verbum contra lollardes' [the best words against the

---

[48] See, for instance, the use that William Taylor finds for Hildegard's prophecy of disendowment in his sermon in Bodleian Library, Douce 53, fol. 9 and fol. 10. (I am grateful to Steven Justice for pointing this out to me). Taylor is likely citing the *Pentachronon* extract from *Liber divinorum operum* (see PL 197, col. 1018ff), though Taylor has softened Hildegard's strident condemnation for his own purposes (in the *LDO* the clergy are certainly not prepared to hand over their goods meekly!) This sermon has now been edited by Ann Hudson, in *Two Wycliffite Texts*, EETS 301 (Oxford: OUP, 1993), see page 9, lines 221 and 244.

[49] 'Cum secundum sanctos spectat ad officium doctoris evangelici prophetare et socii mei prophetant ex dictis Merlini, Hildegardis et vatum similium extra fidem scripture de statibus membrorum ecclesie militantis, motus sum eciam sed fideliori evidencia prophetare'. This is the opening sentence of *De vaticinia seu prophetia*, ed. J. Loserth, *Opera minora* (London: Wyclif Society, 1913), 165.

[50] *Henry IV Part I*, Act III, Sc.1, lines 147 and 150, cited from *The Riverside Shakespeare*, ed. G. Blakemore Evans (Boston: Houghton Mifflin, 1974).

[51] This was an extract from *Scivias* which Gebeno had used in the *Pentachronon*; it begins 'Sicut in tribus personis est deus . . .'; PL 197, col. 490–491. (I have used the PL edition for all citations both because Pitra's partial edition is usable only with PL, but also for textual reasons. See note 22 above).

Lollards]! (fol. 72r).[52] From our vantage point in history these annotations are full of interclerical, intertextual and interreformist ironies – Hildegard was widely known as *the* antifraternal prophet and Dominicans were not known for their interest in prophecy in any case, but clearly this particular friar found the polemical temptation too great to resist. The most disturbing of the ironies comes up in response to Hildegard's Cologne prophecy of how a future heretical group will lead away women: 'Ecce quomodo lollardi seducent mulieres' [Behold how the Lollards will lead away (or seduce) women] (fol. 57v) says the voice in the margin, which looks very like a contemporary condemnation of the Lollard encouragement of women, both as believers and as teachers. One wonders whether the passage that provoked this, which comes from Hildegard's most excerpted prophecy in medieval England, is echoed in the charge against Margery Kempe that she has come 'to han a-wey owr wyuys fro us & ledyn hem wyth þe'.[53] It would be impossible to know, but if so, we would indeed have an instance of the influence of Hildegard on an English woman writer's life – but it is just the kind of politically incorrect influence no one wants to hear about today.

The general conclusion one draws from an examination of the medieval British reception of Hildegard is that the polemical or interpretive community to which a reader belongs is ultimately more important in determining reader response than the simple fact of the writer's gender. In England at least, Hildegard was lionized, vituperated or simply cited on the basis of the polemics she espoused and the genre she represented much more than she ever was on the basis of her gender.[54]

---

[52] The extract is again from *Scivias*, beginning 'Unde ne inspiratio Sp. Sancti . . .', *PL* 197, col. 492.

[53] *The Book of Margery Kempe*, ed. S. Meech and H.E. Allen, EETS 212 (London: OUP, 1940), 116.

[54] I would like to thank the Social Sciences and Humanities Research Council of Canada for providing me with a Research Time Stipend in 1988–9, and thereby allowing me to do the initial research in England on manuscripts of Hildegard there. I would also like to thank the University of Victoria for research and travel support, and both Barbara Newman and Pamela Jouris for their careful reading and comments. An earlier version of this paper was read at the Society for Canadian Medievalists, Carleton University, Ottawa, June 3–4, 1993, and a later version at the Leeds International Congress in 1994. My biggest debt is to Rosalynn Voaden for her endless patience as a session organizer and an editor during the production process for this paper.

Melting into God the English Way:
Deification in the Middle English Version
of Marguerite Porete's
Mirouer des simples âmes anienties[1]

NICHOLAS WATSON

Now herkeneþ bi mekenesse among ȝou atte bigynnynge of þis, a litel ensample of love of þe world, and undirstandiþ it into divine love. There was in oolde tyme a lady, þe whiche was a kynges douȝter of greet worþinesse and of noble nature, þat dwellide in a straunge lond. So it bifelle þat þis lady herde speke of þe grete curtesie and of þe grete largesse of kyng Alisaundre. And anoon sche lovede him for his noble gentilnesse and for his hiȝe renoun. But þis lady was so fer fro þis grete lord in whom sche hadde leid hir love þat sche myȝte neiþir have him ne se him. Wherfore sche was ful ofte discomfortid: for no love but þis ne suffiside unto hir. And whanne sche sawe þis fer love, to hir so nyȝ, was so fer from hir, sche þouȝte to comforte hirsilf of him bi ymaginacioun of sum figure þat myȝte bere þe liknesse of him þat sche lovede, for whom sche felte hir herte ful ofte wounded. And þanne sche lete peynte an ymage þat presentide þat kynges semblaunce as nyȝ as sche myȝte, whom sche so lovyde. And bi þe siȝt of þis ymage, wiþ oþir usages, sche was eesid; and þus sche apeside hirsilf of þe presentacioun of love þat sche was updrawe.[2]

[1] I thank Bernard McGinn and Michael Sargent for sending me copies of materials which have helped considerably in the writing of this essay, and Rosalynn Voaden for the patience with which she coaxed it out of me. My thinking about Marguerite Porete has been fundamentally influenced by Chantal Phan, with whom I am engaged in a wider study of her thought and writing.
[2] Marguerite Porete, ' "The Mirror of Simple Souls": A Middle English Translation', ed. Marion Doiron, *Archivio italiano per la storia della pietà* 5, ed. Romana Guarnieri (Roma: Edizioni di storia e letteratura, 1968), 241–355, 250.24–251.12; here, and throughout, punctuation has been modified, and both u/v and ampersand normalised.

1. Reading the *Mirouer*: the Long Shadow of a Heresy Trial

When Marguerite Porete refused to testify at her trial and so gave ironic endorsement to a process which, in Paris on June 1st, 1310, made her the only medieval woman writer to be burned for heresy, she inadvertently helped create a conundrum which still bedevils the study of her book, even as it guarantees its notoriety.[3] At the same time as this book, the *Mirouer des simples âmes anienties*, was beginning a distinguished, if anonymous, career – which was to see it translated, by various routes, not only into Middle English but twice each into Latin and Italian – statements from it found a way via the council of Vienne (1311) into the decretal *Ad nostrum qui* from where they were influential in forming medieval and modern notions about the 'heresy of the free spirit'.[4] While the *Mirouer* was being read by monks, nuns and many others (perhaps in one of its dozen or so surviving manuscripts, or of the at least thirty-six circulating in fifteenth-century Italy), bastardised versions of its ideas were wrung under torture out of 'heretics' all over Europe by inquisitors using *Ad nostrum* as a guide to the beliefs they should find. As the work's condemnation at Basle in 1439 implies, such ideas became part of a standard ecclesiastical picture of heretical mysticism, and remain so to this day.[5]

---

[3] For accounts of Porete's trial and condemnation see Robert Lerner, *The Heresy of the Free Spirit in the Later Middle Ages* (Berkeley: University of California Press, 1972), 68–84; Paul Verdeyen, 'Le procès d'inquisition contre Marguerite Porete et Guiard de Cressonessart', *Revue d'Histoire Ecclésiastique* 81 (1986), 47–94, which edits the relevant documents; and Ellen Babinsky, ed. and trans., *Marguerite Porete: 'The Mirror of Simple Souls'*, Classics of Western Spirituality (Mahwah, N.J.: Paulist Press, 1992), 20–6.

[4] The French original was translated into Latin and Middle English, the Italian translations being both derived from this Latin version (L1), while a second Latin translation (L2) by the English Carthusian Richard Methley was made from the Middle English. For the circulation of the text, see Kurt Ruh, ' "Le miroir des simples âmes" der Marguerite Porete', in *Kleine Schriften*, II, ed. Volker Mertens (Berlin: De Gruyter 1984), 212–36. Accounts of the Latin (L1) and French manuscripts are in Paul Verdeyen and Romana Guarnieri, eds., *Marguerite Porete, Le Mirouer des simples ames/Margaretae Porete, Speculum simplicium animarum*, Corpus Christianorum, Continuatio Medievalis 69 (Turnholt: Brepols, 1986), 8–12. For the Italian MSS (and a great deal else), see Romana Guarnieri, 'Il Movimento del libero spirito', *Archivio italiano per la storia della pietà* 4, ed. Romana Guarnieri (Rome: Edizioni di storia e letteratura, 1965), 351–708, e.g. 506–8, 640–2: four survive, three of a version attributing the work to the saintly queen Margaret of Hungary, one of a second version. Insular manuscripts of the Middle English and Methley versions are discussed below. For the relationship between 'Ad nostrum' and the articles by which Porete was condemned (most of which are lost), see Lerner, *Heresy of the Free Spirit*, 81–4, citing Guarnieri, 'Il Movimento', 416.

[5] This account is based on Lerner, *Heresy of the Free Spirit*: e.g., 74, drawing in turn (*inter alia*), on Guarnieri, 'Il Movimento'; Guarnieri, 649–61, prints the Basle condemnation.

Despite this fact, however, the paths of the decretal and the book on which it was based largely diverged for six centuries after 1310 (during which time the *Mirouer* mostly circulated unmolested) before being re-united, in 1946, by Romana Guarnieri.[6] Guarnieri's rediscovery of the authorship of the work (two decades after its first modern publication), with her documentation of its remarkable career, precipitated something of a crisis in the study of medieval spirituality. But any hope that Guarnieri's scholarly *coup* would lead to a balanced appraisal of the *Mirouer*'s place in history has been slow to come to fruition. Indeed, despite contributions from Guarnieri herself, Robert Lerner, Paul Verdeyen, and others, the world of Porete scholarship over the last six decades has looked all too like something out of Umberto Eco's novel about conspiracy theories, *Foucault's Pendulum*. Not only has there been the drama of the manuscript that vanished in the post and has not resurfaced; the mystery of another (probably nonexistent) manuscript, whose whereabouts are claimed to be a secret; the comedy of the pretended discovery of a German version of the text by an academic confidence man; and the sorry circumstance of the cessation from publication of the *Archivio italiano per la storia della pietà* (in which both the French and the English versions had appeared) as Colledge and Walsh's edition of the Insular Latin version was in proof.[7] There have also been more mundane problems, as scholarship relevant to the work progresses in three disciplines (theology, philology and history), in five languages (French, Italian, German, Dutch and English), and often in rare publications (like the *Archivio* itself, which cannot be in more than two hundred copies); as misconceptions formed before Guarnieri's discovery have been given new currency; and as the full complexity of the textual problems presented by the *Mirouer* (and not settled even by

---

[6] Guarnieri published her discovery in the Vatican newspaper, *Osservatore Romano*, on June 16, 1946, where it understandably escaped most scholars' attention for a number of years. Despite the condemnations at Vienne and Basle, the *Mirouer* circulated under the name of Margaret of Hungary and Ruusbroec, influenced the poet Margaret of Navarre (see Jean Dagens, 'Le "Miroir des simples âmes" et Marguerite de Navarre', *La Mystique rhénane: colloque de Strasbourg, 16–19 mai 1961* (Paris: Presses Universitaires de France, 1963), 281–9) and was still being read after 1600. See Guarnieri, 'Il Movimento', for the less positive notice the text also received.

[7] The seventeenth-century manuscript Bourges, Bibliothèque municipale 120, disappeared on its way to the Bibliothèque Nationale in Paris in 1961. The putative German and third French MSS were both announced by M. de Corberon in his journal, *Etudes traditionelles* 341 (1957), 211, when he was in the process of bringing out his aborted edition of the French text (which ran to ch. 33 by 1958, when the journal closed). Extensive search has failed to find a trace of a German text and it is now regarded as a hoax; see Ruh, ' "Le Miroir des simples âmes" '. There seems good reason for suspecting the same is the case with the unapproachable third French manuscript as well. The edition by James Walsh and Edmund Colledge, '*The Cloud of Unknowing* and *The Mirror of Simple Souls* in the Latin Glossed Translations by Richard Methley of Mount Grace Charterhouse', was at press with the *Archivio* in 1968 and survives in a few proof copies but was never issued (I am extremely grateful to Michael Sargent for sending me a copy of this rarity).

Verdeyen and Guarnieri's edition for the *Corpus Christianorum* series) have begun to emerge, making the use of any existing edition or translation a perilous affair.[8] Most interestingly, there have been ideological barriers in the way of understanding, as the present repeats the past by working within the same categories as caused the condemnation of Porete's thought in the first place. If Norman Cohn's pioneering study, *The Pursuit of the Millenium*, was wrong to suppose that inquisitorial views of the 'free spirit' heresy had any basis in fact (an error exposed by Robert Lerner), then the demonisation of Porete by a few scholars may not be less so in its assumption that her condemnation was the result of a valid ecclesiastical process, and so must perforce be justified.[9] With its ambiguous French syntax, use of the dialogue form and playful reliance on paradox, the *Mirouer* is a difficult enough text as it is without our reading it within this unhelpfully constrictive framework. It is fortunate that a body of recent work by Barbara Newman and others (much of it inspired by Peter Dronke's *Women Writers of the Middle Ages*) has begun to try to understand the book in its own terms, achieving what is still a tentative view of its structure and meaning based on empirical observation.[10]

As with the whole, so with the part: the story of the Insular reputation

---

[8] It has been difficult even for specialists to keep things straight; the errors into which generalists have fallen are detailed by Michael Sargent in his paper, 'The Annihilation of Marguerite Porete' (forthcoming). A potential bombshell was dropped in 1988 by Povl Skarup in his 'La langue du *Miroir des simples âmes* attribue a Marguerite Porete', *Studia Neophilologica* 60 (1988), 231–6, which argues that the surviving French text is a Middle French translation or version of an Old French original, thus reopening the whole question of the relative textual authority of the different versions. Skarup's article makes large claims which need to be treated with caution. But if he is even partly right, translations based on the French text will need to be reevaluated, as may even Verdeyen and Guarnieri's edition for the *Corpus Christianorum*, whose editorial policy is to select the Latin reading closest to the French wherever possible and only to invoke the Middle English version when all else fails. As I suggest below (and *pace* Skarup's view of the matter), the Middle English version may have more important textual information than this policy assumes.

[9] See Norman Cohn, *The Pursuit of the Millenium*, 3rd ed. (London: Paladin, 1970), and the comments by Lerner, *Heresy of the Free Spirit*, 1–9. The most doctrinaire accounts of Porete since her rediscovery are those of Edmund Colledge and some of his collaborators (see below), though it should be pointed out that more moderate notes are sounded by other scholars from relatively early on; see, for example, Jean Orcibal, 'Le "Miroir des simples âmes" et la "secte" du Libre Esprit', *Revue de l'histoire des religions* 176 (1969), 35–60.

[10] Peter Dronke, *Women Writers of the Middle Ages: A Critical Study of Texts from Perpetua (+ 203) to Marguerite Porete (+ 1310)* (Cambridge: Cambridge University Press, 1984); Barbara Newman, *From Virile Woman to WomanChrist* (Philadelphia: University of Pennsylvania Press, 1995), 137–67. See also my 'Misrepresenting the Untranslatable: Marguerite Porete and the *Mirouer des simples âmes*', *New Comparison* 12 (1991), 124–37. I have not yet seen Bernard McGinn, ed., *Meister Eckhart and the Beguine Mystics: Hadewijch of Brabant, Mechtild of Magdeburg, Marguerite Porete* (New York: Continuum, 1994); or Amy Hollywood, *The Soul as Virgin Wife: Mechtild of Magdeburg, Marguerite Porete and Meister Eckhart* (South Bend: Notre Dame University Press, 1995).

of the *Mirouer* has been hardly less tortuous. After the work had received its first modern notice from Evelyn Underhill in 1911, a modernisation of the Middle English translation by Clare Kirchberger (based on one of its three manuscripts, Bodley 505) appeared in 1927 under the auspices of the Downside Benedictines, complete with archiepiscopal imprimatur, in the Orchard Spiritual Classics series.[11] This series was part of the rediscovery by a newly reinvigorated English Roman Catholic intelligensia of what they saw as their own pre-Reformation heritage. Kirchberger was hence concerned to stress the learning and piety not only of the (yet unknown) French author (whom, like Underhill, she assumed was a man) but of the translator of the Middle English version: known from the glosses appended to some passages of the text only by the initials M.N., and tentatively identified by Kirchberger as Michael of Northburgh.[12] Kirchberger does discuss the 'dangerous' aspects of the book (which she sees M.N.'s glosses and those of the Latin translator, Richard Methley, as reflecting) and occasionally alters the text to bring it into line with formal orthodoxy. But her work is excellent, and must be sharply distinguished from its reissue as recently as 1981 in a version by Charles Crawford, which preserves little of her learning, besides failing (astonishingly) to notice Guarnieri's discovery, thus only contributing to the confusion that surrounds so much to do with Porete.[13] Marilyn Doiron's critical edition (1968) and article defending the *Mirouer*'s orthodoxy are truer testimonies to her predecessor's acumen.[14]

The most formidable interpreter of the Insular versions of the *Mirouer*, however, is Edmund (formerly Eric) Colledge, who has given much of his

---

[11] Evelyn Underhill, 'The Mirror of Simple Souls', *Fortnightly Review* XCV (1911), 345–54 (a note followed by excerpts). Clare Kirchberger, *The Mirror of Simple Souls* (London: Orchard Books, 1927). Underhill's attention was drawn to the work by the British Musuem's acquisition, in 1910, of the Amherst manuscript, BL Add. 37790, which also contains our sole copy of the Short Text of Julian's *Revelation of Love*; the other manuscripts of the English version (Oxford, Bodley 505 and Cambridge, St John's College, 71) and that of Methley's Latin translation of the English (Cambridge, Pembroke College, 221) were discovered by Hope Emily Allen. Kirchberger (xxiv) also knew of four manuscripts of the main Latin translation and of one of the two Italian versions.

[12] For a study of the revival of Catholic mystics scholarship in twentieth-century England, see my 'The Middle English Mystics', forthcoming in *The Cambridge History of Medieval English Literature: Writing in Medieval Britain, 1066–1547*, ed. David Wallace (Cambridge: Cambridge University Press). Michael of Northburgh, who died in 1361, was the bishop of London and a cofounder of the London Charterhouse; it is worth noting that Kirchberger qualifies her guess as 'scarcely conceivable [. . .] unlikely, but not impossible' (xxxv).

[13] See Charles Crawford, *A Mirror for Simple Souls by an Anonymous Thirteenth-Century French Mystic* (New York: Crossroads, 1981), patently derived from Kirchberger. This volume was reissued in 1991 with Porete's name on the title-page, but otherwise unrevised.

[14] See Marilyn Doiron, 'The Middle English Translation of *Le Mirouer des simples âmes*', in *Dr L. Reypens Album*, Studien en Tekstuitgaven van Ons Geestelijk Erf 16 (Antwerp, 1964), 131–52, and 'Mirror'.

energy since 1950 to studying all aspects of the text and its circulation.[15] Colledge has done more than most for the study of medieval mysticism, and our debt to him is profound. But I think it must be said that his work on Porete has always had an inquisitorial quality to it, and that his desire to expose her as a pernicious influence has been a hindrance to impartial discussion of the subject.[16] From the beginning of his career – writing about the *Mirror* in relation to other adaptations of continental texts, *The Treatise of Perfection of the Sons of God* and *The Chastising of God's*

[15] Of Colledge's impressive output, the most relevant studies here are; as Eric Colledge: 'The Treatise of Perfection of the Sons of God, a Fifteenth-Century English Ruysbroeck Translation', *English Studies* 33 (1952), 49–66; an edition, with Joyce Bazire, *The Chastising of God's Children and The Treatise of Perfection of the Sons of God* (Oxford: Blackwell, 1952); as Edmund Colledge: with Romana Guarnieri, 'The Glosses by M.N. and Richard Methley to *The Mirror of Simple Souls*', *Archivio italiano per la storia della pietà* 5, ed. Romana Guarnieri (Rome: Edizioni di storia e letteratura, 1968), 357–82; 'Meister Eckhart: Studies on his Life and Works', *The Thomist* 42 (1978), 240–58; with J.C. Marler, 'Tractatus Magistri Johannis Gerson De mistica theologia: St Pölten Diözesenarchiv MS 25', *Mediaeval Studies* 41 (1979), 354–86; a translation, with Bernard McGinn, *Meister Eckhart: The Essential Sermons, Commentaries, Treatises and Defense*, Classics of Western Spirituality (Mahwah, N.J.: Paulist Press, 1981); with J.C. Marler, ' "Poverty of the Will": Ruusbroec, Eckhart and *The Mirror of Simple Souls*', in *Jan van Ruusbroec: The Sources, Content and Sequels of his Mysticism*, ed. P. Mommaers and N. De Paepe, Mediaevalia Lovaniensia, series 1, studia 12 (Leuven: Leuven University Press, 1984), 14–47; and 'The Latin *Mirror of Simple Souls*: Margaret Porete's "Ultimate Accolade"?' in *Langland, the Mystics and the Medieval English Religious Tradition: Essays in Honour of S.S. Hussey*, ed. Helen Phillips (Cambridge: D.S. Brewer, 1990), 177–83. See also the items cited in the next two notes, and the unpublished edition, with James Walsh, of Methley's translation of the *Mirror*.

[16] See, most explicitly, a statement published in 1968, in the proceedings of a conference whose supposed purpose was to celebrate Vatican II's *renovatio* of Roman Catholicism, with its call for religious freedom: 'Pour ma part, je crois que Marguerite était une hérétique, qu'elle s'est séparée de l'Eglise volontairement et en connaissance de cause, en niant une bonne partie de sa doctrine' ('La Liberté selon l'esprit', in *La Théologie du renouveau*, ed. Laurence K. Shook and Guy-M. Bertrand, 2 vols. (Montreal: Editions Fides, 1968), 60; also published in English as *The Theology of Renewal*). Colledge does praise religious freedom (72–3), in a passage abhorring the incendiary form which the condemnation of Porete actually took and expressing sympathy for Porete, but the drift of his argument is that her inquisitors, after their own lights, were correct. It should be pointed out, in defence of Colledge here, that the picture of medieval heresy painted in books like Cohn's *Pursuit of the Millenium* must have made it difficult for Catholic medievalists to apply Vatican II's liberalism to their own studies; one must also consider his determination to winnow the chaff of heresy from the wheat of orthodox mysticism in the light of the continuing suspicion, in some Roman Catholic circles, of the whole realm of mystical theology (see my 'Middle English Mystics' for more on this point), a suspicion which could make a writer like Porete an acute embarrassment. On the other hand, it is worth noting that Colledge has devoted quite as much energy to exonerating Eckhart (likewise condemned for heresy) as he has to upholding Porete's condemnation (see Colledge, 'Meister Eckhart'; and Colledge and McGinn, *Meister Eckhart*). For a restatement of the idea of heresy in the light of the Council by an author Colledge often cites, see Karl Rahner, *On Heresy*, translated/extracted (from *Häresien der Zeit*) by W.J. O'Hara, Quaestiones Disputatae (New York: Herder and Herder, 1964).

Children – Colledge tried to show how the English response to radical mysticism and 'liberty of spirit' was carefully orthodox. In his presentation, English adaptors of Continental mystical texts were alive to the possibilities represented by writers like Eckhart and Ruusbroec, and thus far from provincial in their attitudes, but were also always careful to repudiate even the potentially suspect: much as the sounder of the English mystics were in his view careful to distance themselves from the enthusiasm of that insular radical, Richard Rolle.[17] In the case of the English response to Porete, of whose heresy he has never been in doubt, this has involved him in the difficult argument that the Insular versions of the *Mirouer* testify to a full awareness that the work was heretical while also demonstrating the orthodoxy of the translators themselves. Such a position, with which I shall be much concerned later, had the virtue of stopping in its tracks what, in the 1960s, seemed a heady line of speculation about the presence of free spirit heretics in medieval England. But, like Colledge's attempt (in a 1984 article, written with J.C. Marler) to make Porete partly responsible for the views which led her successor, Eckhart, into his own heresy trial, the argument he pursues here seems too speculative and fixated on one issue to be useful.[18] As with the study of Porete's thought, so with that of her insular reception, it is time to cultivate a more fluid sense of how she might actually have been read.

This paper is an attempt to do just this, by analysing M.N.'s translation and glosses as a specifically English response to a work whose original theological and rhetorical context was part familiar, part alien. After sketching the *Mirouer*'s structure and preoccupations (section 2) and describing the Middle English version and its background (sections 3–4, where I will be opposing many of the positions taken by Colledge), I ask what it can tell us about insular assumptions concerning mystical theology towards the end of the Middle Ages – focusing on that most startling of mystical topoi, the idea of *deificatio* (section 5). One manuscript of the

---

[17] For Colledge's fullest account of his picture of medieval English spirituality, see the important introduction to his anthology *The Medieval Mystics of England* (New York: Scribner, 1961), 3–55 (under the name Eric Colledge). For the argument that Hilton and the *Cloud*-author's attitude to Rolle was much more complex than mere disapproval, see my 'Middle English Mystics'.

[18] After opining that 'in at least the first half of the work, Margaret shows a marked inability to control her material and to deal with it in orderly fashion' ('Poverty of the Will', 25), Colledge and Marler suggest that what they consider a late and decadent Eckhart sermon, *Beati pauperes spiritu* (46–7), reveals her baleful influence, and conjecture that this fact is noticed by Ruusbroec in his *XII Beghinen* (14, 43); by implication, Porete is responsible for Eckhart's heresy, although he is depicted as much her intellectual and rhetorical superior. In rethinking Colledge's view of the Middle English *Mirror*, I have to an extent been anticipated by Michael Sargent: 'Le Mirouer des simples âmes and the English Mystical Tradition', in *Abendländische Mystik im Mittelalter: Symposion Kloster Engelberg 1984*, ed. Kurt Ruh (Stuttgart: J.B. Metzler, 1986), 443–65, which reinterprets some of the evidence presented by Colledge and Guarnieri, 'Glosses'.

Mirror (BL Add. 37790) juxtaposes the text with Julian's *Revelation* and the translations of Rolle's *Emendatio vitae* and *Incendium amoris* which Richard Misyn made for the nun Margaret. Yet despite this fact, the book seems not to have circulated among the fifteenth-century women readers of Bridget of Sweden, Catherine of Siena, Elizabeth of Hungary and Mechtild of Hackeborn; at least, it did not circulate as a *woman's book*, if only because it was assumed to be by a man.[19] However, while the *Mirror* is an anomaly in relation to some of the works discussed in this volume, I hope my analysis, by raising questions about the relationship between Insular and Continental religious cultures in the late middle ages, may have implications for the study of these works as well.

Throughout the essay my emphasis is on the English translation not on Methley's Latin version of the text, which may postdate it by more than a century and which I have here relegated to a cursory appendix: a move made necessary by the primitive state of Methley studies and the unpublished status of Colledge and Walsh's edition.[20] The religious culture of Mount Grace charterhouse in the late fifteenth and early sixteenth centuries is an important subject for the study of Insular spirituality, but one which cannot be broached here. My concern is simply to bring to more detailed notice an important and relatively inaccessible Middle English text: a text in which we can observe what happens when the world of the late thirteenth-century beguines meets (albeit in drag) the world of late

---

[19] For the way these writers helped to define a specifically female reading community in fifteenth-century England, see Felicity Riddy, ' "Women Talking About the Things of God": A Late Medieval Subculture', in *Women and Literature in Britain, 1150–1500*, Cambridge Studies in Medieval Literature 17 (Cambridge: Cambridge University Press, 1993), ch. 6. Note that the *Mirror* has not yet surfaced in studies of late medieval lay book ownership, and that, unlike the writings of Mechtild, Bridget and others, we have as yet no evidence of its circulating in extract.

[20] James Hogg has promised a collected edition of Methley's and Norton's works for the year 2000. This may be optimistic, but see his *Mount Grace Charterhouse and Late Medieval English Spirituality* 2, Analecta Cartusiana 64 (Salzburg: Institut für Englische Sprache und Literatur, 1978), a facsimile of MS Cambridge, Trinity College O.2.56, a collection of Methley's works (vol. 1 is unpublished): transcribed in 'A Mystical Diary: The *Refectorium salutis* of Richard Methley of Mount Grace Charterhouse', in *Kartausermystik und -Mystiker: Dritter Internationaler Kongress über die Karthausergeschichte und Spiritualität*, ed. James Hogg, band 1, Analecta Cartusiana 55 (Salzburg: Institut für Anglistik und Amerikanistik, 1981), 201–38; 'The *Scola amoris languidi* of Richard Methley of Mount Grace Charterhouse, transcribed from the Trinity College Cambridge MS. 0.2.56', in *Kartausermystik und -Mystiker*, band 2, 138–65; 'The *Dormitorium dilecti dilecti* of Richard Methley of Mount Grace Charterhouse, transcribed from the Trinity College Cambridge MS. 0.2.56', in *Kartausermystik und -Mystiker*, band 5 (1982), 79–103; and Richard Methley's 'To Hew Heremyte, A Pystyl of Solytary Life Nowadays', in *Miscellanea Cartusiensia* 1, Analecta Cartusiana 31 (Salzburg: Institut für Anglistik und Amerikanistik, 1977), 91–119. See also Michael Sargent (to whom I am indebted for these references and generous provision of copies), 'The Self-Verification of Visionary Phenomena: Richard Methley's *Experimentum veritatis*', in *Kartausermystik und -Mystiker*, band 3, 121–37.

medieval England – where *Ancrene Wisse* is still a prescribed text for the beguines's nearest Insular equivalents, anchoresses, and Rolle, Walter Hilton and the *Cloud*-author are the *dernier cri* in contemplative theology. As we shall see, the results, difficult to interpret as they are, are worth attention.

2. The *Mirouer* in Miniature: Theme and Structure

The *Miroeur* consists of a conversation between female allegorical personages – the chief of whom are Amour, Raison and Ame – on the subject of the life of perfection.[21] The conversation is dominated by the idea that there is a state of soul (called at the beginning the 'septieme estat de grace' [F 1: 3–4], but later identified with the fifth and sixth *estaz*) in which the soul achieves 'le plain de sa parfection par divine fruiction ou païs de vie' (F 1: 4–5):[22] a state involving the annihilation of the soul's creatureliness in an experience which can be described equally in terms of absolute fulfilment and absolute deprivation. Thus after the 'quart estat', of delighted enjoyment of Christ's gifts, and the 'quint estat', in which the soul recognises that her own existence is evil (impeding the totality of God [F 118: 66–92, 94–173]), in the 'siziesme estat' (only experienced briefly in this life) the soul 'sees not herself, through the abyss of her humility, nor God, through the height of his goodness; but God sees himself in her by divine majesty' (see F 118: 175–7).[23] This *becoming God's mirror* means that it can only be said of the soul that she experiences God at all because God is all that exists for and in her – so that the 'she' who experiences is nothing but God experiencing himself in her.[24] Such a soul no longer wills, no longer regrets and no longer loves. In her, as at the end of Bernard of

---

[21] Quotations from the French and Latin (L1) versions are taken from Verdeyen and Guarnieri, *Mirouer/Speculum* (with chapter and line references to the French only). I sometimes quote from the Middle English where I suspect it to be closer to what Porete first wrote than either the French or Latin. Where I offer a modern English translation of a passage instead of French, Latin or Middle English, it is a reconstruction from all three.

[22] Compare L1, 'patria uitae'; ME, 'liif of pees' (250: 18).

[23] The French here is more elaborate than either the L1 or ME, suggesting it has been expanded: compare 'l'Ame ne se voit point, pour quelconque abysme d'umilité que elle ait en elle; ne Dieu, pour quelconque haultiesme bonté qu'il ait' with 'anima se non uidet propter abyssum humilitatis, nec Deum propter sublimitatem bonitatis', 'a soule seeþ not hir nouȝt bi depnesse of mekenesse, ne God bi hiȝeful bounte' (ME 342: 10–11, where 'hir nouȝt' may preserve an original reading).

[24] Note that even this paraphrase of F 118, 175–203 (ME 342, 10–30) involves rationalising formulations which are expressed in even more paradoxical terms, since I have here translated the same verb, 'voir', as both 'see' and 'experience'. The effect of the original is a rhetorical fusion of the soul and God in a series of statements which systematically contradict each other.

Clairvaux's *De diligendo deo*, God is 'all in all' and the soul is melted, fused, drowned in his infinity.[25]

Such a state, in which the whole idea of creaturely existence is attenuated to the point of extinction, can only be described in oxymorons, given the createdness of language itself, its inability to do more than tell loving lies about the infinity of God (F 11: 122–56). Much of the *Mirouer* is thus a quest to find ever more intricate ways of saying the unsayable. Indeed, a tension between the need to describe perfection – a need driven by desire, as the famous exemplum of the princess in love with King Alexander quoted at the opening of this paper makes clear (compare F 1: 16–33) – and resistance to any idea that perfection is describable constitutes the book's main source of dramatic interest. Every attempt Amour makes to describe perfection leaves Raison (whose use of language is literalistic [F 8: 3–4]) in worse state, revealing over and over again her inability to understand Amour, and eventually dying of chronic ineffability, in a comic version of a scene from Richard of St Victor's *Benjamin minor*.[26] Raison's troubles are symptomatic of a problem of understanding which Porete assumes will afflict all her readers except for those who have no need of the book (F 119: 5–29). Raison speaks as the mistress of the institutional church, Saincte Eglise la Petite, with its masses, sermons, prayers and scriptures, and its attitude of fearful obedience to the virtues. Only those who transcend her – who bring about her death in their own souls and attain to Saincte Eglise la Grande – can comprehend a state in which the soul, 'aloone in loue, [. . .] doiþ nouȝt for God, ne sche leueþ noutȝt for God, ne noon hir may teche, ne noon hir may ȝiue ne bineme, ne sche haþ nouȝt of wille' (ME 253: 20–2; compare F 5: 8–14). Hence the book is doomed to be misunderstood by almost everyone: 'Beguines dient que je erre,/ prestres, clers, et Prescheurs,/ Augustins, et Carmes, et les Freres Mineurs,/ pource que j'escri de l'estre de l'affinee Amor' (F 122: 98–103). Indeed the book's lack of comprehensibility – which allows Ame to state, 'Verité denonce a mon cueur/ que je suis d'un seul amee' (F 122: 112–13) – is one of the main arguments it adduces for the validity of its picture of the incomprehensible God.

Colledge, agreeing with Porete's imagined opponents that she is in error, in one place explains the difficulty of her book by stating that, as a matter of prudence, 'le *Miroir* fut écrit dans un code ouvert seulement à quelques-uns, capables de comprendre à cause de leur propre expérience

---

[25] For this image, and possible connections between Bernard and Porete, see Robert Lerner, 'The Image of Mixed Liquids in Late Medieval Thought', *Church History* 40 (1971), 399–401. A general survey of the Continental history of this kind of language is the important article by Jean Pépin, '*Stilla acquae modica multo infusa vino, ferrum ignitum, luce perfusus aer*: L'origine de trois comparaisons familières à la théologie mystique médiévale', *Divinitas* 11 (1967), 331–75 (I am grateful to Bernard McGinn for sending me a copy of this article). For what Bernard says, see below, section 5.

[26] See my 'Misrepresenting the Untranslatable', 128.

ses révélations sur les secrets de la communion des 'âmes liberées' avec Dieu; cependant que, pour la plupart des lecteurs, il devait être considéré comme une collection dévote et inoffensive de piété chrétienne'.[27] In such a view, this 'Bible de "la liberté de l'esprit" ' seeks to conceal its audacious inner meanings under a veil of inoffensive language intended to put unprepared readers, especially those in positions of authority, off the scent. Colledge derives this reading model from a link he sees between Porete's 'two churches' and gnosticism, supporting it from statements in the *Mirouer* about the importance of interpretation; as we shall see, this reading has much to do with his presentation of M.N. as the gull of a text whose falsity the translator fails to grasp. Given the elitism of the *Mirouer*, its invocation of the language of class and its status as a work of what Newman terms 'la mystique cortoise', it would not be surprising if it did function in this way;[28] Amour and Ame are haughty enough to Raison and her colleagues to treat them, one might think, with the contempt such a strategy implies. Yet such a Circean view of Porete fits neither what we know of her life nor her strategies as a writer. Despite her silence before the inquisitors, she made strenuous efforts to publicise her teaching and have it approved. This is clear both from the *approbatio* found in many versions of the text (including the Middle English) and from her continuing to disseminate her book after condemnation by the bishop of Cambrai in 1306, a condemnation which (she would have known) paved the way for her execution as a relapsed heretic four years later. Despite the rough treatment it accords Raison, the *Mirouer* itself is equally anxious to explain itself as clearly as it can, for all its emphasis on ineffability. Far from hiding unorthodox statement behind an innocuous exterior, the book does exactly the opposite: begins from a series of extreme statements, then clarifies them and other problems that arise until the process breaks down under the weight of language's inadequacy. If Raison dies midway through the process (suggesting, as a large structural movement within the text does suggest, a progressive elevation of the *Mirouer*'s subject-matter) she does so only after making real gains. Indeed, the last third or so of the book shows a determined effort to describe Porete's teaching as systematically as possible, analysing the seven states, giving seven 'regars' to help the 'marriz' to better understanding, even writing a fictional account of the death of the heart, as the soul progresses from the fourth to the fifth state. And although we could explain this as Porete's response to her worsening situation, I prefer another explanation: that only as the book neared its end did she fully understand herself what it was saying. Ame, who functions in the book as an authorial persona, has not arrived at the highest states of perfection, can only imagine them and know her imaginings to be false; while Amour and Raison can be understood both as universal principles

---

27 Colledge, 'La Liberté selon l'esprit', 60.
28 See Newman, *From Virile Woman to WomanChrist*, ch. 5.

and as Ame's (Porete's) individual faculties (see 119: 15–22). When Raison responds with dismay to another dazzlingly strange remark of Amour's, this thus partly signifies the author's bafflement as she tries to fashion her image of a God she has never seen (1: 28–33). To view the *Mirouer* as a heretical 'Bible,' or a systematic treatise whose aim is to teach a set of preformulated positions, is to fail to notice its performative aspect as a book whose prime intention is not public but personal: a book which exists to convert even its own author to the life it imagines.[29]

3.   The Middle English *Mirror* and its Context

Turning, now, to the Middle English *Mirror*: the first comment that must be made is that the existence of a close English translation of such a work in its entirety is remarkable in itself. Not only is this the only original beguine work we know of in England (and one of a very few texts which are related in any way to a movement which flourished a scant hundred miles across the Channel from London).[30] The *Mirror* is one of a small number of Middle English religious works which advances speculative theological arguments – and in a mode which does not even pretend to work within the safe confines of pastoral theology – and the single one I can think of (apart from the *Cloud* author's strange rendering of Dionysius's *Theologica mystica*, *Denis Hid Divinite*) that is a translation.[31] Indeed, if we except the very different tradition represented by Lollard writings, only Julian's *Revelation of Love* and passages of *Piers Plowman* are as theologically adventurous. Other apparently similar Continental imports (the passages of Ruusbroec translated in *The Chastising of God's Children*; *The Treatise of Perfection of the Sons of God*; or the heavily

---

[29] This point is made repeatedly, e.g. F 1, 16–33, 96.2–27, 119 etc., all passages about how the book seeks to define a state of life of which its author has no experience and about which she is certainly mistaken. See also F 131–2, the book's dramatic climax, a fictional account of the soul's entry into what seems to be the fifth estate.

[30] The only other Middle English works in this category that I know are *The Doctrine of Hert* (see the edition by Sister Mary Patrick Candon, diss., Fordham University, 1963), a partial translation of the *De doctrina cordis* formerly attributed to Gerard of Liège, which was written for nuns but clearly influenced by beguine spirituality (for the authorship, see G. Hendrix, 'Les *Postilles* de Hugues de Saint-Cher et le traité *De doctrina cordis*', *Recherches de théologie ancienne et médiévale* 47 ([1980], 114–30); and the *vitae* of three beguines found in MS Douce 114, edited by C. Horstmann, 'Prosalegenden: Die Legenden des MS Douce 114', *Anglia* 8 (1885), 102–96, on which see the discussion by P. Deery Kurtz, 'Mary of Oignies, Christine the Marvelous, and Medieval Heresy', *Mystics Quarterly* 14 (1988), 186–96.

[31] See *Denis Hid Divinite and Other Treatises On Contemplative Prayer Related to the Cloud of Unknowing*, ed. Phyllis Hodgson, Early English Text Society, OS 231 (Oxford: Oxford University Press 1955).

adapted Suso version, the *Seven Poyntes of Trewe Love and Everlastynge Wisdame*) are all in a firmly pastoral tradition of practical instruction, for all the (from an Insular view) exotic nature of their imagery.[32] The same is true of *The Doctrine of Hert*, the versions of David of Augsburg's *Formula noviciorum*, the *Prickynge of Love* and the Englishing of the pseudo-Augustinian *Soliloquies*, as it is even of a rare work which does involve detailed theological exploration, *The Orcherd of Syon*.[33] As I argue elsewhere, English vernacular theology is far more intellectually varied than its reputation allows.[34] But the *Mirror* is also more of a curiosity in an insular context than elsewhere.

Just when, where and by whom the translation was made remains for now a mystery. Even Kirchberger did not believe her suggestion that M.N. is Michael of Northburgh, whose death in 1361 would place the work several decades earlier than seems likely.[35] Colledge and others have thus inclined towards her second suggestion (following Underhill), that the *Mirouer* entered England with the Carthusians who came from the Low Countries to help in the setting up of Sheen Abbey around 1414 (an explanation which has also been employed to explain the presence of Mechtild of Hackeborn's *Booke of Gostlye Grace* in fifteenth-century England).[36] All three of the surviving English manuscripts of the *Mirror* are of Carthusian provenance, associated with either Sheen or the London

---

[32] See Bazire and Colledge, *Chastising of God's Children and Treatise of Perfection*; and Carl Horstman, ed., '*Orologium sapientiae*, or The Seven Poyntes of Trewe Wisdom, aus MS Douce 114', *Anglia* 10 (1888), 323–89. See also Michael Sargent, 'Ruusbroec in England: *The Chastizing of God's Children* and Related Works', in *Historia et spiritualitas Cartusiensis: Colloquii quarti internationalis acta*, ed. Jan de Grauwe (Destelbergen, 1983), 303–12; Roger Lovatt, 'Henry Suso and the Medieval Mystical Tradition in England', in *The Medieval Mystical Tradition in England: Papers Read at Dartington Hall, July 1982*, ed. Marion Glasscoe (Exeter: Exeter University Press, 1982), 47–62.

[33] For the *Formula noviciorum* (all but brief passages of the English versions of which are unedited), see Michael G. Sargent, 'Bonaventure English: A Survey of the Middle English Prose Translations of Early Franciscan Literature', in *Spätmittelalterliche geistliche Literatur in der Nationalsprache*, Analecta Cartusiana 106.2 (Salzburg: Institut für Englische Sprache und Literatur, 1984), 145–76; and a more detailed treatment, 'David of Augsburg's *De exterioris et interioris hominis compositione* in Middle English' (forthcoming: I am grateful to Dr Sargent for sending me a copy of this article). See also *The Prickynge of Love*, ed. Harold Kane, 2 vols., Salzburg Studies in English Literature: Elizabethan and Renaissance Studies 92.10 (Salzburg: Institut für Anglistik und Amerikanistik, 1983). For the *Soliloquies*, an important unedited translation from the French (with glosses somewhat after the style of M.N.'s), see R.S. Sturges, 'A Middle English Version of the Pseudo-Augustinian *Soliloquies*', *Manuscripta* 29 (1985), 73–85. *The Orchard of Syon* is discussed in detail by Denise Despres elsewhere in this volume.

[34] See my 'Middle English Mystics'.

[35] The period between 1327 – when Michael of Northburgh visited the Low Countries – and 1361 is early for a wellborn English religious to have felt it necessary to translate a work from French into English, unless to meet the needs of specific, English-speaking readers. Existing copies of the *Mirror* also seem to belong to a later period linguistically.

[36] See Kirchberger, *Mirror*, xxxv.

charterhouse; Methley's translation is also a product of a charterhouse (Mount Grace), as is its sole manuscript. Thus if Kirchberger's second suggestion is correct, the *Mirror* might never have been out of Carthusian hands, but have been produced inhouse sometime after 1415, for the benefit of a circle of M.N.'s colleagues. Such a picture is a possibility, though the only evidence I know in its favour is that M.N.'s method of glossing somewhat resembles Nicholas Love's practice in the much better-known *Mirror of the Blessed Life of Jesus Christ*, finished around 1409 at Mount Grace.[37] People and books travelled between England and the Continent all the time, almost always unrecorded, so a specific incident need not be invoked to explain the arrival of the *Mirouer* (a text we know to have been in Paris, hardly an obscure location for English scholars and students). And the fact that a work only survives in copies associated with Carthusians may testify to the high survival rate of their manuscripts, rather than being a sign that the work originated within the order and did not circulate outside; the short text of Julian's *Revelation* and *The Book of Margery Kempe* both survive entirely in Carthusian copies, but this does not imply that either was connected with the order.

Against the theory of Carthusian provenance are the fact that no Carthusians whose initials are 'M.N.' have surfaced, that Methley has no knowledge of M.N.'s identity, and the differences between the *Mirror* and the other Continental texts we know the Carthusians to have translated – not to mention the difference in translation style. Both the *Orcherd of Syon* and the *Seven Poyntes*, produced respectively at Sheen and Mount Grace, for example, are heavily interventionist translations, showing constant concern to articulate their meaning in a way M.N., despite those glosses, does not. Against dating the translation after 1420 is the rarity of vernacular religious writing of all kinds after the promulgation of Arundel's *Constitutions* in 1409, whose drastic effects on English religious writing I explore elsewhere.[38] While the Carthusians found themselves in a privileged position after 1409, it does seem unlikely that they would have embarked on a translation of a text like the *Mirror* at a time when heresy had become a burning matter and when most kinds of vernacular religious writing were under a degree of suspicion. The very kind of project the *Mirror* is – its experimental and speculative nature – suggests that it was

---

[37] *Nicholas Love's 'Mirror of the Blessed Life of Jesus Christ'*, ed. Michael G. Sargent, Garland Medieval Texts (New York: Garland, 1992). Love's system for flagging his glosses is not the same as M.N.'s, consisting of a marginal 'N' (for 'Nicholas'), which is cancelled at the end of a gloss with 'B' (for 'Bonaventure'), whereas M.N. uses 'M' in the text to indicate the beginning of a gloss, 'N' to indicate its end. Even if the two systems are related, we should bear in mind the possibility that Love has borrowed his from M.N., not vice versa.

[38] See my 'Censorship and Cultural Change in Late Medieval England: Vernacular Theology, The Oxford Translation Debate and Arundel's *Constitutions* of 1409', *Speculum* 70 (1995), 822–64.

part of the explosion of vernacular theological writing between around 1370 and 1410 to which *The Cloud of Unknowing*, Julian's *Revelation* and so much else belongs. As such, it may be a Carthusian product (as has been argued for the *Cloud*) but we should not assume this is so. Under the circumstances, indeed, I do not believe we should assume M.N. need have been a monk, or necessarily a man. In an era which produced Julian of Norwich – who identifies herself as a woman in the first draft of her *Revelation* but never in the revised Long Text – and in which a work like *The Chastising of God's Children* could be produced for nuns, a woman could have been responsible for a translation such as this for the benefit of her colleagues. The eccentricity of the text may imply what to us, with our limited picture of the period, seems an equally eccentric point of origin.

Failing clear external evidence for the translation's origin, purpose and intended circulation, we have to infer what we can from M.N.'s prologue, which begins and ends with information about the translation process itself and reveals a certain amount about the translator's interests. In view of the *Mirror's* inaccessibility, I quote this important prologue *in extenso*, before going on to what must be a laborious analysis of what it can (and cannot) tell us:

This boke, þe whiche is clepid þe Myrour of Symple Soules, I, moost unworþi creature and outcast of all oþire, many ȝeeris goon wrote it out of French into Englisch aftir my lewide kunnynge, in hope þat bi þe grace of God it schulde profite þoo devout soules þat schulden rede it: þis was forsoþe myn entente. But now I am stired to laboure it aȝen newe, for bicause I am enfourmed þat some wordis þerof have be mystake. þerfore, if God wole, I schal declare þo wordis more openli: for þouȝ love declair þo poyntes in þe same booke, it is but schortli spoken, and may be taken oþirwise þan it is iment of hem þat reden it sodeynli, and taken no ferþir hede. þerfore suche wordis to be twies iopened, it wole be þe more of audience, and so bi grace of oure Lord, goode God, it schal þe more profite to þe auditoures. But boþe þe firste tyme and now I have greet drede to do it. For þe boke is of hiȝe divine maters, and of hiȝe goostli felynges, and kernyngli and ful mystili it is spoken. And I am a creature riȝt wrecchid and unable to do eny such werk, poore and nakid of goostli fruytes, derked wiþ synnes and defautes, envirowned and wrapped þerinne ofte tymes, þe whiche bynemeþ me my taast and my cleer siȝt, þat litil I have of goostli undirstondinge and lasse of þe felynges of divine love. Therefore I may seie þe wordis of þe prophete: 'My teeth ben not white to bite of þis breed.' But almyȝti Ihesu God, þat fedeþ þe worm and ȝeveth siȝth to þe blynde and wit to þe unwitti, ȝive me grace of wit and wisdom in alle tymes wiseli to governe mysilf folewynge alwei his wille. And sende me cleer siȝt and trewe undirstondynge wel to do þis werk to his worschip and plesaunce: profite also and encres of grace to goostli lovers þat ben disposed and clepid to þis hiȝe eleccion of þe fredom of soule.

O ȝe þat schule rede þis booke, do ȝe as David seiþ in þe sawtere: *Gustate et videte*, þat is to seie, 'taasteþ and seeþ.' But whi trowe ȝe þat he

seide 'taasteþ' first, er þan he seide 'seeþ'? For first a soule moste taaste er
it have verrey undirstandinge and trewe si3t of goostli werkynges of divine
love. O ful nakid and derk, drie and unsaveri ben þe spekinges and
writynges of þese hi3e goostli felynges of þe love of God to hem þat have
not taasted þe swetnesse þerof! But whanne a soule is touched wiþ grace –
bi whiche sche haþ taasted sumwhat of þe swetnesse of þis divine fruycion,
and bigynneþ to wade, and draweþ þe drau3tes to hir ward – þanne it
savoureþ þe soule so sweteli þat sche desireþ greetli to have of it more and
more, and pursueþ þeraftir. And þanne þe soule is glad and ioieful to heere
and to rede of al þing þat perteyneþ to þese hi3e felinges of þe werkinges of
divine love in norischynge and encresynge her love and devocioun, to þe
wil and plesynge of him þat sche loveþ, God Crist Ihesu. þus sche entriþ
and walkiþ in þe wey of illuminacion, þat sche my3te be cau3t into þe
goostli influences of þe divine werk of God, þere to be drenchid in þe hi3e
floode and unyed to God bi ravyschinge of love bi whiche sche is al oon,
oon spirit wiþ hir spouse.

Therfore to þese soules þat ben disposed to þese hi3e felynges, love haþ
made of him þis boke, in fulfillynge of her desire. And often he leieþ þe
note and þe kernel wiþinne þe schelle unbroke. þis is to seie þat love in þis
boke leieþ to soules þe touches of his divine werkis privili hid undir derk
speche, for þei schulde taaste þe depper þe drau3tes of his love and drinke,
and also to make hem have þe more cleer insi3t in divine undirstandinges to
divine love, and declare it hemsilf. And some poyntes love declareþ in þre
dyverse wises, acordynge to oon [= 'which are in accord as parts of a single
meaning']. Oon maner sche declareþ to actifs, the secunde to contempla-
tifes, and þe þridde to comune peple. But 3it, as I seide afore, it haþ be
mystake of summe persoones þat have red þe booke. Therfore, at suche
places þere me semeth moost nede, I wole write mo wordis þerto in maner
of glose, aftir my symple kynnynge as me semeþ is best. And in þese fewe
places þat I putte yn more þan I fynde writen, I wole bigynne wiþ þe firste
lettre of my name, 'M,' and ende wiþ þis lettre, 'N,' þe firste of my
surname.

The Frensche booke þat I schal write aftir is yvel writen, and in summe
places for defaute of wordis and silables þe reson is aweie. Also, in trans-
latynge of Frensche, summe wordis neden to be chaunged or it wole fare
ungoodli, not acordynge to þe sentence. Wherfore I wole folewe þe sentence acordynge to þe matere, as ny3 as God wole 3ive me grace: obeiynge
me evere to þe correccioun of hooli chirche, preiynge goostli lyvers and
clerkis þat þei wole fowchesaaf to correcte and amende þere þat I do amys.

Heere endiþ þe prolog of þe translatour þat drowe þis booke out of
Frensch into Englisch.[39]

Leaving aside for a moment any biographical information we might be
able to glean, some comments about the style of this passage are in order.
By contrast to parts of the translation, the prose here is sophisticated, the
passage as a whole moving within the conventions of 'academic' prologue

[39] ME 247: 3– 249: 9.

form in its loose vernacular manifestations: giving a statement of intent, developing a lengthy humility topos, describing the form and intention of the work to be translated, and stating at the end the translation policy which has been adopted (one favouring the idiomatic over the literalistic).[40] The patina of Scriptural allusion, as well as the exposition of Psalm 34: 8, also contributes to the total effect, as do the invocation of the 'nut and kernel' topos and what (c.1400) would have been a clearly French vocabulary ('fruycion', 'norischynge', 'unsaveri'), deployed here with self-conscious stylistic panache. Of M.N.'s intellectual leanings I say more later, but we can note here the tendency to be influenced by the language of the treatise itself (the image of wading in sweetness is an example), the focus on interpretative problems, and the understanding that these are already encoded in the work. Especially interesting are allusions to the schema of Bonaventure's *De triplici via* in the language of illumination and union (far from ubiquitous in Middle English),[41] and the absence of any terminology clearly deriving from English writers: Rolle's degrees of love, the *Cloud*-author's 'naked entent unto God,' and Hilton's imagery are none of them represented, although there is some relationship (probably by way of an indirect relationship between the original texts) with the language of the *Seven Poyntes*. Yet despite the lack of specifically Insular religious language, the prologue works in ways which would have been familiar to M.N.'s contemporaries – structured as it is on a common vernacular trope which contrasts a 'nakid and derk, drie and unsaveri' response to the text (from those who approach it with *scientia*, not *sapientia*) with a more fruitful way of reading.[42] If the implication of divine inspiration in the third paragraph has a certain audacity, even this is tempered by M.N.'s use of masculine pronouns for 'love' during this preamble (although love is called 'she' in the *Mirror* itself). In short, for all the peculiarities of the project this prologue announces, and whatever

---

[40] See Roger Ellis, 'The Choices of the Translator in the Late Middle English Period', in *The Medieval Mystical Tradition in England: Papers Read at Dartington Hall, July 1982*, ed. Marion Glasscoe (Exeter: Exeter University Press, 1982), 18–46, especially the examples on 26–7.

[41] A relatively rare use of Bonaventure's schema of purgation, illumination and union in Middle English is found in the unedited *Preisinges of Oure Lord God* in Cambridge University Library MS Add. 3042, ff. 116–25r (c.1400–50). See Valerie Lagorio and Michael G. Sargent, 'English Mystical Writings', chapter XXIII of *A Manual of the Writings In Middle English, 1050–1500*, ed. Albert E. Hartung and J. Burke Severs, 10 vols. published (New Haven: Connecticut Academy of Arts and Sciences 1968–) 9, 3049–137, item 60.

[42] For the contrast between *scientia* and *sapientia* in Middle English religious texts as widely dispersed as *Piers Plowman, The Cloud of Unknowing, The Book of Vices and Virtues* and the *Twelve Poyntes* see, e.g., Anne Savage, '*Piers Plowman*: The Translation of Scripture and Food for the Soul', *English Studies* 74 (1993), 209–21; and James Simpson, 'From Reason to Affective Knowledge: Modes of Thought and Poetic Form in *Piers Plowman*', *Medium Aevum* 55 (1986), 1–23.

writing environment it assumes, it is a thoroughly professional piece of work.

What story, then, does this prologue tell? In leading up to this question, I have stressed M.N.'s professionalism and learning because it has proved tempting, knowing what scholars do know about the *Mirouer*'s history, to think of this translator as something of a naïf, trying with dogged stupidity to justify a text which more informed readers saw at once was beyond redemption. To read the work in these terms is, in effect, Colledge and Guarnieri's method of procedure.[43] Colledge and Guarnieri are especially interested in what the prologue says about M.N.'s need to revise a first version of the translation on the grounds that 'it haþ be mystake of summe persoones þat have red þe booke', and in the translator's decision to meet this problem by providing the reader with glosses. After first suggesting 'that the passages in the text which are glossed by M.N. represent the places, and the topics, which had most offended his critics', they go on (in what is a substantial speculative leap) to offer the theory that 'M.N.'s critics may have been familiar with the list of propositions, now lost, extracted from the *Mirror* which were condemned at Paris in 1310' (and part of which, as we saw, may have gone into the making of *Ad nostrum*).[44] Assuming their theory is correct, they then reconstruct the list by analysing the fourteen glosses where M.N. explains difficult passages of the *Mirror*, treating these glosses as evidence that the work's heretical content was well understood by M.N.'s readers (to whom they consistently refer as 'critics'). In this view, the glosses become proof not only of the translator's own orthodoxy but of the presence of a more informed orthodoxy in M.N.'s environs, to which the translation is a defensive response. Far from being (as it seems) simply a Middle English devotional treatise of an unusually speculative kind, the *Mirror* emerges as yet another site for the battle between orthodoxy and heresy: as evidence for sophisticated Insular awareness of the dangers of some of the religious teachings being disseminated on the Continent.

Even after Sargent's tactful critique a decade ago,[45] Colledge and Guarnieri's argument has continued to hold sway as part of what is still an influential version of relations between English and Continental spiritualities. Yet the argument assumes (without ever stating) a series of events so unlikely that simply to make them explicit is probably enough to refute them. For the argument to be right, we have to accept that M.N., told that a

---

[43] See Colledge and Guarnieri, 'Glosses', 381.

[44] Colledge and Guarnieri, 'Glosses', 358.

[45] Sargent, '*Le Mirouer* and the English Mystical Tradition', 461–2. Sargent notes that Colledge and Guarnieri are influenced by a note which appears in Pembroke 221 (in a hand different from the main hands in the MS), which states '*De Beguardis In clementinis de Religiosis decretalibus. capitulum Ad nostrum*' (f. 40v). But this note was written in the sixteenth century and has no bearing on what M.N. may have known more than a hundred years earlier.

list of errors from a heresy trial in Paris (somehow circulating in England) was drawn from the *Mirror* (which M.N. had already translated in innocence), responded not by suppressing the book but by revising it: defending passages which had been condemned in the most solemn terms and then capping things off by *signing* the result with those initials. Even if the prologue indicated that M.N.'s glosses responded to specific readerly objections (instead of being written 'at suche places þere me semeth moost nede', a clause which emphasises M.N.'s control of the process of glossing), this would be improbable.[46] As the prologue stands, the argument seems to me without any foundation.

What we can conclude about the translator's relationship with the *Mirror* and the context in which it was made is less exciting and more general. First, M.N. was writing for colleagues, not for either institutional superiors or spiritual dependents: so much is clear from the lack of specific direction given readers, and the lack of alarm generated by what might seem the worrying situation of their failure to understand the translation's first draft. (The submission at the end of the prologue to the Church, scholars and lovers of God is a topos, not any sign of panic.) Second, despite this, M.N. thought that the translation might circulate widely, or at least beyond the immediate environs in which it was written: this is why a whole new copy of the translation was thought to be necessary, and why the source of the letters 'M.N.' had to be stated (for readers who did not know the translator personally). Third, and most interesting, the possibility that the *Mirror* was a heretical work with a long, sad history had never (*pace* Colledge and Guarnieri) entered M.N.'s head. Even when one gloss warns 'not oonli þese wordis but also many mo oþir wordis þat ben writen bifore and aftir semen fable or errour or hard to undirstonde' (ME 256: 17–18), we should not take it that the word 'errour' is charged with any awareness of heresy: M.N. would not have used this word if heresy had actually been in question. The 'greet drede' to which M.N. confesses (ME 248: 13–14) has to do with the book's elevated content and nothing more. Far from testifying to the cosmopolitan nature of English religious writers and readers, and their wide knowledge of the controversies surrounding mystical writing on the continent, the *Mirror* evokes an Insular environment which was still firmly local, even parochial, and to which news of such controversies had never penetrated: one in which the work could be read without any of the aura of fear and suspicion with which Colledge and Guarnieri try to surround it.

---

[46] In one gloss, M.N. does say 'I have answerid to þo poyntes þat have be mystake aftir my lewid kunnynge' (ME 305: 26–7); this may suggest that M.N. has a set of 'poyntes' in mind and even that it grew out of heated discussion (hence 'answerid'), but it does not support the idea that these are attached to certain places in the text, let alone that the translator was handed a formal list.

4. The Translation and its Glosses

M.N.'s policy in glossing the translation is to protect the reader from some of the consequences of Porete's provocative tendency to work outwards from gnomic and purposely shocking statements to more readily comprehensible restatements, made in the face of Raison's queries. The account M.N. gives of this tendency in the prologue is the clearest I know. Love 'leieþ þe note and þe kernel wiþinne þe schelle unbroke' not for frivolous reasons but to help readers understand love's message more feelingly, with 'more cleer insi3t in divine undirstandinges', by being made to expound this message ('declare it') themselves (it is much the defence that Boccaccio makes of poetry's obscurity in the *Genealogia deorum gentilium*).[47] Such an understanding of the *Mirror*'s difficulty as purposeful is both perceptive and in part surely correct. On a practical plane, it is this understanding which allows M.N. to gloss the text so little, clustering most of the text's fourteen glosses in the first part of the work (before ch. 70 of the French text), and proceeding after that to add further glosses only where absolutely necessary, on an interestingly *ad hoc* basis. As we shall see, however, on a more abstract level, this understanding also works in another and perhaps less benign way, for it allows M.N. to accept without ever having to confront the large theological and rhetorical gap between Porete's speculative mysticism and M.N.'s very different views.

The interpretation of Porete's language which M.N. urges on us has various aspects to it, but chief among them are two theological points and one point, closely tied to these others, which we might term rhetorical. The first two points are self-consciously made at the outset in a carefully organised gloss, structured like a brief homily, to a passage after the Alexander *exemplum*:

> **M.** 3ee auditoures of þis boke, takeþ kepe of þese wordis þat seiþ, *not we lordis fre of al*. For whiles we ben in þis world we may not be fre of al; þis is to seie, to be departid contynuelli from alle spottes of synne. But whanne a soule is drawe into hirsilf from al outward þing, so þat love werkiþ in þe soule, bi whiche þe soule is for a tyme departid fro al synne and is unyed to God bi unyoun, þanne is þe soule fre, as for þe tyme of unyoun. Ful litel tyme it is; and whanne sche comeþ doun þerfro, þanne is sche þralle, fallynge or fadynge. To þis acordeþ hooli writ, where þat it seiþ: *septies in die cadit iustus*. But þis fallinge of þe ri3twise is more merit þan synne bicause of þe goode wille þat stondiþ unbroken, and is unyed to God. A creature may be enhabited bi grace in fredom forevere. But to stonde

---

47 See Book XIV, ch. xii, 'The Obscurity of Poetry is not Just Cause for Condemning it', translated in *Medieval Literary Theory and Criticism, c.1100–c. 1375: The Commentary Tradition*, ed. A.J. Minnis and A.B. Scott with the assistance of David Wallace (Oxford: Clarendon Press, 1988), 428–31.

contynuelli in fredom wiþoute synne it may not, for þe unstabilte of þe sensualite þat is alwei flittinge. And þerfore it is arettid þe fallynge to þe sensualite, and not to þe hooli soules þat parfiitli have sett her wille in God, bi whiche love makeþ hem fre for þe noblei of his werk. þerfore it may wel be seid: *not we lordis fre of al, but love of him for us.* **N.**

(ME 251: 22–252: 4)

The verb-less sentence which occasions the gloss may be the result of missing words in the text's exemplar, and misrepresents Porete's sense.[48] Be that as it may, M.N.'s theological points are, first, that references to perfection in the *Mirror* only apply to moments of union; second, and perhaps more important, that such moments are brief, and that all statements in the text which appear to imply the contrary are to be interpreted in light of that fact – so that words like 'alwei' do not mean what they seem (ME 283: 6). M.N. is clearly concerned to derive these hermeneutic principles from the text as early as possible and couch them in familiar terms: terms which will bring the spiritual exercise of *The Cloud of Unknowing* to modern readers's minds and which are often assumed to constitute the mainstream Insular position on the issue of deification, though we shall see that the situation is more complex than this. To make these points, M.N. first brings Porete's reference to Proverbs 24: 16 forward from almost the end of the work (see F 103: 4); second, describes the state of *vicissitudo* in which even 'perfect' souls live between sin and sinlessness in terms we could parallel both in Bernard and Rolle; and third, distinguishes between the holiness God attributes to the perfect and the sins they will in practice continue to commit while *in via*, a distinction found in Rolle and (in a different sense but startlingly similar language) Julian of Norwich.[49] It is M.N.'s contention throughout that everything the

---

[48] ME here is a mixture of F and L1 with some missing elements: compare F: 'Et pource nous vous dirons comments Nostre Seigneur n'est mie du tout enfranchi d'Amour, mais Amour l'est de Lui pour nous' (1: 45–7); with L1: 'Et dicemus uobis qualiter dicuntur totaliter liberi. Non nos tamen, sed amor de se pro nobis'; and ME: 'Heere I schal seie ȝou hou not we lordis fre of al but love of him for us' (251: 20–1). F here seems itself an attempt to deal with a difficult original by expansion, while L1 probably offers the closest to what Porete wrote, along the lines of: 'And we will tell you they are (or are said to be) wholly free – not us, though, but Love of Him on our behalf'.

[49] See ch. 11 of Rolle's *Emendatio vitae*, in *Richard Rolle: 'Emendatio vitae' and 'Orationes ad honorem nominis Ihesu'*, ed. Nicholas Watson, Toronto Medieval Latin Texts 21 (Toronto: Pontifical Institute of Mediaeval Studies, 1995), 55–6, an account of the meaning of the word *puritas* itself ultimately dependent on, among other texts, Hugh of Strasbourg's *Compendium theologicae veritatis*. Compare Julian's development of her proposition, 'In every soule that shal be savid is a godly wil that never assentid to synne ne never shal', in the statement 'God shewid that synne shal be no shame but worship to man', as well as her use of the term 'sensualite' (Julian of Norwich, *A Revelation of Love*, ed. Marion Glasscoe [Exeter: Exeter University Press, 1986], 39, 7–8, 20).

Mirror says is in effect an elaboration of these relatively simple ideas: a contention which is far from being self-evidently absurd (Porete often is talking of an *estat* which can only be felt as mere intimation in this life), but which does have the effect of much reducing the intellectual tension and complexity of the original.

The rhetorical point which supports M.N.'s main theological observations involves the status of the words of the *Mirror* themselves, words which readers are repeatedly told they must examine with care to understand. In a gloss on a passage where the soul laments the impossibility of saying anything true about God, concluding 'I wole no more heere gabbe of ʒoure divine goodnesse' (ME 264: 10; compare F, ch. 11), M.N. reveals a belief that parts of the *Mirror* were written in, or at least represent, a state of ecstasy, and thus cannot be taken at their face value:

> **M.** This is an usage in loves daliaunce, bi whiche þese soules have þanne so cleer siʒt in divine biholdynges þat it semeþ hem al þat þei or oþire seien it is but gabbynges as in regarde of þe hiʒe goodnesse and greet noblesse þat is in God, þe whiche may not be knowe for multitude of greetnesse but of himsilf. And þerfore þei þenken þat þei ne oþire kunne ne mowe not seie but al is gabbinge, for as myche as þei may not areche to a poynt of þe fulhede of sooþfastnesse. **N.** (ME 264: 11–17)

By understanding certain passages as transcripts of inspired love-talk, M.N. can explain why the *Mirror* tends so readily towards not just difficulty but (as M.N. would see it) the exaggeration of the literal truth. When the text refers to permanent states, sinless souls and so on, it is not representing mundane reality but should be interpreted as a record of how states of ecstasy actually *feel*. M.N.'s voice here resembles that of Chaucer's narrator in *Troilus and Criseyde* who, as an expert on love from a solely theoretical viewpoint, can stand both outside the events of the poem and in a sense above his deeply unworldly hero despite the elevation of soul Troilus attains. Being reportedly unapt for divine love (as the prologue insists), M.N. presents the persona of a kind of voyeur, whose interest in the *Mirror* is that it offers indirect access to experiences which most can never have. This aestheticised view both of religious experience and of that of reading the *Mirror* is partly a humility topos. But it is of a piece with the prologue's insistence that the *Mirror*'s difficulty is there to be appreciated, and may go far towards explaining M.N.'s fascination with the work.

The translation itself certainly provides plenty of evidence of this fascination, both in its care and length, and in its lapses and willingness to soldier on with material that has not been well understood. The prologue notes that M.N.'s exemplar is less than satisfactory, which may explain some problems with the translation; and if one compares the Middle English with the Continental Latin version as well as the French, it becomes clear that some apparent errors in the English are original readings corrupted in the sole surviving French manuscript.[50] But even when all this is taken into account, problems remain that are caused by M.N.'s struggle with ideas that are simply unfamiliar to Insular traditions and habits of thought. Perhaps the most interesting such problems are those that reveal the translator's failure to identify the Ame, not Amour, with the *Mirror*'s main narratorial standpoint, despite the explicit references early on to 'þis soule þat þis boke lete write' (ME 251: 13): a failure which (besides concealing the fact that the author is a woman) robs the book of much of its subjectivity and drama for the sake of the authority inscribed in the figure of Amour. A clear example (the product of who knows what combination of corruption in the exemplar and guesswork by the translator) is in the rendering of an autobiographical passage, which Porete originally wrote as an account of how the book came into being:

> He, pour Dieu! ne laissons nulles choses de nous ne d'autruy jamais entrer dedans nous, pourquoy il conviengne Dieu de sa bonté hors mectre! Une foiz fut une mendiant creature, qui par long temps quist Dieu en creature, pour veoir se elle luy trouveroit ainsi comme elle le vouloit, et ainsi comme luy mesmes y seroit, se la creature le laissoit oeuvrer ses divines oeuvres en elle, sans empeschement d'elle; et celle nient n'en trouva, mais ainçoys demeura affamee de ce qu'elle demendoit. (F 96: 5–14)

In the English, this has been transformed into the following:

> And if eny seie þus, 'A, for God, lete we noþing of us, ne of noon oþir þan of him, hennesforward be wiþynne us, þat it bihovede God wiþ his bounte out putte,' þis is a beggynge creature, þat bi hir emtinesse sekiþ God in creatures. Soþeli sche fyndeþ þe dede þat sche willeþ and þat sche hirsilf doiþ. But truli sche þat fyndeþ him suffreþ him do his wille and his divine werkis in hir wiþoute werkinge of hir; but oon þat sekiþ and nou3t ne fyndeþ dwelliþ enfamyned of þat þat sche askiþ. (ME 324: 25–31)

By adding a clause at the outset, shifting the tense from past to present and making other changes (though I suspect 'emtinesse' may be right), M.N. transforms Porete's confession into an analysis of a generic state of soul, and thus forces the text back into an instructive paradigm from which it was threatening to escape. What is produced makes marginal sense – better sense than the passage later on where several leaves seem to have gone missing without M.N. noticing[51] – but hardly constitutes a clear piece of religious instruction: I am not clear even whether the 'beggynge creature' here is being held up as an exemplum of proper or (as I suspect) improper behaviour. Space forbids a proper examination of M.N.'s

---

[50] Verdeyen and Guarnieri give examples in the apparatus of their edition, but notice only about a third of the possible examples.
[51] See ME 345: 1–23, which skips from F 122: 52 to 126: 17. The break in sense has been tidied up so far as possible, perhaps by M.N., perhaps by the exemplar.

procedures as a translator, which are generally as crabbedly literal as possible (almost as literal as the Early Version of the Wycliffite Bible), occasionally to the point of failing to make sense even on the level of syntax. But while I would reiterate that this passage displays a lively intelligence, we have to conclude from it, I think, that a view of the text's obscurity as a good thing in itself allowed M.N. – faced with a myriad of unfamiliar terms and concepts, as well as a messy French manuscript – to resign much of the control that Middle English translators of religious works usually exercised. For reasons carefully described in the prologue and glosses and that have to do with the value to the reader of glossing the text for themselves, M.N. thus produced a version of the original that meets lower standards of comprehensibility (even sometimes in terms of syntax) than were usually felt acceptable. Like the glosses themselves, the translation gives us a version of Porete which seldom actively travesties her but which regularly fails to make real, intimate contact with her thought.

5. Conclusion: Melting into God the English Way

Seynt Poul seiþ, 'It is not two spiritis, God and þe soule þat is þus unyed to him, but it is al oon spirit,' in tyme of þis unyon. Wherof, þanne, in þe tyme of þis unyon, schulde hir inwardnesse fele, or sche hirsilf meve? O, sche may not do it, for sche is al molten in God for þe tyme. (ME 313: 32–5)

Sic affici deificari est. Quomodo stilla aquae modica, multo infusa uino, deficere a se tota uidetur [. . .], et quomodo ferrum ignitum et candens igni simillimum fit [. . .], et quomodo solis luce perfusus aer in eamdem transformatur luminis claritatem [. . .], sic omnem tunc in sanctis humanam affectionem quodam ineffabili modo necesse erit a semetipsa liquescere, atque in Dei penitus transfundi uoluntatem. Alioquin quomodo 'omnia in omnibus erit Deus'?[52]

Like Porete herself (as we have seen), M.N. drew on a tradition of thinking about *deificatio* which, while it is both complex and very ancient, in a proximate sense derives from a famous passage of Bernard's *De diligendo deo*, a passage to which M.N.'s gloss above clearly alludes. But whereas M.N. accepted at face value Bernard's view that this experience is reserved for the next life (apart from momentary anticipations of it in this)

---

52 Bernard, *De diligendo deo*, in *Sancti Bernardi opera*, ed. Jean Leclerq, C.H. Talbot and H.M. Rochais, 6 vols. (Paris: Editiones Cistercienses, 1957–77), III, 119–54, X.28: 'To become this is to be deified. Just as a drop of water placed in a great quantity of wine seems to lose itself entirely, and as fiery, glowing iron becomes like a fire, and as air pervaded by the sun's light is transformed into the same luminous clarity, so every human affection in the saints must in an unspeakable manner melt from itself, and the will be wholly transposed into God. Or how else will *God be all in all*?' (I Cor. 15: 28)

Porete was at least prepared to speculate about a state (the fifth) in which the soul has so far been transformed into love that she lives only for such intimations of her coming annihilation (moments in which she is swept up into the sixth *estat*). As Newman points out, in so doing, Porete defied Richard of St Victor's emphasis (in the *De quattuor gradibus violentae charitatis*) on the perfect soul's return to the world to assist her neighbour in the state of *amor insatiabilis*, in favour of a doctrine of passivity which much later came to be identified as quietism.[53] By this means, the *Mirouer* – with the support of Eckhart, and drawing on traditions developed by Hadewijch and Mechtild of Magdeburg – helped to precipitate a heated Continental discussion of the whole relationship between God and the soul as it is experienced in this life: a discussion which, after 1300, at once popularised and threatened to hereticate much of the radical strain of Christian neoplatonism derived from pseudo-Dionysius.

It is this discussion of which the Middle English *Mirror*, I have argued, is unaware. Despite occasional phrases which indicate familiarity with negative mysticism (see especially a gloss which begins 'forȝetel is hir name' [ME 260: 20–9], another place in the text in which the *Cloud of Unknowing* comes to mind), M.N.'s glosses can indeed leave the impression that English spirituality was stuck in a backwater, repeating two-hundred-year-old positions as though there was nothing more to be said, and rejecting the sophisticated speculations present in Continental writings by Porete and others out of an instinctive sense of pragmatism and caution. Even after opposing the view that M.N. is merely a naive reader of Porete, it would be easy, in other words, to use the kind of analysis I have presented here to represent the translator as doing no more than to foreclose reading possibilities, as bringing nothing distinctive to Porete's book. To do this would be to find our way back towards a familiar view of Insular spirituality as endemically conservative and reactive, a view put forward by scholars such as David Knowles, Colledge and (more recently) Wolfgang Riehle.[54] But this is a view which does scant justice to the interest, engagement and curiosity that a translation such as this evinces, for all M.N.'s lack of complete comprehension at certain moments. In ending this paper, I thus want to look at the Middle English *Mirror* in a more general light in order to ask if any other way of looking at it presents itself. Does this text, for all M.N.'s excitement, exemplify no more than a

---

[53] Newman, *From Virile Woman to WomanChrist*, 158–64.

[54] For a discussion of the scholarly topos which assigns to late medieval insular spirituality the qualities of pragmatism and conservatism, see my 'Middle English Mystics'. The topos finds powerful expression in David Knowles's book, *The English Mystical Tradition* (London: Burns and Oates, 1961), in the introduction to Colledge's anthology, *The Medieval Mystics of England*, and in a number of more recent works. For example, Wolfgang Riehle's useful study of mystical imagery, *The Middle English Mystics* (London: Routledge, 1981) is built on a series of contrasts between the 'daring' language of German mysticism and the 'caution' of Insular diffidence about using such language.

stolidly parochial, automatically conservative response to Continental radicalism, whose lack of a sense of danger is a product of incomprehension? Or is there more to be said? To put the same question much more broadly, reaching out into a number of other works which we might see as providing M.N. with a context: is there, here or elsewhere, anything we could legitimately call an 'English way' of melting into God?

The answer I want to give this question is of the 'no and yes' variety. On the one hand, I suggest that English religious writers (including M.N.) have no organised response (whether conservative or otherwise) either to late medieval Continental mysticism *per se* or to the idea of *deificatio* found in Bernard, Richard and other twelfth-century writers, whose thought had been an integral part of Insular spirituality from the late twelfth century on. While it is true that Insular mysticism in general is often as cautious in its approach to deification as M.N. is in particular, it is far from being so in any systematic or self-consistent way – so that there is no necessity to see M.N. as *typical* of Insular spirituality as a whole. On the other hand, however, M.N. does have something important in common with the variegated approaches many English mystical writers take: something which is not easily assimilable to the term 'conservative,' but is indicative, rather, of what needs rather to be seen as simple difference from Continental concerns.

I believe that such differences could be exemplified even in the early English Cistercian writers (Aelred, John and Baldwin of Ford, Gilbert of Hoyland and others) who had immediate links with their Continental colleagues, Bernard and William of St Thierry.[55] But they also emerge much closer to M.N.'s time in two heirs of the Insular Cistercian tradition from the first half of the fourteenth century, Rolle and the Monk of Farne. As I have shown elsewhere, in Rolle's *Expositio super aliquos versos Cantici canticorum* we can trace a remarkable struggle between Bernard and Richard's notion of transitory deification and Rolle's own home-cooked belief that the mystical experience of *canor* (for him the highest experience that is attainable by souls *in via*) can be had continually. Rolle even uses the brevity of the experiences Bernard and Richard describe as

---

[55] I am aware of no study of Insular Cistercian writing *per se*, but an obvious place to start is with the continuations to Bernard's sermons on the Song of Songs by John of Ford and Gilbert of Hoyland, or the treatises of Baldwin of Ford: all of the above now being available in excellent translations. See John of Ford, *Sermons on the Final Verses of the Song of Songs*, tr. Wendy Mary Beckett, with intr. by Hilary Costello, 5 vols. (Kalamazoo, Mich.: Cistercian Publications, 1977–83); Gilbert of Hoyland, *Sermons on the Song of Songs*, tr. Lawrence J. Braceland, 3 vols. (Kalamazoo, Mich.: Cistercian Publications, 1978–81); Baldwin of Ford, *Spiritual Tractates*, tr. David N. Bell, 2 vols. (Kalamazoo, Mich.: Cistercian Publications, 1986). For a more synthetic study which includes several Cistercian writers and texts, see Malcolm Robert Moyes, *Richard Rolle's 'Expositio super novem lectiones mortuorum'*, 2 vols., Salzburg Studies in English Literature (Salzburg: Institut für Anglistik und Amerikanistik 1988), 1:25–67, with much relevant material and bibliography.

evidence that their accounts are of a lower stage of the spiritual life than continual *canor*, which is reserved not for the *perfecti* themselves but that *crème de la crème* of the *vita contemplativa*, the *perfectissimi*. Yet even while doing this he reveals his covert discomfort with the images of fusion and melting used by Bernard, and in effect rewrites the *De diligendo* to make it assert that the soul remains in its own substance, instead of melting into God at all.[56] That is, far from developing a theology which is even in any close sense related to Continental understandings of Bernard, Rolle's thinking proves tangential to the concerns articulated by writers like Porete, Eckhart and Ruusbroec. While he is deeply influenced by Bernard and Richard, his indifference to aspects of their mysticism which to us and Rolle's Continental contemporaries seem fundamental is as great as M.N.'s indifference to some of Porete's principal themes. We find a similar situation in the final parts of the Monk of Farne's *Meditatio ad crucifixum*, an account of the grades of love similarly indebted to Bernard, which becomes (via the English Cistercian hymn, *Dulcis Ihesu memoria* and John Pecham's *Philomena*) a meditation on how love causes the soul to long for death. In an idiosyncratically literalistic reading of this topos, the meditation concludes that Bernard's insistence that the height of love cannot be experienced in this life means that it actually kills those who attain to it: 'Necesse est ergo ut mors interueniat ad hoc quod Deus ab aliquo "ex tota uirtute" diligatur, que sepius ex nimio amore causatur.'[57] This view, which is stoutly maintained over several chapters (with numerous examples), reveals, as with Rolle, at once a deep involvement in the thematics of late medieval affective mysticism as it grew out of Bernard and the Victorines, and a lack of awareness of how affective theology was developing elsewhere in Europe. Once again, this writer is at a tangent to his Continental contemporaries, and reads their common predecessors in a way they would have found eccentric, but hardly 'conservative' – after all, this is as extreme a doctrine of passionate love as anything in Porete. And no more than either Rolle, or M.N., could the Monk of Farne be called 'pragmatic'.

The Monk of Farne and Rolle seem no more aware of each other than they are of their Continental contemporaries; and while M.N. has an advantage over them with respect to the latter, we have seen that the

---

[56] Nicholas Watson, *Richard Rolle and the Invention of Authority*, Cambridge Studies in Medieval Literature 13 (Cambridge: Cambridge University Press, 1991), ch. 6, 147–59. See 'Richard Rolle's Comment on the Canticles', ed. Elizabeth M. Murray (dissertation, Fordham University, 1958). Rolle's picture of eternal felicity is not one of absorption into God but of communal rejoicing in the heavenly court, and he is thus uninterested in imagery that has to do with the dissolving of the boundaries of identity.

[57] 'The Meditations of the Monk of Farne', ed. Hugh Farmer, *Analecta Monastica* 4 (1957), 141–245, ch. 82 (207): 'So death must intervene if a man is to love God with his whole strength, and in fact it often does result from intense love' (*The Monk of Farne*, trans. A Benedictine of Stanbrook (London: Burns and Oates, 1961), 98–9).

Mirror's glosses and prologues do not evoke any particular tradition of Insular mysticism. The isolation of all three writers (and we could add the *Cloud*-author, among others) is suggestive of how unsystematic and local was the development of religious writing in England before the last years of the fourteenth century, how much less organised around a body of themes and arguments than the speculative Continental tradition to which I have compared it. Yet despite their contrasting treatments of mystical union, M.N. does have one large thing in common with Rolle and the Monk of Farne, in which, I suggest, resides something especially characteristic of affective Insular religiosity and in which I would seek to locate a major source of the translator's attitude to Porete's book. Like Rolle and the Monk of Farne, M.N. is deeply interested not in the complex theology surrounding the ineffable experience of mystical union but in the *rhetoric* of ecstasy, in the ability of words to convey the feelings which accompany elevated states of soul, and, on a more theoretical level, on the subjective component of all religious language when it is being used in an affective context. Both the Monk of Farne and Rolle are deeply indebted to an old Insular tradition of meditative writing and religious soliloquy which goes back at least to Anselm's *Orationes sive meditationes* and finds its expression in a remarkable outpouring of meditative writing in Latin and later French and English.[58] The Monk of Farne quotes John Pecham's *Philomena*, a major poetic exercise in devout soliloquy from the late-thirteenth century, while Rolle was clearly familiar with John of Hoveden's slightly earlier poem of the same name: a poem in the broadly Bernardine tradition (much influenced, for example, by the hymn *Dulcis Ihesu memoria*), which has divine love as both its muse and ostensible *auctor*.[59] Indeed, Rolle's doctrine of *canor*, in which the soul attains the highest possible state precisely by singing of its love in a mode inspired by love, can be seen as no more than a conscientiously elevated version of themes which had long been at large within this tradition. In his *Melos amoris*, Rolle presents readers with a literary version of mystical ecstasy, in which the subject matter is not God or the theology of union with God but the literary work and the experience of *canor* with which it corresponds themselves.[60] In Rolle's writing and (in a more diffuse way) in many other works in the affective meditative tradition, souls melt into God not in the

---

[58] For this body of literature, see Thomas H. Bestul, 'Devotional Writing in England between Anselm and Richard Rolle', in *Mysticism Medieval and Modern*, ed. Valerie Lagorio, Salzburg Studies in English Literature, Elizabethan and Renaissance series 92/20 (Salzburg: Institut für Anglistik und Amerikanistik, 1986), 12–28, and 'The *Meditationes* of Alexander of Ashby: An Edition', *Mediaeval Studies* 52 (1990), 24–81. See also many sections of A.G. Rigg, *A History of Anglo-Latin Literature, 1066–1422* (Cambridge: Cambridge University Press, 1992).

[59] See *Johns Hovedens Nachtigallenlied*, ed. Clemens Blume, Hymnologische Beiträge (Leipzig: Reisland, 1930); Rigg, *Anglo-Latin Literature*, 208–15.

[60] See my *Richard Rolle*, ch. 7.

brief moments of ineffable silence Bernard calls *deificatio* but in another way altogether: by talking about it.

I am not suggesting that M.N. knew Rolle's works – although it would hardly be surprising if this was so – and there are clearly a number of more or less specific theological influences on the *Mirror*'s prologue and glosses. But I do think it is likely that M.N.'s understanding of Porete was inflected in an important way by the Insular tradition of passionate religious soliloquy of which Rolle's writings constitute some of the best-known examples. In their emphasis on the difficulty of the *Mirror* – the need to learn to penetrate the veil of its apparently misleading terminology and imagery – as well as on the work's status as a labour of rhapsodic passion, composed by Love, M.N.'s glosses appear to assimilate the work to a mode of writing somewhat akin to that practised by Rolle or by John of Hoveden: to suggest that the work should be read as Rolle invites us to read *Melos amoris*, as an inspired outpouring which resembles *canor*. Like Rolle and many others, M.N. has a tendency to use the same language for aesthetic and devotional experiences. Not only does M.N.'s narratorial persona maintain what I suggested was an aestheticised attitude to the work's subject, seeing the elevated souls it describes as themselves a source of devotion and interest. Both the work and the experience it describes are discussed in terms of the same images of sweetness and taste (see Rolle's experience of *dulcor*); the prologue's use of such imagery to delineate a proper reading of the book (a reading that 'sauoureþ þe soule so sweteli') is directly comparable with one gloss's account of souls who, well on their way to perfection, 'have taasted of þe swete drawtes of hevenli fluences' (ME 258: 25). (This is, of course, not surprising, since – despite M.N.'s own disclaimers in this regard – only such souls are said to be able to understand the book.) For all M.N.'s awareness of the notion of ineffable union with God (though the glosses' version of even this is not, so far as I can see, much like the specifically imageless union described by the *Cloud*-author), the spirituality presupposed in the apparatus to the Middle English *Mirror of Simple Souls* is for the most part of the rhapsodic, essentially talkative kind found in Rolle and the Monk of Farne. As with Rolle's strange rereadings of Bernard and Richard, speculative theological language is here reinterpreted as subjective devotional affect.

We cannot describe M.N. as (in Harold Bloom's term) a 'strong reader' of Porete: there is too much awe, enthusiasm and muddle in the translation, and not enough forceful redirection to be able to claim that Porete's thought has been channelled in any decisively new direction by being reconsidered through Insular categories. But I hope it is clear that those categories have had their effect, and that this is not wholly a negative one whose result is merely to corrall Porete's thought, but does have, however indistinctly, its own agenda. The Middle English *Mirror* may, in a sense, be more valuable to us for what it tells us about Insular ignorance of and indifference to some of the more controversial issues surrounding mystical writing on the Continent than it is for what it says, in a positive way, about Insular spirituality in itself. But for all that, it does need to be seen as part of a broad Insular mode of thinking about the summit of the spiritual life that is not merely less daring or interesting than its Continental equivalent, and which there is still room to learn to understand in its own terms.

Appendix: Richard Methley's Latin Version of the *Mirror*[61]

Cambridge, Pembroke College MS 221 contains heavily glossed Latin translations of *The Cloud of Unknowing* and *The Mirror of Simple Souls* (the latter from M.N.'s English version) by the Mount Grace Carthusian, Richard Methley, author of a number of partly autobiographical treatises on the spiritual life (e.g., the *Scola amoris languidi* and the *Experimentum veritatis*, see note 20).[62] The manuscript is early sixteenth-century and in the hand of the Sheen Carthusian scribe William Derker, but the translation of both works was done in 1491, for Methley's confrère Thurstan Watson, and are clearly intended as a pair. Both works are carefully translated and painstakingly annotated, each section of the text concluding with a series of notes to sentences in the section, distinguished by letters (A, B, C) which also occur at the relevant place in the margins of the sections themselves. The translation of the *Mirror* (which Methley calls *Speculum animarum simplicium*), like that of the *Cloud*, opens with a prologue describing the work – that it was written in French and translated into English, in both cases by people unknown – going on to discuss Methley's divisions of the work and concluding with a sample of his distinctive affective Latin which, as so often, recalls Rolle: 'Ooo, agh, agh, amore langueo, Jhesu gracias ago, dissolui desidero', and so forth. The translation excludes M.N.'s apparatus, but Methley's glosses may have been influenced by them; at any rate, they make a number of the same points. Despite this fact, however, Methley's whole style and reason for glossing is different from M.N.'s, his purpose being much more clearly aimed at reaching a correct understanding of his original in a scholarly sense, and his assumption being that this original is a theological treatise, not a devotional effusion as M.N. sometimes appears to think. Thus, glosses refer the reader to sources, most frequently the Bible or pseudo-Dionysius's *Mystical Theology*, and focus on the choice of imagery, turns

---

61 The information contained in this appendix is mostly taken from Walsh and Colledge unpublished edition (cited in note 7). The few analytic observations made are not, however, theirs.

62 For a useful discussion of Methley, see Karma Lochrie, *Margery Kempe and Translations of the Flesh* (Philadelphia: University of Pennsylvania Press, 1991), ch. 6.

of phrase, difficulties in the Latin (not inconsiderable, given the nature of Methley's source text), in much the style of a literal commentary on a book of the Bible; while, to make the process of glossing easier, Methley divides the text not only into chapters but into groups of chapters he revealingly calls *distincciones*. Unlike the Middle English version, the glosses here continue all through the text, though there is a marked reduction in their number and length after the opening third or so (where the glosses are almost as long as the text) to the end (where many long passages pass unglossed). Methley's view of the original is similar to that of M.N., in that he considers Porete to be referring at all times to moments of union, not permanent states of soul, and takes pains to counter the apparent quietism of certain sections: in both of which endeavours he was doubtless also influenced by the fact he had just been translating the *Cloud*. Walsh and Colledge take the view that Methley's translation has an undertone of awareness that his source text is not orthodox, although I have not been able to agree here, even when his concluding prayers begs, 'Obsecrans vos, eterne deus, si vobis placeat, quod qui hunc legerint librum nec vnum male intelligant verbum'. It is true that one marginal note in the manuscript actually refers the reader to *Ad nostrum*; on the other hand, however, another such note attributes the original work to Ruusbroec and claims him as a Carthusian prior. On the whole, like M.N., Methley seems fascinated but wholly unalarmed by the text.

The Company She Keeps:
Mechtild of Hackeborn in Late-Medieval Devotional Compilations

ROSALYNN VOADEN

In the Prefatory Note to *The Book of Margery Kempe*, Hope Emily Allen wrote in 1940: 'I now believe that the three books of revelations [of Bridget of Sweden, Catherine of Siena and Mechtild of Hackeborn] had been translated into English before Margery Kempe finally succeeded in getting her own revelations recorded (1436–38).'[1] While a considerable amount of scholarship has subsequently been devoted to the dissemination of the works of Bridget and Catherine in medieval England, the Insular presence of Mechtild of Hackeborn has been rather neglected; the little research which has been done tends to be scattered and difficult to track down, often buried in commentaries on other mystics, on female piety, or on women writers.[2] In this chapter, I intend to redress the balance, by assembling evidence testifying to the popularity and circulation of Mechtild's revelations in certain circles in England. My method is

List of Manuscripts

Cambridge, University Library MS Dd. xiv(3)
Downside Abbey MS 26542
London, British Library MS Egerton 2006
London, British Library MS Harley 4012
London, British Library MS Harley 494
London, British Library MS Lansdowne 379
London, British Library MS Sloane 982
London, Lambeth Palace MS 3597 (formerly Coughton Court)
Oxford, Bodleian Library MS Bodley 220

[1] Sanford Brown Meech, ed., *The Book of Margery Kempe* (Oxford: EETS, 1940), lxvii.
[2] For example, there are brief allusions to Mechtild in Hope Emily Allen's Prefatory Notes to *The Book of Margery Kempe*, see n. 1, above; in Alexandra Barratt, ed. *Women's Writing in Middle English* (London: Longman, 1992), 49–60; and in Karma Lochrie, *Margery Kempe and Translations of the Flesh* (Philadelphia: U of Pennsylvania P, 1991). In the edition of *The Booke of Gostlye Grace* by Theresa Halligan (Toronto: Pontifical Institute, 1979) a section of the introduction examines the dissemination of the revelations in England (46–59), as does Norman Blake's brief article, 'Revelations of St Matilda', *Notes and Queries* 218 (1973), 323–5. The most informative general work to date on Mechtild of Hackeborn is Caroline Bynum, 'Women Mystics of the Thirteenth Century: the Case of the Nuns of Helfta', *Jesus as Mother: Studies in the Spirituality of the High*

twofold: one is to gather together information on the reception of Mechtild's revelations, both by making available material which has not previously been published and also by summarizing, or pointing the way to, earlier work in the area. The second is to use that evidence to speculate about the nature and significance of Mechtild's reception in late-medieval England. In so doing I hope also to lend support to Hope Emily Allen's claim that a translation of Mechtild's revelations was in circulation before 1436.

Mechtild of Hackeborn was a nun at the Bendictine/Cistercian convent of Helfta at the end of the thirteenth century. The *Liber specialis gratiae*, the record of her revelations, was written, in Latin, during the last years of Mechtild's life by two other nuns of Helfta, one of whom was Gertrude the Great (c.1256–1302).[3] The book was completed soon after Mechtild's death in 1298 with the addition to the first five parts of a further two, recounting her death, her posthumous visitations to the convent, and describing the community and its remarkable abbess, Gertrude of Hackeborn.[4] It is easy to appreciate why the *Liber* was widely disseminated and well received; it is spiritually orthodox and aesthetically pleasing, and, although lengthy, the vivid descriptions of her visions make compelling reading or listening. The *Liber* circulated extensively on the Continent, both in its original form, and in a shortened form which eliminated the last two parts and abridged the first five.[5] This abridged version was available there by the mid-fourteenth century.[6] Curiously, given Mechtild's orthodoxy and Continental popularity, and the generally positive reception of visionary works, it is not until well over a century after the completion of the work, that is, until the end of the first quarter of the fifteenth century, that there is evidence for its presence in England.[7]

There are four Latin manuscripts of the *Liber* extant in England, although it is important to remember, as Norman Blake points out in his

Middle Ages (Berkeley: U of California P, 1979), 170–262. However, this does not consider the English reception of Mechtild's revelations.

[3] The correct title was *Liber specialis gratiae*, but it was frequently corrupted to *Liber spiritualis gratiae*. On the orthodox nature of the *Liber*, and its consequent popularity with ecclesiastical authority, see Halligan, 55–8.

[4] The abbess was elder sister to Mechtild, and should not be confused with Gertrude the Great. Another Mechtild, also a visionary, Mechtild of Magdeburg (d.1282), was in residence at Helfta for the last ten years of her life, and made a major contribution to this period of intense visionary activity and writing at Helfta.

[5] Dom Ludwig Paquelin, ed., *Revelationes Gertrudianae ac Mechtildianae*, 2 vols. (Paris: H. Oudin, 1875–7), 2: viii–xi. This edition is based on the Guelferbytanus codex, dated 1370; it is from this edition that all references in this chapter to the *Liber* are taken.

[6] Halligan, 8.

[7] In contrast, there was a manuscript of the revelations of Elizabeth of Schönau in England soon after her death in 1165, and Latin copies of the revelations of Bridget of Sweden were in England before her death in 1373. See: Ruth Dean, 'Elizabeth, Abbess of Schönau, and Roger of Ford', *Modern Philology* 41:4 (May 1944), 210; William Patterson Cumming, *The Revelations of Saint Birgitta* (London: EETS, 1929), xxix.

review of Halligan's edition, 'because manuscripts are in England now it does not follow that they were in the fifteenth century'.[8] The most reliable evidence for reception of a Continental work is to be found in translations of that work, or its inclusion in manuscript *compendia* of works in both English and Latin. This chapter first examines the inclusion of excerpts from the *Liber specialis gratiae*, in either Latin or English, in a number of late medieval collections of devotional and spiritual works.[9] Second, it outlines the type of material which was drawn from Mechtild's revelations. Where the manuscript excerpt has not been previously edited, or where it seems useful to have the excerpt readily available, a transcript is given. Third, this chapter considers the other works included along with Mechtild's in the collections, and attempts to draw some conclusions about the distribution network for the *Liber* and its reception. Most notably, it assembles further evidence for a Carthusian/Brigittine connection with the English dissemination of Mechtild's revelations, evidence which makes the case noted by some previous scholars even more compelling.[10]

The Middle English translation of the *Liber* was entitled *The Booke of Gostlye Grace*.[11] Both extant copies are translations of an abridged version of the *Liber*. These copies are Oxford Bodleian Library MS Bodley 220, and British Library MS Egerton 2006. MS Bodley 220 contains *The Booke* (ff. 1r–101r); a treatise on meekness (ff. 101r–103r); a treatise on the vices and virtues attributed to Isidore (ff. 103r–106r); and two English poems (ff. 106r–107r). On f. 103r, at the end of the treatise on meekness, is found *Deo gracias Amen, quod Wellys I. et cetera*. Halligan speculates that this scribal signature could possibly be that of John Wells, a Carthusian monk whose existence is first noted in records in 1425, and who might be the John Wellis whose death is recorded at Hinton Charterhouse in 1445.[12] Although Halligan argues correctly that the name is too common for certain identification, this tentative attribution does raise the possibility that MS Bodley 220 dates from the second quarter of the fifteenth century, and has a Carthusian connection.

---

[8] *Speculum* 56 (1981), 387. The manuscripts are: Oxford, Bodleian Library MS Trinity College 32, Oxford Bodleian Library MS Digby 21, Oxford Bodleian Library MS Laud Misc. 353, and Cambridge, University Library MS Ff. 1. 19. The Laud manuscript is incomplete, containing only two prologues and the first two parts of the work; it was once part of the library of the Cistercians of Erbach. The other manuscripts are all of the abridged version. The Bodleian manuscripts are all mid- to late-fifteenth-century; the Cambridge manuscript is the work of John Whetham of the London Charterhouse, and is dated 1492. For further information on these manuscripts, see Halligan, 8–10.

[9] 'Excerpt' is probably a misleading term, since in most of the cases under discussion the passages purporting to be from Mechtild's work are reworkings, or paraphrases, of passages in the original full text, rather than exact, or sometimes even close, copies.

[10] See Halligan and Blake.

[11] Throughout this paper, *Liber* will refer to the Latin text, and *The Booke* to the Middle English translation.

[12] Halligan, 2 n. 4.

MS Egerton 2006 contains only *The Booke*; this is the version which Halligan chose to edit.[13] The hand is mid-fifteenth-century. On the first flyleaf is written, in a contemporary hand, the names 'Anne warrewyk' and 'R Gloucestre'; the latter is repeated on the last flyleaf. These refer to Richard III and his wife, Anne Warwick.[14] The pair were married in 1471, and died in 1485, which places the latest possible date for the creation of the manuscript as 1485 – more probably 1483, the year of Richard's accession to the throne. Of course, it could well have been written considerably earlier. Halligan suggests that both manuscripts are independent descendants of a common antecedent, one stage, at least, removed from the autograph translation.[15]

Apart from these two complete versions of *The Booke*, excerpts by, or attributed to, Mechtild of Hackeborn appear in a number of devotional works and collections.[16] Perhaps the best known of these is *The Myroure of Oure Ladye*.[17] This work was written for the nuns of Syon Abbey, established in 1415, and provides an English translation of the Brigittine Breviary, Hours, Masses, and Offices, together with an account of how their service was revealed to Bridget of Sweden by an angel, and written in Latin by her confessor, Master Peter. The date of composition of *The Myroure* is uncertain, since the only surviving manuscript is a copy dating from the late-fifteenth or early-sixteenth century.[18] However, it seems probable that the original work was written certainly no earlier than 1408, and most likely between 1420 and 1448.[19]

The Myroure contains two excerpts from the work of Mechtild of Hackeborn, and one reference to 'saynt Mawde' receiving her revelations during divine service.[20] It is impossible to tell whether the excerpts were

[13] For complete manuscript descriptions, see Halligan, 1–6.

[14] For the association of *The Booke* with Cecily, Duchess of York, mother of Richard III, see below. Since women's ownership of compilations containing works by Mechtild is remarked in this chapter, it is worth noting that the names of five women beside Anne Warwick are written in the Egerton manuscript: Bessy Harrimons of Wenlock, seventeenth-century hand, last flyleaf; Elizaabeth Maior, Eneanor ffruene, Eliz M, sixteenth- or seventeenth-century hand, f. 85r; Marget Thorpe[?], fifteenth-century hand, f. 127r (Halligan, 4).

[15] Halligan, 7.

[16] Mechtild's name is variously translated in Middle English as Mawde, Moll, Molte, Molde, Maude, Maute, Matilde.

[17] See John Henry Blunt, ed., *The Myroure of Oure Ladye* (London: EETS, 1873). References to *The Myroure* in this chapter are to this edition.

[18] *Myroure*, vii–viii. However, for more recent information on the date of composition, see Ann Hutchison, 'Devotional Reading in the Monastery and in the Late Medieval Household', *De Cella in Seculum: Religious and Secular Life and Devotion in Late Medieval England*, ed. Michael Sargent (Cambridge: D.S. Brewer, 1989), 220.

[19] Hutchison, 219–20.

[20] *Myroure*, 33. Claiming that a visionary received her or his revelations in some sanctified place, or in the course of devout activity, for example, during the mass, while at prayer, or in church, was a means of establishing the divine origins of those revelations, and thus the credentials of the visionary.

based on the *Liber* or *The Booke*; they are not direct translations or transcriptions of any extant source, and could well have been corrupted during the descent of the work from the autograph copy to the extant manuscript.[21] The first excerpt is found in a section of *The Myroure* which explains the purpose of divine service.

> And hereof ye haue a notable example in saynt Maudes reuelacions, bothe for diuine seruyce, & for howslyng. That lyke as a man agenst a lordes comyng to hym maketh clene his house, & yf he may not for hast, cast out all the vnclennesse before his entrey, then he swepeth yt vp togyther in to a corner & castyth yt oute afterwarde. Ryghte so when a persone goyth to dyuyne seruyce, or to the howslynge, & felyth grudgeyng in conscyence, yf he may not get his gostly father to shryue hym, then he ought to sorowe hys synnes in his harte by contricion, and to shryue him therof to god and so swepe yt in to a corner of hys mynde tyll he may gette hys confessour, and trustynge in oure lordes mercy go to hys seruice or to hys howslyng. (*Myroure*, 38–9)[22]

The second excerpt is in the section of *The Myroure* which deals with each day's service. It is introduced as 'a shorte lesson that oure lorde iesu cryste taughte to saynt Maute, whyche ys ful good to vse in the begyn-nynge, & at the ende, of eche howre of youre seruice' (*Myroure* 276). Following this are three prayers which Christ commended to Mechtild, but without the narrative context of the revelations.[23] All three prayers are given their Latin *incipits* with an English translation in *The Myroure*, whereas in *The Booke* only one, *Deus propicius esto michi peccatori*, is in Latin. This suggests not only that the writer of *The Myroure* used the *Liber* as his source, but that he considered his audience capable of understanding a (very) little more Latin than did the translator of *The Booke*.

The *Speculum devotorum* is a meditative compilation written between 1420 and 1440 for a religious woman, a 'gostly syster', by a monk of the Carthusian order, possibly a member of the community of Sheen. The author's purpose, stated in his preface, was to provide a devotional work for 'sympyl & deuot soulys þat cunne not or lytyl vndirstonde latyn' (2: 5). Among his sources he lists 'the boke þat is called the Orlege of Wysedom' (6),[24] Nicholas of Lyra, various doctors of the Church, and 'sum reuelacyons of approuyd wymmen' (9–10). These approved women are

---

[21] See Hutchison, 220–21, on the textual variations of *The Myroure*.

[22] The equivalent passage in the *Liber* is 2: xiv; in *The Booke* it is 348: 11–350: 6. Note that Halligan's reference for this passage (50 n. 30) actually refers to the second excerpt from Mechtild in the *Myroure* (276–7). The domestic imagery of this passage is echoed in one of Bridget of Sweden's revelations: 'For it is skyll þat the house be clensid into þe whilke þe kynge sall entir . . .' (Roger Ellis, ed., *The Liber Celestis of St Bridget of Sweden* (Oxford: EETS, 1987), 280: 8). Although this may be a coincident commonplace, it could also indicate that Bridget was familiar with Mechtild's revelations.

[23] *Liber*, 3: xxxi–xxxii; *The Booke*, 473: 10–475: 19.

[24] Suso's *Horologium sapientiae*. For the Carthusian role in the dissemination of this work

Bridget of Sweden, Catherine of Siena and Mechtild of Hackeborn.[25] Presumably the approbation refers to the orthodox nature of their visions; in case anyone should be in doubt, the writer includes 'a lytyl techynge how a man or a woman mygth knowe goode vysyonys fro badde aftyr the techynge of oure lorde to a blyssyd vyrgyne that ys called Kateryne of Sene' (13).

The principal reference to Mechtild's work is a description of a vision of a wall of angels reaching from earth to heaven.

> And atte thys gloryus resurreccyon ȝe maye thynke was a gret multytude of angyllys for hyt ys conteyned in a reuelacyon of Seyint Mawte that hir semede sche seygh sueche a multytude of angyllys aboute the sepulcre that fro the erthe vp to the skye they wente aboute oure lorde an hyt hadde be a walle. (316)

The image of a wall of angels is a favourite with Mechtild: *The Booke* also describes a wall of angels at the Annunciation (80); in Mechtild's heart, surrounding a vineyard there (219); and defending Holy Church (331). This particular vision of angels around the sepulchre corresponds to *The Booke*, 181: 2–6.[26]

Mechtild's inclusion in the *Speculum devotorum* and *The Myroure of oure Ladye* is testimony that her revelations were familiar and acceptable enough to the Carthusians and Brigittines to rank alongside Bridget and Catherine. Indeed, it is possible that Mechtild's works were nearly as well known in these circles as those of the other two; the catalogue of the Syon library reveals at least five copies of her revelations among its holdings at various times.[27]

---

see Roger Lovatt, 'The Imitation of Christ in Late Medieval England', *Transactions of the Royal Historical Society* 18 (1968), 113–14.

[25] See Norman Blake, 'Revelations', 324; Halligan, 50. Michael Sargent, in his survey of Middle English devotional writing, states that the author of the *Speculum devotorum* drew heavily on the revelations of both Mechtild of Hackeborn and Bridget of Sweden ('Minor Devotional Writings', *Middle English Prose: a Critical Guide to Major Authors and Genres*, ed. A.S.G. Edwards (New Brunswick: Rutgers UP, 1984), 160). The *Speculum devotorum* has been edited by James Hogg, although so far only two volumes of text have been published; the volumes containing the Introduction and the Conclusion and Glossary are still, hopefully, to come. See *The Speculum Devotorum of an Anonymous Carthusian of Sheen, edited from the Manuscripts Cambridge University Library Gg. 1. 6 and Foyle*, 2 vols. (2+3) (Salzburg: Institut für Anglistik und Amerikanistik, 1973–4). For a brief description of the *Speculum devotorum* see Ian Johnson, 'Prologue and Practice: Middle English Lives of Christ', *The Medieval Translator: the Theory and Practice of Translation in the Middle Ages*, ed. Roger Ellis (Cambridge: D.S. Brewer, 1989), 75–80.

[26] *Liber*, 1: xix.

[27] Roger Ellis lists five copies of Mechtild's revelations; see *Syon Abbey: The Spirituality of the English Bridgettines* (Salzburg: Institut für Anglistik und Amerikanistik, 1984), 120 n. 65. Halligan cites a total of seven: three early sixteenth-century printed versions and four in manuscript form (51:17). See also Blake, 'Revelations', 323, for information on a lost translation of *The Booke*.

The Myroure and *Speculum devotorum* are both full-length works drawing on a number of different sources. Extracts from Mechtild's work, or passages attributed to her are also found in several compilations of devotional writings, for which there was a growing lay audience in the late Middle Ages.[28] One such manuscript is London, British Library MS Harley 4012. This is a collection of religious writing, in English, in both prose and verse. The manuscript was owned by Anne Harling (c.1426–1498), a wealthy Norfolk woman who had some connection with Syon, possibly as a member of a lay confraternity there. It is probable that the manuscript was made for her; internal evidence suggests its composition in the 1460s or 1470s.[29] The passage attributed to Mechtild is the fifth item in the manuscript.[30]

Theis be the wordis that oure Saueoure Ihesu spake to his holy spouse and virgen sent Moll in al thi werkis kepe iii thingis in thi mynde.

Oone is what seruice or benifice or humanite be donne vnto þe of ane creture receue hit soberli & mekeli with gladnes of sprite ʒilding al þankingis to me as hit were donne to me in þe saing with mouþe and herte deo gracias that is to saie to þe my lord god be hit þanking presing or worship. The secunde is whateuer þou doo doo hit with a meke intencion to þe worship and plesans of me, and þink þat I am worcher and ordainer in þe and þou but as an instrument not knawing wheþer þou be thanke worthi or reproue, hatered or loue. ffor all goodnes cometh of mee and not but wrachidnes of thee. The iiide is what adversite sicnes or disses of bodi or of sprit þat falleth vnto þe, gurche not þerwith but committe it to mee as I sufferd hit in pec and thinke þat hit mai not falle soo to þe but bi my will and my sufferance. Com therfor first to me and compleine þe to me of all þi dissease shewing openli þi hert as I were ther with þe present for I am soueren leche and ther mai noon help þe in þi dissease but I or bi mee. Therfor trust faithfulli to me þat I wil help þi dissease and then I shal strengh the to paciens þat whateuer þou suffer hit shalbe frutefull and profitable to þe. Trobill the not ne tare not þi liue striuing therwith as þou woldist ouercom hit bi mistrie or bi awne wit or strengh for þat is

---

[28] Vincent Gillespie discusses the use of spiritual miscellanies by lay audiences in '*Lukynge in haly bukes: Lectio* in some Late Medieval Spiritual Miscellanies', *Analecta Cartusiana*, 106:2 (1984), 1–27. See also Sargent, 155–6.

[29] For a complete description of this manuscript and its ownership, and of Lambeth Palace Library MS 3597 (formerly Coughton Court, Throckmorton Collection) with which it is compared, see Edward Wilson, 'A Middle English Manuscript at Coughton Court, Warwickshire, and British Library MS Harley 4012', *Notes and Queries*, NS. 24 (1977), 295–303. I am grateful to Anne M. Dutton for allowing me to read her article, 'Piety, Politics and Persona: MS Harley 4012 and Anne Harling', forthcoming in *Prestige, Authority and Power: Studies in Later Medieval Manuscripts*, ed. Felicity Riddy (Cambridge: D.S. Brewer).

[30] Listed in P.S. Jolliffe, *A Check-List of Middle English Prose Writings of Spiritual Guidance* (Toronto: Pontifical Institute, 1974), I. 31(b). In all my transcriptions from manuscripts in this chapter, I have silently expanded abbreviations, and regularized punctuation.

presumcion and pride. But aftir þou hast complained þe to me and wrought after discrete counsell and findiste no remedie, wete þou well þenne þat hit is ordained in my prive counsaill þat thou shalt suffire for þe best in ponisshing of thi sinne & clensing of þi saule and if hit be soo greuous too þe þat þou arte were of þi lif and desire to die orels to fall in dispaire þat þe thinkith þat þou arte reprouid me and art not of my chosen saules it com to mee as I haue saide with full trust and hope of help, and thorowe doune at my fete all þi heue burden and worship my passion and think faithfulli þat I of my awne frewill and for thi loue sufferid so gret paines will not suffer þe to be ouer com with my enmy þe deuill. Therfor kepe feith and worche þou mekeli and all shalbe to þe grete profet and merite to thi soule with me and my aungell in þe kingdom of heuyn. That blis he ne graunt þat is endles god in trinite AMEN. (ff. 77v–78r)

This passage is not taken directly from *The Booke*. The image of Christ as a 'leche' appears there (197: 10; *Liber*, 1: xix), as does a much shorter, and more benign, listing of the three points Mechtild should keep in mind (436: 17–437: 6), which is a close translation of the passage in the *Liber*, 3: xiii. The writer is taking some license with his source by amalgamating or expanding various passages. This often occurred with the extracts from Mechtild's revelations; such adaptation was certainly not unusual in devotional collections. Michael Sargent, in his discussion of 'The Seven Points of True Love and Everlasting Wisdom', the Middle English abridgement of Suso's *Horologium sapientiae*, confirms this.

We can see in the popularity of the *Seven Points* from before the end of the fourteenth century the degree of penetration of continental devotional literature in England; but we can also see that this penetration was achieved by adaptation and alteration of the literature for a different audience.[31]

The other items which appear in Harley 4012 are largely of a penitential nature. They include *The Clensyng of Man's Sowle* (ff. 1r–68v); *The Charter of our eritage* (ff. 69r–72r), a tract taken from *Pore Caitif*; *Foure thingis be nedefule* (f. 73r); *The Mirroure of Sinnes* (ff. 73r–77r); *A Tretes of mekenes* (ff. 79r–83r), specifically addressed to a woman ('And þerfor sister' (f. 79v)); *The Artikell of the faith* (ff. 83v–100v); and *The Mirror of St. Edmund* (ff. 101r–103v) [imperfect, ends at c.iii]. Harley 4012 also contains *The Pardon of the Monastery of Shene, whiche is Syon* (ff. 110r–113r), further testimony to the connection of this manuscript and its owner with Syon. Other contents are a devotional poem, a prayer, another penitential treatise and four saints lives: Katherine, Margaret, Anne and Patrick.

The first eight items in the manuscript – which includes the passage from Mechtild – have been listed here in detail because they all also appear in Lambeth Palace MS 3597 (until 1992, Coughton Court

---

[31] Sargent, 161.

(Throckmorton)).[32] This manuscript, dating from the third quarter of the fifteenth century, also belonged at one time to a woman; her name, Elyzbeth, appears on f. 95r. It may even have been made for a woman. As in Harley 4012, the *Treatise of Meekness* is addressed to a woman: 'And therfore systere' (f. 7r). In his comparison of the two manuscripts, Edward Wilson points out that the majority of texts of this treatise are addressed to a brother.[33] He also suggests a common composite volume as ancestor for both manuscripts, pointing out that the Lambeth version of *The Mirror of St Edmund* is noted by Ian Doyle to be the same translation as that in Harley 4012.[34]

The Mechtild passage in Lambeth MS 3597 is attributed to Saint Molte. Apart from minor variants in spelling, it does not differ from the passage in Harley 4012. Wilson states that this extract is extant only in these two manuscripts.[35] As far as I am aware this is the only case of exact duplication of an extract from Mechtild's revelations in any extant manuscripts.

Another compilation of devotional works belonging to a woman and containing a treatise attributed to Mechtild is British Library MS Harley 494. Largely consisting of Marian devotions in both English and Latin, this is a strange little manuscript, only 15.5 x 11cm, consisting of 110 folios; it is obviously designed to be portable for everyday use. It is written in a variety of cramped late-fifteenth-or early-sixteenth century hands, and is very plain and quite amateurish in appearance. On the verso of the first folio is written 'One Anne Bulkeley ATTINET Liber iste'. On the facing page, in fancy box-printing with lacy designs, is written 'domina anna bulk/le' – the edge of the page is torn where the middle 'e' and final 'y' would be. A prayer then starts immediately.

On f. 33v of the manuscript, at the end of a series of prayers for the souls in Purgatory, is written 'And of your charite forget not hym þat daily praieth for yow ye wreche of Syon'. This manuscript is thereby definitely linked with Syon.[36] The links with Mechtild are somewhat more tenuous. Certainly the *incipit* on f. 26r reads 'A short meditacion and informacyon of oure lord Jhesu shewyd to Seynt Maude be reulacon'. However, what follows bears little direct relation to anything Mechtild wrote. There are prayers and blessings for the rituals of life: for rising and sleeping, for

---

[32] The excerpt from Mechtild's revelations is listed in Jolliffe, 1. 31(b). Note that the folio is 6r–v, rather than 5r–v, as Jolliffe has it.

[33] Wilson, 299.

[34] Wilson, 303.

[35] Wilson, 300.

[36] Harley 494 is connected with Syon in yet another fashion. Ian Doyle has pointed out that the main hand of this manuscript appears to be identical with that of the only manuscript of the *Myrrour of Oure Ladye*, Aberdeen UL 134 + Bodley Rawlinson C.941, signed by the writer Robert Taylor for sister Elizabeth Montoun – presumably the Elizabeth Mountayne in the 1518 Syon list. I am most grateful to Dr Doyle both for his information and for his generous response to my query.

hearing and speech, for various hours and for members of the family. This last is personalized, and certainly didn't find its source with Mechtild: 'then begynne þe with yer parentz Symen and Alysoune þat bene dede and then for yer benefactors' (ff. 32v–33r). Neither was Mechtild likely to have been responsible for the prayer for the 'realme of englande' which is found on f. 33r.

It seems that for the scribe, and presumably for Dame Anne Bulkeley, the attribution to 'Seynt Maude' lent authority to some very common prayers. It was Mechtild's name that mattered, rather than what she wrote. This suggests that she was a familiar figure of orthodox piety to those connected with Syon, to the extent that her name became a kind of free-floating talisman, to be attached to various devotions and prayers in order to add to their *gravitas* and signal their orthodoxy. In this, Mechtild joins a long tradition of deliberately spurious attributions; perhaps we should label the passage in Harley 494 'pseudo-Mechtild'.

A much more impressive collection, and one in which the authenticity of the attribution to Mechtild is in no doubt is British Library MS Sloane 982. This manuscript is entitled *Extracta de libris Revelationum Dei Beate Birgitte, principesse Nericie de regno Suecie*. It is a mid- to late-fifteenth-century work: virtually all of the manuscript is in Latin, apart from a brief prayer in English which has a marginal attribution to 'Molte', and a short passage immediately following an excerpt in Latin from the *Liber*. The manuscript consists mainly of a number of extracts from St Bridget's Revelations, arranged as *libelli*, interspersed with material by Anselm, Augustine, Gregory, and Mechtild. Much of the Brigittine material is revelation and prophecy, rather than prayers or devotional material. The passage from Mechtild is also much more vivid and compelling than those extracts from her works usually found in devotional compilations.[37] The inclusion of this more serious, and potentially more controversial, material from the two women visionaries could have been facilitated by the authority of the other writers included in the collection, by the profound nature of the issues addressed by them, and by the fact that most of the manuscript is in Latin. It could well be that this collection was intended for study in a monastery, as opposed to devotional reading for pious gentlewomen. Certainly the readership would have been Latinate, which argues for a higher level of religious education.

The excerpt from the *Liber* begins:

> *Hec sequencia scripta sunt in libro sancte Matildis, virginis devotissime, quem Dominus Noster Jhesus Christus nominavit Librum Spiritualis Gratiae*

---

[37] Roger Ellis discusses the Brigittine extracts in MS Sloane 982 in '*Flores ad fabricandam . . . coronam*: an Investigation into the Uses of the Revelations of St Bridget of Sweden in Fifteenth-Century England', *Medium Aevum* 52 (1983), 172, 176–81.

The extract runs from f. 54r to f. 60v (with the exception of the misplaced folio 57).[38] It consists of a graphic description of the Passion, instruction in the devotion of tears, and then of a fascinating section in which Mechtild is taken by Christ to face judgement before the court of Heaven. She is accused of various sins by all the orders of angels in turn, by the apostles, and martyrs, and so on. Christ then takes her sins on himself and pleads for her before the court. There is also a description of devotion to the holy wounds, and of Christ giving his heart to the sisters at communion.[39]

Immediately following this extract, on f. 60v, is a brief passage in English with the rubric 'How a man may cum to clennesse of sowle'. It begins:

A devowt woman preyede to Criste for clennesse of sowle and crist apperede to hyr and seyde . . .

Jolliffe identifies this item as a variant of a passage from the *Documento* of Catherine of Siena which he has found in ten manuscripts.[40] Only in MS Sloane 982 is a women specified as the subject. It is significant that this extract should appear in conjunction with works by Bridget and Mechtild, and that in this context its association with a woman should be noted. It is, however, difficult to say why this particular item has been translated into English, when virtually all the rest of the manuscript is in Latin.

The only other passage in MS Sloane 982 in English is attributed to Mechtild, although only in a marginal gloss. On f. 133v, in the margin beside the rubric, the same hand has written in the same red ink, 'Molde þe þe[sic] holy nonne'. The passage is as follows:

Here folowes an askynge of our lordes blessynge.
Thy godhede blesse me, þi manhede comforte me, þi pyte noryshe me. Deer lorde make me repentante and reconceyle me. Mak me þi frende þat y may receyf of the alle gyftes whiche oo frende may gyf to a noþer. Mak me þi broþer þat y may haf heuenly heritage with þe, which þou purchesdest with þi precios blode. Mak me þi spouse þat y may haf þi godhed in me.

The first sentence of this fragment corresponds to *The Booke*, 517: 16–18; *Liber*, 4: xxvi. The remainder is similar to *The Booke*, 196: 15–197: 18; *Liber*, 1: xix, especially in its use of the phrase 'heuenly heritage', although

---

[38] Halligan's note on this manuscript is a trifle misleading (47: 1). The Mechtild material is quite distinct from the Brigittine extracts. A passage from St Bridget begins on f. 50v, but then on f. 54r the extract from Mechtild begins, with the clear *incipit* quoted and it is material from Mechtild alone which constitutes this section of the manuscript.

[39] This material corresponds to *The Booke*, 160–80; *Liber*, 1: xviii. The part listing six ways to achieve the devotion of tears (*The Booke*, 164: 10–165: 22; *Liber*, 1: xviii) is also found, also in Latin, in MS Downside Abbey 26542, see below.

[40] Jolliffe, I. 7(a–c).

in the source material Christ is described as a father who shares the heavenly heritage with his child. Here he is described as a brother. As observed earlier, translations often took greater liberties with the source material; unlike the earlier Latin excerpt in the manuscript, which remains close to the *Liber*, here the writer has amalgamated and adjusted passages from the source. It seems likely that the marginal attribution was an afterthought, which supports the argument that it was Mechtild's name which was familiar to the late-medieval audience, rather than her words. The writer could be confident that attaching her name to his patchwork would validate the prayer and, quite literally, convey authority.

Downside Abbey MS 26542 is a devotional compilation written about 1430. Like several of the manuscripts examined in this chapter there is evidence that it was owned by women. On the blank folio at the beginning of the book is written in a late fifteenth-century hand 'This boke is gove to Betryce Chaumbre. And aftir hir decese to sistir Emma Wynter and to sistir denyse caston nonnes of dertforthe for ever'. In the early sixteenth century it is listed in the will of Betryce Chaumbre, bequeathed to the two nuns.[41] On f. 53v a sixteenth-century hand wrote *Ellen haburlaie est verus possessor*, and 'Marye haburley'.[42] The manuscript is described by Colledge and Walsh as 'an anthology of the less popular spiritual classics'.[43] They point out similarities with BL MS Add. 37790, the manuscript containing the short text of Julian of Norwich, and suggest that both collections would have appealed to the same mid-fifteenth-century readership.

Among these less popular spiritual classics in the Downside manuscript are, in English, *The Pricking of Love* (ff. 1r–90r), commonly attributed to Hilton, the complete *Pore Caitif* (ff. 94r–168v), and a treatise attributed to Bernard (ff. 90v–92v). A series of meditations on the Passion, in Latin, includes excerpts from Suso's *Horologium sapientiae* and from Mechtild's *Liber* (ff. 171v–172r).[44] Halligan points out that these two excerpts 'correspond exactly with part of the *Speculum spiritualium*, a collection ascribed to a Carthusian of Sheen early in the fifteenth century'.[45] This information is important both because it testifies to the Carthusian/Sheen-Syon connection, and because of the early dating. The *Speculum spiritualium*, *The Myroure of Oure Ladye*, and the *Speculum devotorum* provide the

---

[41] Felicity Riddy, 'Women Talking About the Things of God: a Late Medieval Subculture', *Women and Literature in Britain, 1150–1500*, ed. Carol Meale (Cambridge: CUP, 1993), 108–9, 119 n. 14. See also Aelred Watkin, 'Some Manuscripts in the Downside Abbey Library', *The Downside Review* 59 (1941), 75–92.

[42] Watkin, 77.

[43] Edmund Colledge and James Walsh, eds., *A Book of Showings to the Anchoress Julian of Norwich*, 2 vols. (Toronto: Pontifical Institute, 1978), 1: 2.

[44] *Liber*, 1: xviii; *The Booke*, 164: 10–174: 5. Part of the Mechtild passage, dealing with the devotion of tears, is also found in the Latin excerpt in Sloane 982.

[45] Halligan, 49.

evidence for the earliest known presence of Mechtild's revelations in England, that is between 1414 and 1430. All three works are strongly connected with Syon or Sheen. It therefore seems valid to assume that the Carthusians were responsible for the introduction of Mechtild's revelations into England, as well as for their translation, and that they played a major part in their dissemination.[46]

The Carthusian connection is also apparent in a rather odd collection of miscellanea, British Library MS Lansdowne 379.[47] Here, among sermons, carols, a recipe to break the stone in a man's body, a tract on the temperaments of the human body, a note of the years elapsed since the creation of the world and a remedy for toothache ('Take a clove of garlycke . . .') is a section of Carthusian prayers and devotional material which includes a reference to Mechtild. The manuscript is a strange patchwork of hands and papers, mostly in manuscript but including a copy of a tract, *Exormatorium curatorum*, printed by Wynkyn de Worde. It is impossible to date with any exactitude; the printed tract is obviously post-1500, but the other sections could have been collected over a number of years, or excised from other collections.

The Carthusian section (ff. 47r–64v) is in a mid- to late-fifteenth-century hand; it is the most damaged of the whole manuscript. It consists largely of meditations on the Passion for each day of the week. The passage from Mechtild comes at the end of a section on the devotion of the Hundred Pater Nosters, and follows a personal testimony to its effectiveness.

> A monk of the chartre hous of london sent in wryting the rule and reuelacion of the forsaid prayer to a brother of the same ordre atte mountgrace in the northe countre. Withyn sevyn dayes after he wrotte to hym to London thankyng god & hym that euer he knewe or herde of þe forsaid prayer for he said by þe merite & grace of þe same prayer he felt more of gostly joye & consolacion in hys saule with hertly loue to God than ever he did afore and beside all this he used to say this lytell prayer folowyng afore euery hundred pater noster which litel prayer the holy virgyn saint mawde used to say thus in latyn. *Domine Jhesu filii dei viui suscipe hanc orationem in amore illo super excellentissimo in quo oram vulneram tui sanctissimi corporis sustinuisti et michi miserere et omnibus peccatoribus cunctis que fidelibus tam viuis quam deffunctis amen.* That ys to say my lorde Jhesucrist þe sone of almyghty god receyve this prayer in

---

[46] Norman Blake makes this suggestion ('Revelations' 325), and is supported by Michael Sargent (150–1). Halligan notes the Carthusian connection but she maintains that although it seems a valid assumption that the Carthusians introduced Mechtild's revelations to England and that the translation was done at Sheen or Syon, this, in fact, remains only 'a possibility' (53).

[47] Halligan identifies this manuscript as a Book of Hours, which it most evidently is not (48).

that most excellent love in the which thou souffred all the woundes of thy most holy body and have mercy of me and all synners and on all crysten people qwyk & dede Amen. (ff. 52r–53r)[48]

Following this the writer delivers an even more enthusiastic and convincing testimonial, and one which offers evidence of the informal spread of Mechtild's name and fame, quite apart from either the *Liber* or *The Booke*. He recounts that the monk from Mount Grace wrote that he had sent copies of the Revelation of the Hundred Pater Nosters and of Mechtild's prayer to his friends. Among these friends was one, a good husbandman of virtue, who said the prayer daily as devoutly as he could. One day, one of his servants smote his ox so sorely that the beast fell to the ground and could not get up. Despite all manner of efforts, nothing availed, 'and so the sely beste lay stille on þe ground withoute eny mete or drynke from Saterday noone till monday after noone'. At this point the goodman, 'full sory of the grete losse of hys oxe for he was but apore man', gave up on human efforts and prayed to God, using the 'aforesaid prayer'. Lo and behold, when he returned to his ox, he found the animal 'hooll, & sounde stondynge on his ffeete etyng his mete . . . lustily' (ff. 53r–54r). This raising of an ox from the (near) dead just may be the most practically effective use of the revelations of Mechtild of Hackeborn in late-medieval England.

The efficacy of the Paternoster is one of the themes of another passage attributed to Mechtild, found in Cambridge University Library MS Dd. xiv. 26(3), although it lacks the homespun drama of the Lansdowne narrative. The manuscript is a collection of devotional works in Latin and English, prose and verse. Jolliffe lists the Mechtild excerpt, which is in English, in the same section of his *Checklist* as Harley 4012 and Lambeth Palace 3597 (formerly Coughton Court), which are virtually identical tracts.[49] However, although the incipits are similar, the content of the Cambridge MS passage is quite different from that of the other two.

Domino dixit sanctam me[chtildem] virginem sue
Owre lorde god seyd to seynt mawde his blessyd virgyne & holy spowse. yf þou wylle be to me a dere doȝter study euer to haue a restfulle herte and pesabulle þoȝtes. And þat þou gyf solas & comforthe to þose þat be in tribulatioun & temptation and alwey study to be meke [&] obedyente ȝa to þe dethe yf nede be. for swythe vertu of mekenesse & obedyens thorowe þe vnyon & vertu of my mekenes and obedyens schalle be more nobulle and acceptabulle then a thowsand vertuse whyche be not do be swythe

---

[48] *The Booke*, 538: 20–539: 9, where the Latin prayer is followed by a short summary in English, rather than a verbatim translation as it is in Lansdowne, 379; *Liber*, 4: lvi. Part of this prayer is also included in the material from Mechtild's revelations which appears in Cambridge University Library MS Dd. xiv. 26; see below.
[49] Jolliffe, I. 31.(a).

intencioun.[50] *Scriptum est enim. Cristus dominus factus est obediens vs ad mortem. Vnde Augustinus cuius exauditur vna oratio obedientis quis decem milia contemptoribus.* Also oure lorde seyde to hyre. I telle þe þer may neuer pore almesman be made more gladde when [he] takys almes as I wythe gladnes & ioy [re]ceyue a prayer þat is ȝouen to me in worchyppe of my wownddes.[51] After v. Pater noster [a]man schulde pray to oure lorde Ihesu cryste þat he take þos prayers in werchyppe of alle his wowndes, and he haue mercy of hym and on alle synfulle bothe quyke and dede.[52] Also oure lorde seyde to hyre, when a man here telle that ony crysten man is dede, yf he say v. pater noster to my wowndys for that sowle þat [es pas]sydde be affeccioun of compassion and [charite] he schalle be partynere of alle þe good dedys that be doun in holy chyrche and specially of þat same that is dede. And in þe day of his passynge he schalle fynde þem redy to þe remedy of his owne sowle.[53] Also [þ]e good aungelle seyd to hyre, thou schalt know for sothe that as oft as a man wythe standys his euille thoȝtes and desyres & purposys a none rether to suffure dethe then wylle to do synne [a] none þat is acceptede to god as þoȝ þat vertu of gostly martyrdome had bene performyd in dede.[54] Also when disciplyne is takyn for þe quyke and for þe dede aungels eneȝou fendys fle and sowlys be relesydde of payne and ther cheynes brokyn. (ff. 45r–46r)[55]

The Latin reference does not appear in either *The Booke* or the *Liber*. The interpolation of Scriptural (Philippians 2: 8) and Augustinian authority, in Latin, functions as a validation of Mechtild's vision, and of its inclusion here. The remainder of the tract is an amalgamation of extracts from Mechtild's revelations. The wording of these extracts is fairly close to that of *The Booke*, although it is not *verbatim*; this suggests that the writer was drawing directly from *The Booke*, rather than relying on his memory. This being so, it is interesting that he felt the need to validate Mechtild's revelations, when he was himself taking considerable editorial license with those same revelations, patching together extracts to form a relatively homogenous homily to suit his own didactic purpose. However, as we have seen, such editorial license was certainly not unusual, and is an indication that for both writers and readers the reputation and the revelations of Mechtild of Hackeborn were familiar and acceptable.

This close examination of nine devotional works and spiritual compilations suggests several conclusions about the reception of Mechtild of Hackeborn in late-medieval England. It is clear that her revelations were popular with the Brigittines and Carthusians; most of the compendia have some connection with Syon, Sheen, or with other charterhouses, and many of them incorporate other works with a Carthusian or Brigittine

[50] *The Booke*, 531: 10–16; *Liber*, 4: xxxiii.
[51] *The Booke*, 538: 5–10; *Liber*, 4: lvi.
[52] *The Booke*, 539: 2–9; *Liber*, 4: lvi.
[53] *The Booke*, 581: 13–20; *Liber*, 5: xix.
[54] *The Booke*, 428: 21–429: 6; *Liber*, 3: viii.
[55] *The Booke*, 381: 22–382: 5; *Liber*, 2: xxvi.

connection, such as those by Bridget of Sweden, Catherine of Siena, Suso, and Walter Hilton.[56] It is most probable that the *Liber* came to England through the offices of these orders, and that *The Booke* was translated by Carthusians. This speculation is borne out by the fact that despite its completion in the early years of the fourteenth century, and its reasonably wide distribution on the Continent by the middle of that century, there is no sign of either the *Liber* or *The Booke* in England before the first quarter of the fifteenth century, just after the foundation of Syon. Although lack of evidence is not conclusive proof that the revelations were not known in England at an earlier date, the apparently complete absence of any mention, anywhere, of either Mechtild or her revelations is a significant indication.

A brief survey of other manuscripts containing excerpts from, or references to, the revelations of Mechtild of Hackeborn provides further support for these conclusions about the Carthusian/Brigittine company Mechtild keeps. Cambridge Peterhouse MS 276 is an early fifteenth-century psalter, also containing prayers and devotional material, which belonged to the Charterhouse of St Anne in Coventry. It identifies two Latin prayers as taken from the revelations of 'blessed Matilde' (ff. 6v–7r); these are followed by a prayer from the revelations of Bridget of Sweden.[57] John Rylands MS 395 is a devotional miscellany dated after 1480. It includes two extracts in Latin from Mechtild's revelations (f. 90r),[58] as well as excerpts from Catherine of Siena, Bridget of Sweden, Richard Rolle and Bonaventure.[59] Dublin, Trinity College MS 277 includes excerpts in Latin from the works of St Bridget, Bonaventure, Richard Rolle and, on f. 16r, two passages from the *Liber specialis gratiae*.[60]

Records of manuscripts left in wills or donated by individuals also demonstrate this tendency of Mechtild's works to travel in convoy with those of Bridget of Sweden, Catherine of Siena, and other Syon favourites, through Carthusian or Brigittine networks. On the last folio (f. 104v) of Cambridge, King's College MS 18 (*S. Ambrosii Quaedam*) is written a list of seven books which were given by Peter, the vicar of Swine in Yorkshire, to the Cistercian nunnery there in the first half of the fifteenth

---

[56] For a discussion of the Carthusian role in the dissemination of devotional works, see Michael Sargent, 'The Transmission by the Carthusians of some Late Medieval Spiritual Writings', *Journal of Ecclesiastical History* 27 (1976), 225–40; see also Lovatt, 97–121.

[57] M.R. James, *A Descriptive Catalogue of the Manuscripts in the Library of Peterhouse* (Cambridge: CUP, 1899), 348–51.

[58] *The Booke*, 251: 3–8; 168: 22–170: 22; *Liber*, 1: xxvi; 1: xviii. The second passage, in which Mechtild appears before the court of Heaven, also appears in MS Sloane 982, see above.

[59] Ian Doyle, 'The Work of a Late Fifteenth-Century Scribe, William Ebesham', *Bulletin of the John Rylands Library* 39 (1956–7), 319; Moses Tyson, 'Hand-List of Additions to the Collection of Latin Manuscripts in the John Rylands Library 1908–1929', *Bulletin of the John Rylands Library* 12 (1928), 604.

[60] *The Booke*, 466: 2–17, 453: 7–12; *Liber*, 3: xxvi, 3: xix. Halligan, 49: 10.

century. One of them is *liber beate Matildis virginis vocatus liber spiritualis gracie*; another is *liber S. Brigide regine cuius prologus sic incipit Inueniet*; a third is a copy of the *Historia scolastica*, a work which the author of the *Speculum devotorum* lists among his sources (9).[61]

In the mid-fifteenth century John Blacman donated books to the Witham Charterhouse, which he later joined. Among these were works by Bridget of Sweden, Catherine of Siena, Elizabeth of Schönau, Richard Rolle and Mechtild of Hackeborn.[62] John Blacman also gave a copy of Suso's *Horologium sapientiae* to the Witham Charterhouse; this manuscript is now Lambeth Palace MS 436.[63] On the third folio marked 10 (52 in modern foliation) there is a notation in the bottom margin referring to chapters in Suso's work, to *divina matildi parta quinta c. 10*, and to *divina Katerina c. 38, 39*.[64]

The earliest known record of *The Booke of Gostlye Grace* is in the 1438 will of Alianora Roos, of York, where it is identified as *Maulde buke* and left to Dame Joan Courtenay, who may have been a nun.[65] Alianora Roos was buried at the Carthusian monastery of Mount Grace, which suggests that she may have had a connection of some sort with the order. Later in the century, a record of the devotional reading which took place in the household of Cecily, Duchess of York includes the works of Bridget of Sweden, Catherine of Siena, Mechtild of Hackeborn, Bonaventure and Hilton.[66] When she died in 1495 she left her *Boke of Saint Matilde*, a life of Catherine of Siena, and a copy of the *Legenda aurea* to her granddaughter – who was also her god-daughter – Brigitte, a nun at Dartford.[67] To another granddaughter, Anne de la Pole, who was prioress at Syon, she

---

[61] M.R. James, *A Descriptive Catalogue of the Manuscripts Other than Oriental in the Library of King's College, Cambridge* (Cambridge: CUP, 1895), 33–5.

[62] Halligan, 50: 15. Norman Blake points out that E. Margaret Thompson, in *The Carthusian Order in England* (London, 1930), lists the copy of Mechtild's revelations in Blacman's donation and also mentions that the London Charterhouse had a copy of a book called *Revelociones Sancte Matildis*. Thompson identifies this as a work of Mechtild of Magdeburg; Blake argues that it is more probably a copy of the *Liber specialis gratiae* (Blake, 'Revelations', 325 n. 11). I agree with Blake.

[63] In the margin at the bottom of f. 1r is written *Liber cartusiae de Witham. orate pro iohanne blacman*.

[64] *The Booke*, 575: 10–580: 18; *Liber*, 5: xviii. This section is a commentary on the Pater Noster.

[65] Halligan, 51: 20; Riddy, 108. Felicity Riddy notes that Alianora Roos also owned a copy of the first part of Hilton's *Scale of Perfection*; this was another writer whose works were often found in conjunction with Mechtild's. For a discussion of Hilton's possible influence on communities of pious gentlewomen, see Riddy, 106–11.

[66] C.A.J. Armstrong, 'The Piety of Cecily, Duchess of York: a Study in Late Mediaeval Culture', *For Hilaire Belloc. Essays in Honour of His 72nd Birthday*, ed. Douglas Woodruff (London: Sheed and Ward, 1942), 79–80. Cecily, Duchess of York, was the mother of Richard III, whose name appears, along with that of his wife Anne of Warwick, on the fly leaf of the Egerton manuscript of *The Booke of Gostlye Grace*; see above.

[67] This is the same house where Beatryce Chaumbre, owner of what is now Downside Abbey MS 26542, was a nun. It seems likely therefore that at least one full-length version

left a book containing Hilton and Bonaventure, and a copy of the revelations of St Bridget.[68] Again, these records of devotional reading and book ownership reveal the frequent conjunction of the works of Mechtild with those of Bridget of Sweden and Catherine of Siena, and of Carthusian or Brigittine houses.

It seems unlikely that anything was known of Mechtild of Hackeborn in England independent of her revelations. However, the manuscript evidence indicates that she was perceived as an orthodox visionary, whose prayers and revelations were worthy of dissemination. Women seem to have been particularly drawn to her work; a large number of the compilations show evidence of female ownership, and records demonstrate a considerable female readership. To return to Hope Emily Allen's assertion cited at the beginning of this chapter: it is almost certain that a translation of Mechtild's revelations was in circulation before Margery Kempe completed the composition of her *Book* in 1436–8. The fact that Alianora Roos left one copy of *Maulde buke* in her will of 1438 argues for the probable existence of other copies of *The Booke of Gostlye Grace of Mechtild of Hackeborn* around this time. In addition, *The Myroure of Oure Ladye*, and the *Speculum devotorum*, with their references to Mechtild, could well have been in circulation, or at least in use at Syon. Margery did not visit Syon until 1434.[69] Although Mechtild is not mentioned by name in *The Book of Margery Kempe*, Margery could well have heard of her, or have heard material read from her revelations during her visit to Syon.

Like a lady, a medieval visionary was known by the company she kept, literary as well as literally. As the devotional works and records examined in this chapter indicate, the revelations of Mechtild of Hackeborn were frequently found in compilations and libraries along with the works of the more widely known Bridget of Sweden and Catherine of Siena. Indeed, she seems to have travelled on their coattails, entering England through the auspices of the Carthusians and their association with Syon.[70] Even more specifically, it can be argued, in part due to the apparent absence of Mechtild's revelations in England during the fourteenth century, that it was the foundation of Syon in 1415 and the establishment of the Brigittines in England which were responsible for the arrival of Mechtild of

---

of Mechtild's revelations and one excerpt were available to the Dartford sisters at the beginning of the sixteenth century.

[68] Riddy, 122 n. 41.

[69] Meech, 245: 31–2.

[70] This raises the interesting questions of how, when and where the initial adoption of Mechtild's revelations by the Carthusians, and her connection with Bridget and Catherine, occurred. The copying and distribution network of the order was impressive, and, as Roger Lovatt points out in relation to the English charterhouses, their libraries showed great uniformity, and were systematically stocked (112). Therefore, once Mechtild had become part of the Carthusian canon, the dissemination of her works was assured.

Hackeborn on alien shores. However, once in England, Mechtild soon found herself at home, a familiar and acceptable visionary whose revelations enhanced many a devotional work, and whose prayers raised the spirits of the faithful and the felled ox of a poor husbandman.

The Visionary and the Canon Lawyers:
Papal and other Revisions to the
Regula Salvatoris of St Bridget of Sweden

ROGER ELLIS

A volume entitled 'Prophets Abroad', some of whose papers were first heard at a seminar entitled 'Continental Holy Women in England',[1] invites consideration, under a number of headings, on the role of prophecy in the Middle Ages, particularly as embodied in women. It could consider ways in which European holy women provided role models for their English counterparts, or, as the seminar did, how these women's revelations were received in and adapted to English situations. It could also consider ways in which, as Jesus had said they would be, prophets were often held in low esteem in their own country, and, by implication, more highly regarded abroad. We might think of the way Margery Kempe's gifts were often recognised more easily by foreigners, German priests, for example, or the Franciscans at Bethlehem, than by her own companions – even if her fame was such as to draw an Englishman to Italy in pursuit of her.[2] Similarly, St Bridget, whose *Regula Salvatoris* is the subject of this paper, may have left Sweden for Rome, in part, as a reaction to the hostility her prophetic mission was provoking in some Swedish circles.[3] Nevertheless, neither St Bridget nor Margery was without friends at home or enemies abroad, and we should not define the prophetic charisma solely in respect of the hostility it can generate among those close to the prophet. In any case, we

---

[1] At the Leeds International Medieval Congress, 4–7 July 1994, session chaired by the editor.

[2] See *The Book of Margery Kempe*, ed. Sanford Brown Meech and Hope Emily Allen, EETS 212 (London: Oxford University Press, 1940), hereafter *Book*, 73:28–33, 75:11–15, 83:21–27, 96:19–33 (chs. 29–30, 33, 40).

[3] On hostility to St Bridget in Sweden, see *Acta et Processus Canonizacionis Beate Birgitte*, ed. Isak Collijn, SFSS Ser. II, Bd. I (Uppsala: Almqvist & Wiksell, 1924–1931), hereafter *A et P*, 313, and brief comment in Roger Ellis, 'The Swedish Woman, the Widow, the Pilgrim and the Prophetess: Images of St Bridget in the Canonization Sermon of Pope Boniface IX', in *Santa Brigida Profeta dei Tempi Nuovi*, Proceedings of the International Study Meeting, Rome 3–7 October 1991 (Rome: Tipografia Vaticana, 1993), 112.

can hardly talk, except during the troubled years of the papal Schism, of a literal 'abroad' in Catholic Europe – other, that is, than in the lands inhabited by the pagans on its eastern, and by Muslims and Orthodox on its southern, borders.

A more fruitful line of enquiry, though one largely unexplored in this paper, might have looked to the prophet's experience of failure to provide the real key to her message. Consider, in particular, how central a part prophecy plays in the life of St Bridget. She is marked out from the beginning by confident declarations of divine purpose (*A et P*, 74–76). She is similarly marked out in adult life, prior to the decisive spiritual experience in which God declares her his spouse, the so-called summoning revelation of 1344–5 (*A et P*, 80–81), by a number of revelations which prophetically anticipate their own fulfilment: one in particular predicts that she will go to the Holy Land, where she will receive revelations about the Passion of Christ (*A et P*, 81). Then, in the aftermath of the summoning revelation, she is told to go to Rome, where she will see Pope and Emperor together and announce God's words to them (*A et P*, 94); and directed to found a new religious Order, whose Rule Christ gives her in a revelation, and whose creation will arrest the decline in religious life. These projects, which interweave in a programme of personal sanctification and ecclesiastical reform, occupy St Bridget for the rest of her life. Periodically reconfirmed by revelation (*A et P*, 95–96, 266), they nevertheless leave her waiting for their fulfilment: understandably anxious that vindication is not immediately forthcoming, even when repeatedly promised in revelations to her (cf. *Liber*, I.xxxii, II.xxviii).[4] And when at length the Pope and Emperor do appear in Rome together (1368), the fulfilment of the earlier prophecy proves short-lived: by 1370 Urban V is back in Avignon. Worse is to follow. In a Bull of 1370, hereafter θ, Urban V approves the Rule of the new Order in a form very different to that in which it was submitted to him for approval, hereafter π.[5] Here, as in the previous episode of the return of the Pope to Rome, a starkly simple question confronts the prophet: can God be in error or change his mind? If not, what purposes are served by this apparent failure of his prophecies?

---

4 *St Birgitta Revelaciones Book I*, ed. Carl-Gustaf Undhagen, SFSS Ser. II, Bd. VII:1 (Uppsala: Almqvist & Wiksell, 1978), 332:23–25 (I.xxxii) and *Revelationes Sancte Birgitte*, impressit Bartholomaeus Ghotan (Lubece, 1492), II.xxviiiA.

5 The versions of the text studied here are edited, with others, in *Den Heliga Birgitta Opera Minora I: Regula Salvatoris*, ed. Sten Eklund, SFSS Ser. II, Bd. VIII:1 (Lund: Berlingska Boktryckeriet, 1975), hereafter Eklund, whose sigla I have followed and whose numbered subsections are given, by number alone, in the body of this paper when the texts are cited or quoted. The following discussion assumes (i) that the version of the Rule presented to Urban V for authentication was an early π manuscript, since π is the earliest stage of the tradition that can be reconstructed with certainty, and (ii) that π represents St Bridget's original reasonably faithfully (see further below 75). As Eklund notes, π was probably based on an earlier version of the text, ω, and possibly it was a copy of this latter that Urban V saw. For further discussion, see Eklund, 21, 64, 72–73.

The contrast, that is, between the certainty of the promised outcome and the uncertainty of its actual realisation lies at the heart of the prophet's role. The domestic and rather trivial version of prophecy, where people approach the prophet for information about their own situations – amply recorded in Margery Kempe's *Book*, as well as in the life and writings of St Bridget – obviously produces its own immediate proof and justification.[6] But the larger exercise of the prophetic function has no such certainty. It follows, as the present paper will argue, that prophecy is more an attitude of mind than a set of propositions, and addresses rather final than intermediate ends.

In the light of the foregoing remarks one can sympathise with the Saint when, aged nearly seventy and now in failing health, she is directed by God, in fulfilment of those earlier promises to her, to prepare herself for a pilgrimage to the Holy Land (*A et P*, 95–96). This time the prophet jibs at carrying out the message, and has to be told that she will be given strength enough for the journey and be brought safe back to Rome.[7] One of the results of that journey was a revelation of the birth of Christ which rapidly became normative in western art.[8] Here, then, though the prophet did not live to see the 'proof' of her vision in its immediate widespread circulation, we may feel justified in reading her story, as her disciples did, as a prophecy fulfilled.[9] Admittedly, the failure of her more ambitious politico-religious projects, including a project, also initiated in the aftermath of the summoning revelation, to bring about an end to the Hundred Years War between England and France, must weigh more heavily in any assessment of the prophet's significance than her success in what one might call the domestic religious sphere.[10] It might also make us wonder whether the prophet is not likely to be better regarded when his or her gifts remain safely within the latter sphere, and when the laity rather than the establishment can take up and make use of those gifts.

The foregoing observations provide a context, and, I hope, a defence,

---

[6] For two examples in the life of St Bridget, see *A et P*, 251–253, 359, the former discussed in Roger Ellis, 'The Divine Message and its Human Agents: St Birgitta and her Editors', *Studies in St Birgitta and the Brigittine Order*, ed. James Hogg, 2 vols., *Analecta Cartusiana*, 35:19 (Salzburg: Universität Salzburg, 1993), 1, 209–211, the latter in Ellis, 'The Swedish Woman', 107 and n. 40.

[7] We might compare Margery Kempe's reluctance as a woman of sixty to go overseas to Germany in response to a command from God to do so (*Book*, 226:30–227:16 [Bk II ch. 2]).

[8] The standard work on this subject is Henrik Cornell, *The Iconography of the Nativity of Christ* (Uppsala: A.-b. Lundequistksa bokhandeln, 1924), 1–45.

[9] On this point see further Eric Colledge, '*Epistola Solitarii ad Reges*: Alphonse of Pecha as Organiser of Birgittine and Urbanist Propaganda', *Mediaeval Studies* 18 (1956), 19–49 *passim*.

[10] Sister Julia Bolton Holloway has similarly stressed the importance of failure in the career of St Bridget in her *Saint Bride and her Book: Birgitta of Sweden's Revelations* (Newburyport, Massachusetts: Focus Texts, 1992), 20.

for the narrow focus of most of this paper: a study of the θ form in which *Regula Salvatoris*, the Brigittine Rule, first received papal approval. Not the least of the ironies of this limited focus, for students of the religious scene in late medieval England, is that the Rule appears not to have survived in this θ form in any manuscript with English connections.[11] Moreover, far fewer copies survive of this than of the other versions of the Rule, and those that do survive normally accompany a copy of the Rule in one of the other versions.[12] We can readily infer that, whereas the other versions of the Rule were used routinely as part of the Order's day-to-day running, the θ form of the Rule was preserved only as part of a complete record of papal dealings with the Order – so, for instance, in the important Vadstena manuscript, the *Liber Priuilegiorum Monasterii Vadstenensis* (Eklund, 50, 64). Urban VI's reinstatement of π, in a modified version, ε, in 1378 (Eklund, 25–26), meant that thereafter the day-to-day running of the Order would depend not on θ but on π or on ε or on other versions deriving from π or ε or a combination of both, varying according to local preference.

We have, nevertheless, a good reason for concentrating on θ, short-lived as it was. Whenever we talk about holy women in the Middle Ages, we have sooner or later to consider their relation to male religious authority: to the priests who examined and authorised women who left no written record of God's dealings with them (for example, St Marie of Oignies); to the priests who examined and/or produced such written records.[13] With striking and notable exceptions, a priest, when publishing the text of a woman's words, may be adapting those words to the expectations and understandings of an establishment whose approval he must secure on her behalf, even as he claims, and is sometimes directed, to publish the woman's words, since they are divinely inspired, unchanged.[14] And since the visionary is usually well aware of the claims of the establishment upon

---

[11] Nor is it listed in the *Catalogue of the Library of Syon Monastery Isleworth*, ed. Mary Bateson (Cambridge: Cambridge University Press, 1898).

[12] In four instances, the copy of the θ version accompanies a copy of the ε version of the Rule; in one instance, a copy of the π version; and, in one instance, a copy of the φ version (the manuscripts designated B^e, D^e, I^e, M^f, U^f, and p: Eklund, 11–12, 15–16).

[13] Of course, in female religious communities female authority may also have played a part in the matter of authorisation: on this point see, for example, Caroline Walker Bynum, *Jesus as Mother: Studies in the Spirituality of the High Middle Ages* (Berkeley: University of California Press, 1982), ch. v. Even in such contexts, though, the ultimate power to prove the visionary's gifts remains with the male religious on whom the nuns depend for the sacraments.

[14] So, for example, the scribes of St Bridget's revelations: on this point see Ellis, 'The Divine Message', 209–211. A ready parallel can also be drawn, as it was by St Bridget herself, who used the evangelists in support of her position (*art. cit.* 211), with medieval translators' professions of fidelity to the texts they were translating even as they often subjected them to wholesale revision; on this point see *The Medieval Translator*, ed. Roger Ellis *et al.*, 5 vols. so far (Cambridge: D.S. Brewer, 1989; London: Centre for Medieval Studies, Queen Mary and Westfield College, 1991; *New Comparison* 12, 1993; Exeter:

her, she may have undertaken a sort of self-censorship even before presenting her work for authorisation.

This 'translation' of an original voice can render its recovery intensely problematical. We can determine the role of the priest-scribes in the finished product only when we have extant copies of the visionary's original work, often in the vernacular, to set against their version of it, usually in Latin. Traces of written sources in the writings an unlettered visionary dictated to a priest-scribe might point to the latter's exercise of an editorial function, but might equally point to the former's highly developed memory (admittedly, of texts usually written by men).[15]

Or, to draw closer to the point of this paper: the recovery of St Bridget's original texts from Latin versions in which they have survived has been rendered all but impossible by the way in which, making a virtue of necessity, St Bridget is told by God to accept revisions to those texts by those divinely authorised to publish them (see n. 14 above). In particular, as noted elsewhere, the earliest surviving form of the Rule itself, π, witnesses to editorial interference which may throw in doubt the recovery of the Saint's actual words (cf. n. 5 above). Nevertheless, even as edited by the Saint's priest-companions, π arguably bears very clear traces of her words.[16] Moreover, and more importantly, we have, in the form in which the Rule was promulgated by Urban V, θ, clear signs of an establishment view of a text which was to be crucially important for the Order's development (it is recited on a regular basis in the Order): a text therefore at the heart of the Order's realisation of the Saint's prophetic instincts.

Comparison with the Rule as finally approved by Urban VI, ε, provides a useful introduction. A central feature of π was its insistence on its own divine inspiration. It includes prefatory material (Prologue, ch. 1) which describes how the Saint received the Rule 'in oracione rapta in visionem spiritualem et intellectualem' (1) [ravished in prayer into a spiritual and intellectual vision].[17] It further tells how St Bridget's revelations,

University of Exeter Press, 1994; Turnhout: Brepols, 1996)), or *Medieval Translators and Their Craft*, ed. Jeanette Beer (Kalamazoo, Michigan: Western Michigan University, 1989), *passim*.

15 For the view that such traces in Margery's *Book* may point as well to 'a source open at a page [as to] . . . a memorial reconstruction or general indebtedness', see David Lawton, 'Voice, Authority and Blasphemy in *The Book of Margery Kempe*', *Margery Kempe: A Book of Essays*, ed. Sandra McEntire (New York: Garland, 1992), 99. The consensus of critical opinion on this question favours memorial reconstruction as the best way of explaining the traces: we know that Margery was read to for a period of years from devotional and theological works (*Book*, 143:25–35 [ch. 58]).

16 On these points see further Roger Ellis, *Syon Abbey: the Spirituality of the English Bridgettines*, Analecta Cartusiana 68 (Salzburg: Universität Salzburg, 1984), 4–7.

17 On the distinction between spiritual and intellectual visions, see Alphonse of Jaén's *Epistola Solitarii*, ch. 5: parallelisms in phrasing suggest that Alphonse was responsible for the prefatory material of the Rule. For a recent edition of the *Epistola*, which doubts his authorship of this prefatory material, see *Alfonso of Jaén: His Life and Works*, ed. Arne Jönsson (Lund: Lund University Press, 1989), esp. 64; for an edition of the Middle English

including, by implication, the Rule, were examined and approved by the Archbishop of Uppsala and three other bishops. And it has Christ as speaker throughout the Rule. ε, by contrast, refers twice in the preamble to the Rule's divine inspiration, but in such a way as to leave the question open, Urban by means of the phrase 'vt creditur' (45d) [as it is believed], and Cardinal Elziarius, to whom he had entrusted its examination, in the parallel phrase 'vt dicitur' (46e) [as it is said]. ε reinforces the sense that the work's claim to divine inspiration is either unproven, or inappropriate in the context of the creation of monastic legislation, by suppression of the prefatory material; by cutting the important opening chapter in which Christ declared that the he would himself dictate the rule of the new Order, which was to be established, first and foremost for women, in honour of his blessed mother (44); and by the suppression of all reference in π to Christ's dictation of the Rule, so that, whereas π reads 'mea/meum/mei', or 'egoipse Deus', spoken by Christ, ε, by contrast, reads 'Domini', 'Dei' or 'Christus' (88, 212, 234, 237, 240: cf. Eklund, 72 n. 126). These suppressions indicate that Urban's approval of the Rule implies no automatic endorsement of its claims to divine inspiration.

ε made other changes to the original, too, so as to situate the Rule more clearly in relation to the authority of the Church and existing monastic observance – as, to be sure, π itself had done (cf. Ellis, *Syon Abbey*, 21). Thus, for example, the account of the fasts to be observed by the Order carries the added comment that, in fasts prescribed by the Church, as opposed to those peculiar to the Order, 'forma ecclesie seruetur' (92) [the practice of the Church is to be followed].[18]

A more significant change, for our purposes, concerns the matter of speech with seculars, where π's permission to the nuns to speak with seculars at certain times (84) now carries the added comment in ε that the nuns require the Abbess's permission and must always be accompanied by other sisters: 'semper sint tamen associate' [let them always be accompanied]. This change – one which, we shall see, ε shares with the earlier, θ, version of Urban V – appears to shift authority away from the Rule, as interpreted by each sister for herself, and towards the Abbess, who will interpret it for her. And the change has further and greater significance for our investigation: it simplifies St Bridget's thinking on the matter. At issue in π, and obliterated in ε, that is, is a significant distinction between the sister's relations with the outside world, and her relations with her fellow religious, especially the monks.

translation in MS British Library Julius F II, Rosalynn Voaden, 'The Middle English *Epistola Solitarii ad Reges* of Alfonso of Jaen', *Studies in St Birgitta*, 1, 142–179.
[18] At Syon the fasts peculiar to the Order were the responsibility of the Abbess, while those prescribed by the Church fell to the confessor general to supervise: see *The Rewyll of Seynt Sauioure*, ed. James Hogg, vol. 4: *The Syon Additions for the Sisters*, Salzburger Studien zur Anglistik und Amerikanistik (Salzburg: Universität Salzburg, 1980), 9:10–13 (cited hereafter in the body of the paper by page and line number alone).

Her relations with the latter are fenced around with prohibition. At the wheel, a medieval dumb-waiter between the monks' and nuns' quarters through which each side can exchange necessities with the other, sisters are forbidden to engage in conversation with the brothers, or to give or receive anything, without the knowledge or permission of the Abbess ('sine scitu vel licencia abbatisse'). Everywhere, except when at confession, no sister may hear or speak to anyone without other sisters present to hear all that is said ('sine presencia aliquarum sororum . . . que omnia verba audient sicut ipsa'). Similarly, none of the brothers may enter the nuns' enclosure except when the confessor administers the sacraments to the sick: and he must always be accompanied by others (249–250, cf. 81).

Speech with seculars is presented in an altogether more positive light. Permitted times and places are nominated: from nones to vespers on Sundays and major saints' days, at the windows deputed for the purpose. And the sister has the option, if she is requested to do so by family or friends, to open the window so as to be seen by them: the Rule encourages her not to do so, for the sake of the greater reward she will gain in heaven as a result (84–85).

I read these permissions, and the partnering exhortation, as meaning that St Bridget, confident that religious of her Order would share her own high standards, was prepared to give them some room to manoeuvre on the matter of speech with seculars.[19] Seculars, it seems, pose no threat to one as committed as St Bridget imagines her nuns to be to the rigours of her new monastic régime. Temptation may, however, be generated inside the convent, perhaps as a reflex of that very commitment. Hence the contrast between the permissions on the one hand, and the prohibitions on the other.

ε appears to have found this position altogether too idealistic: in the real world, temptation is as great outside as inside the walls of a convent.[20] Consequently, ε obliterates the distinction, and legislates for speech with seculars in the same terms as St Bridget had used in π to legislate for speech inside the convent. One can appreciate the need for the change, but one must also regret the loss of the original distinction, and the loss of confidence that it reveals in the idealism and dedication of religious of the Order.

That said, it is also true that, for the most part, the changes to π's wording in ε are minor. In particular, the priority which the Rule accorded to women in the Order is still clearly evidenced by the preservation of the

---

[19] For further comment on ways in which the Rule expected high standards of religious of the Order, see Ellis, *Syon Abbey*, 8–16.

[20] The 'real', as opposed to the 'ideal', monastic environment, in which, for example, nuns absconded or were forcibly removed from the convent, is implied at a number of points in the additional legislation produced for the Syon nuns (Ellis, *Syon Abbey*, 73–76, 82–92) and features regularly in Eileen Power, *Medieval English Nunneries c.1275 to 1535* (Cambridge: Cambridge University Press, 1922).

Rule's original form. Admittedly, in fleshing out the formal promise of obedience to be made during the profession ceremony by the newly professed, and in creating a speech which the newly professed, male or female, will make ('monialis vel frater recipiendus respondeat sic: Ego soror, vel frater, N facio professionem . . .') (113) [the nun or brother to be admitted will reply thus: I sister, or brother, N make profession], ε does more than π had done to give male religious an equal voice and presence in the Rule. π had merely said that the sister would make such a promise ('promittente illa se ista facturam'), and had explained in ch. 13 that the rite of male profession was to be modelled on its account of female profession in chs. 10–11 (162–164). Yet ε's creation of this male presence and voice does not accompany any wholesale rewriting of the ceremonies of profession, much less of the rest of the Rule, so as to adapt to a male readership the female reference used throughout π, though rewriting of material in a few manuscripts of the Rule shows that such an adaptation was intermittently attempted (Eklund 28–29).[21]

The situation is very different in the case of the Rule first approved, twenty-five or so years after it was first revealed to St Bridget, by Urban V. Urban will not even consider the Rule's claim to divine inspiration: his preamble credits St Bridget with divine inspiration only in respect of the monastery she has determined to found, where work has already started on the buildings for the nuns (318d), and where she is proposing to enter as one of them ('infra dictarum monialium numerum', 318 h).[22] Inevitably, the original revelation-experience disappears. But, by contrast with ε's modest rewriting of the original, the version in θ undergoes a thorough and systematic rewriting. Some of the changes probably represent an effort to tidy up a text which had presented its material in a fairly haphazard way: a possible reflex of the original revelation-experience, though one unlikely to appeal to canon lawyers.[23] Other changes, though, went to the heart of the original vision.

Whether by accident or design – and I have argued in *Syon Abbey* (3, 19–26) that the feature seems to characterise most monastic legislation – the original had walked a narrow line between asserting its conformity with, and declaring its independence of, monastic tradition. To be sure, the

[21] For fuller comment on ε and reasons for its other changes to π, see Ellis, *Syon Abbey*, 50–52.

[22] St Bridget's desire to enter her new Order not as Abbess but as one of the nuns is worth lingering over for the light it throws on her understanding of the Order and her place in it (cf. comments below, 82–86, on the roles of Abbess and nun in the Rule). It can be compared with the way in which St Dominic situated himself relative to the members of his Order; see David Haseldine, 'Early Dominican Hagiography and the Canonization of St Dominic', *New Blackfriars* 75 (September 1994), 400–414, esp. 407–408.

[23] I have noted this feature of St Bridget's writing elsewhere: see 'The Mystic and the Many-Faceted Image: Book VIII, Chapters 48 and 56 of the *Liber Celestis* of St Bridget of Sweden', in *L'Image Pluridimensionelle*, Actes du Colloque, 23–25 Juillet 1982 [ed. Roland Maisonneuve] (20 Rue Fiol, Lyon, IRIS Association Internationale, 1982), 50.

new project was something of a novelty: an Order created especially for women was a departure from tradition in the simple sense that most new Orders were founded by and for men.[24] Female branches of these Orders were usually separate, dependent and later creations. And even when those female branches had distinctively different charisms to those of their male counterparts – I am thinking particularly of the contemplative Dominican and Franciscan sisters – they were nevertheless accommodated to existing religious structures.[25] Thus, for example, St Augustine's rule for monks, given by Urban V, and confirmed by Urban VI, as the Rule for the Brigittine Order, also circulated in a version adapted for female religious; so did the Rule of St Benedict.[26] So Urban V's canon lawyers must have supposed, as they began to read the Rule, that they were about to enter familiar territory: a supposition confirmed by the way in which the following chapters, however distinctive their visualisation of Brigittine observances (the habit, the Office, régime of fasting, rites of entry), seemed to be operating within a familiar frame of reference. Thus, the Order's establishment on the three virtues of humility, chastity and poverty (50) must have seemed close enough to the traditional vows of poverty, chastity and obedience to need no alteration or even glossing.

More to the point, in those early chapters the Rule was studiously silent about the presence and role of Brigittine monks. They first appear in ch. 12 as the providers of Mass for the sisters (150), and might even have been mistaken for priests brought in from the outside to provide this service, since they are directed to sing not the distinct Office prescribed for the sisters (67–72) but the Office obtaining in the diocese where the monastery is situated (150). More contentious might have been the sense that they are present, almost literally, to make up the number: counting priests, deacons and laybrothers together there will be twenty-five of them to supplement the sixty sisters allowed for by the Rule (153). Their implied subordination is reinforced by material in ch. 13, which describes only those aspects of their religious dress (156–161) and, as earlier noted, rites of profession (162–164) which cannot be readily paralleled in the earlier account of the sisters' dress and profession, this last taken up and repeated by θ (339). Thereafter, their role is distinguished from that of the sisters only when they are directed to preach in the vernacular (174) and to hear confessions (177–178, 185). The former activity grows out of their life of

---

[24] On this point see C.H. Lawrence, *Medieval Monasticism* (London: Longman, 1984), ch. 11 ('sisters or handmaids').

[25] On this see further Lawrence, *Medieval Monasticism*, 214–215.

[26] On versions of the former adapted for female religious, see *The Rule of St Augustine*, trans. from the Dutch version of Tarsicius J. van Bavel by Raymond Canning (London: Darton, Longman and Todd, 1984), 3–5; for a version of the latter adapted for female religious, *Les monuments primitifs de la règle Cistercienne*, ed. Ph. Guignard (Dijon: Imprimerie Darantiere, 1878), 584–642.

study and prayer (173), but that life is as available to the women as to the men.[27]

Yet more contentious than this overt subordination of men to women in the Order is an item lodged in the middle of the chapter where they first appear. The monks are not priests brought in from outside, but members of the same community, housed within its walls. They are to be housed separately, with access only to the convent church, where a separate choir for each group will ensure that the monks cannot make direct contact with the sisters (151). Given that π surrounds this item with uncontentious material describing the monks' Office and the numbers of male religious in the convent, and despatches it as quickly as possible, and given also that π has to consider the topic again, in more detail, shortly before the end of the Rule (247–252), I cannot help feeling that the compiler of π was uneasily aware how much of a hostage to fortune the item might represent if viewed out of context, or without sympathy.

The double monastery, a way of ensuring a regular and religiously informed priestly presence for the nuns, was as central to Bridget's vision as it was generally uncommon in the later Middle Ages.[28] And there were two distinct differences between other instances of the practice and that proposed by the Rule. The former had been accommodated explicitly or implicitly to an existing Rule; and they had usually been founded by men.

We cannot determine which, if any, of these considerations weighed most with the commission that Urban V set up to examine the proposed Rule. The outcome should hardly have surprised contemporary Vatican-watchers. Taking his lead perhaps from the fact that work had already started on the nuns' quarters, but not on those of the monks (318e, k), Urban V directed the episcopal recipients of the Bull to situate the monks' cloister in the same town but physically remote from that of the nuns (318e, k). The monks would therefore require a complete set of monastic buildings to match that of the sisters, so that we must now speak, as the Bull does, with great regularity, of two monasteries. There must also be two identical sets of officers to see to each convent's relations with the outside world (345).

The revisers' difficulties with the idea of the double monastery may have had something to do with imprecisions of expression in the Rule submitted to them. π describes the monastery as existing on a number of levels simultaneously, which it does not completely distinguish: as an ideal construct guaranteed by observance of the Rule; as the collection of buildings in which men and women practise their religion; and as the

---

[27] Thus another passage (228) which, in context, looks to be referring only to priests and emphasising their commitment to study, has been regularly understood to refer to the sisters as well.

[28] On double monasteries, see F. Luigi de Candido, 'The Double Monasteries: an Idea, an Experience, an Interpretation', in *Santa Brigida Profeta dei Tempi Nuovi*, 607–639, esp. 609, 616–623.

separate cloisters of the monks and the nuns. π had tacitly identified the Rule with the Order and the buildings in which it would be housed.[29] Though the monks' quarters were only ever described as a 'curia' (151, 164, 201), the term 'monasterium' could indicate the convent as a whole, or the nun's quarters, the latter by contrast with other monastic buildings, such as the church (197) or the monks' quarters (251). Similarly, the term 'conventus' might refer to the female religious in the convent (118, 143) or to the complete community, male and female, under the one roof (165, glossed by the phase 'cum omni congregacione sororum et fratrum', 168). Such ambiguities of expression the Bull of Urban VI would pass over without comment; θ gave much greater care to the matter of labelling. Thus it regularly indicates the precise application of the term 'monasterium' to one or other convent by use of the phrase 'monialium' or 'fratrum'; and when it uses the word 'conventus', it sets it in such close proximity to a reference to monks or nuns (340, 345) as to remove ambiguity. It further symbolises the physical separation of the two communities by two separate sections devoted to each of them (319–335, 354–357, the nuns; 336–353, the monks).[30]

It would seem that Urban V was hoping by these changes to demonstrate that the monks and the nuns were distinct but equal. What this meant in practice we can see from θ's change to the minimum age for entry for the men. According to π, women were not to enter before their eighteenth year, men not until they were twenty-five (231). The latter argues clearly for the high level of religious knowledge and dedication which St Bridget expected of the priests in her Order, and the high hopes she had for the sisters whom they would be serving: not even the Carthusians demanded as much of their men.[31] θ brought the minimum age for entry by the men into line with that for the women (319, 337): which had the consequence of bringing the former more into line with what obtained in other orders, and of undermining one of the most important features of the original Rule. In practice, it seems, Urban expected less, both intellectually and religiously, of priests entering the Order than St Bridget had done.

The physical separation of the two religious establishments from one

---

[29] According to the rubrics to prologue chs. 1–2, the Order was to be a 'religio nova' (13, 22); according to the rubric to Rule ch. 1, the Rule itself was 'nova' (42). Similarly, the rites of entry used the phrases 'recepcio ad religionem' and 'introduccio ad monasterium' almost as equivalents (96, 110).

[30] Admittedly, the section given over to the monks defines them in large measure by the work they are to do for the nuns – daily Mass (338), weekly sermon (341–342), Eucharist (343), confession (343–344) – and by the restrictions it imposes on their other relations with the nuns (349–351).

[31] Candidates for admission to the Carthusians were expected to be at least twenty years old: see the Carthusian *Consuetudines* (PL, 153, cols. 691–692 [ch. 27]). Compare the age of fifteen for admission to the Cistercian Order, as noted in Jean Leclerq, *The Love of Learning and the Desire for God*, trans. Catharine Misrahi (New York: Fordham University Press, 1961, repr. 1988), 144 n. 6.

another made Urban's task simpler when he came to legislate for the powers of the chief officers of the convent, the abbess and the confessor general, the latter called, throughout the Bull, a 'prior'. The relationship of these two officers to one another was left unclear enough in the original legislation to provide fertile breeding grounds for debate and dissension, as happened more than once in real life.[32] Urban short-circuited the problem by physically separating the two convents, and restricting the powers of the two officers, for the most part, to their respective establishments.

The heart of the problem remained, however, in π's account of the powers and duties of the Abbess. According to π, she was to be the chief officer of the whole community: her rule symbolised, and was authorised by, the supposed rule of the Virgin Mary over the post-Ascension, pre-Pentecost, church (167). Just as the local Bishop is to be consulted when the Convent elects her (167), she is herself to be consulted by the confessor general of the convent on all matters other than those that directly concern the spiritual direction of the monks and the conservation of the Order (170, where the phrase 'consilio abbatisse' echoes that used of the Bishop, 'consilio episcopi', in 167). The sisters were to obey her as absolutely as the brothers obeyed the confessor general (169). Yet, outside of the section from which these quotations come (ch. 14), π makes little of her role, and that little is largely symbolic or ceremonial. Consider, for example, the rites of entry. It is for the Abbess, probably (the actual speaker is not named), to instruct the candidate to return in three months' time, after her request has been duly deliberated by the community as a whole. When she returns, the Abbess will question her on her motives. Yet when, at the end of the year, after a further meeting, the decision is taken to admit her, it is the whole convent of the sisters who must give consent (98–101). Here a largely ceremonial role is being created for the Abbess in relation to the life of the community. Or consider what happens when gifts are offered to the monastery, and when extreme need forces the acceptance of the gifts. Once again, the Abbess speaks in the name of the community (217–218: cf. 221 'dicatur . . . a conventu'), and invites the donor to return with proof that the donations are entirely above board. Should there be doubt about the probity of the gifts, 'aliis sencientibus sic, aliis vero [non]' (220) [some in favour, others not], they are not to be

---

[32] On this point, see esp. Hans Cnattingius, *Studies in the Order of St Bridget of Sweden. I. The Crisis in the 1420s*, Stockholm Studies in History 7 (Uppsala: Almqvist & Wiksell, 1963), and, relating to Syon Abbey, *The Incendium Amoris of Richard Rolle of Hampole*, ed. Margaret Deanesly (Manchester: Manchester University Press, 1915, repr. Folcroft, Pennsylvania: Folcroft Library Editions, 1974), 111. The Syon Additions for the sisters note the possibility of discord between the Abbess and the confessor general but only, in the context of their list of more grievous faults (ch. 4), as something which a sister might 'sowe' between them (11:8–10).

accepted. The quoted phrase shows clearly where, for St Bridget, discernment operates in a religious community: in the total life of the sisters.[33]

Regularly, then, π presents the Abbess, and implicitly defines her, in relation to the community on whose behalf she exercises power. In π she is, most notably, the point at which the outside world meets the convent. But π also defines her in relation to the Rule itself. Sisters may look to her for the meeting of their needs, but may not have what the Rule does not permit (52): specifically, they are forbidden to have any private property at all (50). Consequently, the Abbess must not on any account accept gifts from seculars on behalf of any of the sisters (194). Thus at the same time that π recognises the Abbess's powers, it subordinates them to the teachings of the Rule (196). Hence, as noted earlier, when the Rule licenses speech with seculars, the Abbess initially has no direct part to play in the process (75–78, 84).

I am arguing that the picture of the Abbess presented by the π version of the Rule needs to be understood in relation to the more important picture of the devout Brigittine sister who has internalised the teachings of the Rule and can be trusted to carry them out. An obvious counterclaim suggests itself: the role of the Abbess is so traditional in religious life that St Bridget took for granted as normative of her own Order practices that obtained in other Orders. Hence, the various impersonal constructions, especially passives, in which many of the regulations of the Rule were cast, including many of those features noted in previous paragraphs, might as well have the Abbess as agent as the individual sister. The Rule, that is, might have implied that the permissions it conceded to the sisters were in fact to be authorised by the Abbess.

In support of this contrary view we note evidence from the Rule itself. Its account of the sisters' manual labour – specifically, their embroidery (51) – and of their dealings with male religious of the Order, notes their need to secure the Abbess's permission ('licencia') beforehand (236, 249). Similarly, when the newly-professed sister is handed over to the community by the Bishop, it is the Abbess who, in her own name, and not on behalf of the community, assumes charge of the new sister, and is made personally responsible by the Bishop for preserving and augmenting her holiness (144–146). The speeches created at this point for the Bishop and the Abbess contain slight but clear echoes of passages in the Rule of St Benedict describing the duties of the Abbot: a work which lays great stress on the powers and responsibilities of the chief officer of the convent, not least in the way it frames its account of monastic life by chapters on the Abbot near the very start, and again near the end, as a way of symbolising

---

[33] On this point, see further Ellis, *Syon Abbey*, 36–37.

his all-embracing authority over the community (chs. 2, 64).[34] Such details suggest a more traditional view of the Abbess's powers and duties.

Nevertheless, as earlier noted, St Bridget seems to have envisaged her Rule and Order in a number of ways as distinguishable from, and opposed to, existing religious observance; so it is at least arguable that her vision of the Abbess's role was also distinct and subtly nuanced. In a community with as highly developed a spiritual sense as St Bridget seems to have hoped for, the individual sister, the subject of so many chapters of the Rule, could readily be taken as the heart of the new Order.[35]

Of the two images of the Abbess that can be inferred from the pages of the π version of the Rule, it is, unsurprisingly, the more traditional one that θ chose to develop. The most notable instance of this comes in θ's account of the ban on private property. As earlier noted, the Rule had placed both the Abbess and the individual religious under ban in respect of private property. The gravity of this ban is well indicated by the fact that no other crime is mentioned by name in the account of the workings of the chapter: hence θ notes private property as a transgression to be raised 'presertim' among the lapses in observance of the Rule during the weekly chapter (357). At the same time, θ moves towards a simpler Benedictine model and away from the more subtly nuanced Brigittine one by giving the Abbess powers of interpretation and dispensation which St Bridget's Rule had forbidden her.

Even in θ, of course, the ban on private property is still a weighty matter: witness the way it brings together, near the start, a number of scattered references to the subject in the Rule. But it also modifies them, in slight but significant ways. It envisages the possibility that a postulant may have brought private property with her or been given gifts during her year of novitiate. Such private property she may dispose of as she wishes: she can give it to the poor, much as the community in the original Rule was directed to dispose of gifts to itself, and of the food and clothing assigned to religious who had died, but whose place no new sister had as yet taken (321 [cf. π 208, 215], 348). Once professed, though, as in π, the sister may have no private property. She may not even handle the gold and silver thread she needs for her embroidery without the Abbess's permission (323, cf. π 51), nor receive gifts of any sort (323, cf. π 194). This latter, though, comes with a qualification which, while seeming to reinforce the original ban, robs it of its force. As earlier noted, π had forbidden the Abbess to permit anyone to receive such gifts; θ merely states that sisters may not receive gifts 'sine ipsius abbatisse licencia' (323) [without the licence of the Abbess].

---

[34] I have used the edition by D. Oswald Hunter Blair (Fort Augustus: the Abbey Press, 1886, repr. 1934), hereafter RSBen.

[35] Admittedly, the Rule also recognises that this high ideal may not always be realised in practice: cf. Ellis, *Syon Abbey*, 37–38.

The Abbess's powers are much to the fore, too, in the following section of θ, on speech with seculars. Such speech, as earlier noted, was restricted to the period between nones and vespers on Sundays and high feast days (84). θ keeps this restriction but fences it about with discouragement. Where π envisaged a window which could be opened, to allow the sister to be seen if she wished, θ insists on a closed iron grate between the speakers ('crate ferrea clausa mediante') so that neither speaker can see the other, and bans such speech 'nisi vrgens necessitas aliud suaderet' [unless some compelling reason suggests otherwise]. The difference between the two versions can be seen if we trace the phrase 'urgens necessitas' back to its origins in π. In π, the parallel phrase 'intollerabilis necessitas' explains and justifies the receipt of gifts (217). In both cases, the action licensed – speech with seculars, receipt of gifts – directly concerns the sisters' relations with the outside world. But the picture given by θ, in respect of speech, is rather less trusting of the sister than what we get in π. As in ε, θ requires two sisters to be present to hear what is said; and the Abbess's permission must have been secured beforehand. In θ, that is, speech with seculars becomes as potent an occasion for temptation as, in π, the reception of gifts from the outside world had been.

In thus heightening the powers of the Abbess and slotting her into a simpler and more traditional role than the Rule had done, θ also, and inevitably, simplified the Rule's presentation of the individual sister. The changed attitude towards speech, previously noted, focuses this point clearly: as does the next section, on the rule of silence. According to θ, strict silence is to be observed outside of the performance of the liturgy ('saluis ecclesiasticis lectura et cantu ac aliis tangentibus celebracionem huiusmodi' (329) [except for the reciting and singing of the liturgy and other things germane to liturgical celebration]). π had been much more relaxed about speech, licensing periods of each day for speech and also allowing for exceptions in the name of reasonableness: in consequence it had to legislate against 'scurrilia vero et ociosa' [lewd and idle words] and in favour of spiritual conversation ('de collacione spirituali') to do with the upholding of the Order and of 'veris necessariis' (75–77) [things truly necessary].[36]

One small sign of the changed view of the individual religious comes even as θ is reinforcing one of the directives of π on the reception of the Eucharist. In π the whole community is to receive the sacrament on a set number of feast days; other sisters, whom God has inspired with greater devotion, may, if they seek the privilege with fervent desire, and after consulting their confessor, receive communion once a week, on Saturdays, in addition, presumably, to the feast days already noted (181–182).[37] θ

[36] On the interpretation of the phrase 'de collacione spirituali', see Eklund, 232. The phrase 'scurrilia . . . et ociosa' derives from RSBen, 40 (ch. 6).
[37] In addition to Maundy Thursday, Easter, the Ascension, Pentecost and Christmas Day,

directs that all male members of the community who are not priests, and all the sisters, are to receive the Eucharist at least ('saltem') every Sunday and on the principal feasts of the year (343). Weekly communion is rare in the later Middle Ages, as the added permission in π implies: for θ to legislate for weekly communion therefore paradoxically implies a recognition of the high standards that the Order has set itself. Sadly, θ seems to have found irrelevant to the creation of a book of rules π's reference to the devotion of the sisters: that quality which the original Rule had taken so much for granted as the norm, and legislated to encourage.[38]

Another small but significant change concerns the year which precedes profession, when the community is testing the candidate's vocation. In π the candidate spends this year outside the monastery, and, after her first meeting with the community, when she formally requests admission, she returns twice during the course of the year so that she and the community may learn more about each other before reaching a final decision.[39] If the community is formally testing her vocation by this means, she is also, and more importantly, testing her own vocation, in the rough-and-tumble of the world outside the walls. θ envisages a very different situation, a year of proof *inside* the walls of the convent, where the candidate is obviously testing herself but where the principal agents of testing are, equally obviously, convent officers. Admittedly, θ is not explicit on this point, but its earlier-noted permission to the postulant to dispose of gifts by giving them to the poor would be meaningless unless it envisaged a postulant in close and regular contact with professed sisters, especially, as in the Syon Additions, a novice mistress. And ε helps to confirm the picture by distinguishing what it calls the year of proof – a phrase first used in θ (319) – from that obtaining 'in aliis religionibus infra monasterium' (ε 103) [in other Orders inside the convent]. Once again θ is modifying a distinctive element of π so as to bring it into line with current practice. The change is of a piece with others we have noted: it is less trusting of the individual religious than St Bridget had been, and legislates for a lower level of commitment.

With this sense of a more traditional picture of the individual religious in θ comes a sense of much greater recourse to authority: a sense reinforced in the section dealing with the fasting régime of the Order. Four times in this section the text situates the fasts of the Order in relation to the fasts instituted by the Roman church. This feature would also figure, as earlier noted, in ε, but θ takes it very much further; it reappears, for

these are the days whose vigil requires a bread and water fast, the latter listed in the chapter on fasting (90–91).

[38] On this point, see Ellis, *Syon Abbey*, 11–12; and see further below, 89, on developments of this item of legislation at Syon.

[39] The Syon Additions allow for the candidate to be dispensed the second and third visits if she spends the year in close proximity to the convent, 'in the courte withoute' (82:23–83:4 [ch. 15]).

example, in the account of the election of the prior 'secundum canonicas sancciones' (340) [according to canon law]; again (344), when confession is allowed for 'in casibus sedi apostolice vel episcopo minime reseruatis' [in cases not reserved for Pope or Bishop]; and again, in the account of how the priests' vestments are to correspond in respect of their colours to the 'usum et ritum Romane ecclesie' (352) [the use and custom of the Roman church].

These details reveal an unmistakable change of emphasis. The early version of the Rule, π, always presupposes the authority of the church as a backdrop against which to set its own innovations (see above 76). For Urban V, the innovations are to be absorbed into, and accommodated to, an ecclesiastical mainstream. That is, the Order has to come into line with existing practice and legislation, and must be seen to do so.

In respect of a few details, as earlier implied, the Rule itself had invited the very rewritings that it was now receiving. Recognising, as the rubric to the final chapter of the Rule of St Benedict has it (ch. 73), that 'non omnis justitiae observatio in hac sit regula constituta' [the whole observance of perfection is not set down in this Rule], the penultimate chapter of the *Regula* allowed for the creation of additional legislation, including 'quomodo excessus emendandi sunt . . . et qualiter visitabit episcopus et pro quibus casibus ingredietur monasterium' (260) [how excesses are to be corrected . . . and how the Bishop shall make his visitation and for what causes he shall enter the monastery]. The diocesan Bishop had appeared twice before in the Rule, once to conduct the rites of profession (104–146), once to give advice concerning the election of the Abbess (167). St Bridget's view of his role can be well summed up in a phrase at the head of the chapter under discussion: he is to be the whole community's father and visitor, as well as the judge of all causes or cases touching the sisters or the brothers (256). This formulation combines both idealism (father) and a realistic awareness that cases may arise in which the Bishop needs to exercise a judicial function (visitor and judge). The developments of this latter point in θ are very interesting. θ allows for an annual visitation, more than many convents actually received, and more than the triennial visitation Syon legislated for.[40] The Bishop and his followers are not to be admitted into the enclosure, but must see the sisters at the grate. Two sisters must accompany those being examined by the Bishop, so positioned that they can see what is going on but not hear anything (354). Since the meeting has something of the character of a confession, the two sisters may not eavesdrop on the conversation. These sisters, though, recall those who were to be present to hear what a sister said to seculars, and suggest that not even the relation between the Bishop and individual members of his flock could be taken for granted, unsupervised. On

---

[40] For the practice at Syon, see *Syon Additions*, 39:2, 48:10–13 (chs. 10–11, the latter translated from the *Bulla Reformatoria* issued in 1425 by Pope Martin V).

occasion, it appears, both Bishop and sisters might need protecting against each other.

θ, then, is of considerable interest in showing the changes which the clerics who edited and authorised the texts of women visionaries could make to their texts. θ's revisions seem to indicate (i) a greater awareness of the difficulties of male-female religious relationships, especially in a situation where a woman is head over men; (ii) a greater awareness of the real world in which religious had to live out their observance, as opposed to the ideal world in which St Bridget had set them in the Rule; (iii) impatience with an untidy and unfinished set of regulations. The pity is that instead of trying to work with – or take their cue from – a complex and potentially enriching, genuinely visionary, text, Urban's revisers set about tidying it up, so as to reinforce simpler, safer, more traditional patterns.[41]

I said near the start of this paper that its narrow focus was a necessary consequence of the absence of surviving copies of θ in England. A few words, by way of coda, can show, though, that, even inside Syon Abbey, some of the more distinctive elements of the Rule, noted in previous paragraphs of this paper, were themselves subjected to an interpretive filter and subtly modified, even as their authority was publicly affirmed by regular recitation. The interpretive filter, of course, was the Syon Additions. As previously noted, the Rule had foreseen the need for such additional legislation, and had allowed for its creation by Benedictine or Cistercian monks (260), who might well bring subtly different, non-Brigittine, understandings to bear on the questions of religious observance, and might well, in consequence, replace some of the Rule's more distinctive emphases with others more familiar to themselves.[42]

Of course, the Additions were produced in the shadow of the modest revisions to π and the confirmation of the Order published by Urban VI, the canonization of St Bridget by Boniface IX, and their subsequent confirmations by Pope Martin V. Consequently, several features of the original Rule which Urban V had tried to modify had been reinstated and established beyond all possibility of debate by the time of the Syon Additions: most notably, the idea of the double monastery. Nevertheless, the Additions are sometimes subtly other, as well as more, than the original Rule, even when they appear to be following it to the letter.

We can see this, for example, in the way the Additions for the Sisters legislate for their relations with seculars (ch. 14). As in both π and ε, the

---

41 Similar changes had to be made to documentation sent from Sweden in support of the canonisation process: see Ellis, 'The Swedish Woman', 115.

42 The creation of the Additions is discussed by Deanesly, 121–123, and Ellis, *Syon Abbey*, 131. The debt of Brigittine to Benedictine and Cistercian traditions is, of course, of long standing, given that one of St Bridget's chief confessors was Peter Olavson, Cistercian subprior, later prior, of Alvastra, and that both St Bridget and her husband had close links with the Alvastra community.

Additions allow for the sister to be seen at visiting times by her friends: they twice quote the passage which, in the original Rule, encourages her not to open the window at such times so as to secure herself a greater reward in heaven (75:10–12, 16–19); they take from the Rule its account of the 'grete festes' when sisters may speak with seculars (74:26–28); and they owe to the Rule, as approved by Urban VI, the comment that the Abbess must license the opening of the window (74:30–75:1). At the same time, they introduce a number of qualifications. In the first place, ε had allowed for the sister to be seen 'aliquociens in anno' (85) [several times in the year]; the Additions require the privilege to be granted 'seldom in the yere' (75:1) and, when granted, to be accompanied by warnings to the sister to behave 'godely and religiously, in countynaunce, in chere, and in al [her] meuynges' (75:9–10). Moreover, the Abbess is not to allow the window to be opened without first consulting with the confessor general, since, as 'conseruatour of the order', a title deriving from the Rule itself (170), he has the responsibility of seeing that the Rule is observed in its entirety (75:3–7). Lastly, there is the endearing qualification, peculiar to the Additions, that the sister might herself wish to be seen by her friends (75:2–3). In the Rule, such innocently human desire has no place: though the sister may open the window in response to the desires of her friends, her own desires must be directed heavenwards, or, as ch. 17 implies, focused upon the reception of the sacrament.

In these few details we can see the Additions, like the Bull of Urban V, legislating for a lower level of religious observance than the Rule had done. Similar modifications occur – to take a final example suggested by the concluding words of the previous paragraph – when the Additions treat of the Eucharist. They list as grievous faults, second in an ascending scale that goes from light to most grievous, the failure of a sister to receive communion on the days set down in the Rule unless her absence has been licensed, and, similarly, her reception of communion on any other day without permission (9:1–9). In so doing, they appear to be legislating not only against too little devotion but also against a devotion which does not keep to the rules. The latter point marks a clear, if subtle, shift of emphasis from the original Rule. There, we remember, the devout sister was to be permitted, so long as she consulted with her confessor ('cum consilio confessoris'), to receive communion on Saturdays. The Additions require her not to consult but to be licensed: and licensed not by her daily confessor, though he can license her to withdraw from communion on one of the days set down in the Rule, but by the confessor general himself. As earlier noted, licensing features regularly in the Rule (77, 83–5 above). Consultation also occurs in the Rule (82, 87 above), with this difference: that whereas consultation takes place between figures of approximately equal standing, licensing characterises the relations of superiors and subordinates. Consequently, when the Additions turn counsel into a requirement to be licensed, and make the chief officer on the men's side the one who does the licensing, we may well feel they have gone some way towards reinstating the traditional role models which θ had set up, against St Bridget's wishes.

Some stories have a happy ending – not every visionary gets herself burned and her book banned – though, as I have noted elsewhere, it is difficult to resist the conclusion that other considerations than the simple merits of the case weighed on Urban VI when he restored to the nascent Order the Rule in very much the form its foundress had created for it.[43] But most such endings are temporary, even if they last for two centuries and more. Witness the changes forced upon the Order by the Council of Trent,[44] to say nothing of new developments in the Order since.[45] Witness – to take stories of visionary men, who also founded new Orders – the way in which St Dominic had planned for the lay brothers in his Order to handle the finances, leaving the friars free to study and preach, and the friars, unwilling to accept so bold an innovation, opposed his plans so as to ensure that they remained in control of the purse strings:[46] or the way in which the first version of St Francis's Rule 'did not receive papal sanction and therefore remained inoperative'.[47] Which reminds us of a point earlier made, that the prophetic charism is not a matter of truths set in stone, but more like trying to write on water: and may also remind us that the problems facing women visionaries in the Middle Ages differ in degree but not necessarily in kind from those facing their male counterparts.

---

[43] See Ellis, 'The Swedish Woman', 114.

[44] For a brief account of these changes, see Ellis, *Syon Abbey*, 124–131.

[45] For developments in the Brigittine Order in the seventeenth century, see Ulla Sander Olsen, 'The Revival of the Birgittine Order in the Seventeenth Century: What Happened after the Reformation?', paper heard at a Conference on St Bridget in Buckfast Abbey, Devon, 18–21 July 1994 and kindly communicated to me by the author. For other developments see relevant articles in *Santa Brigida Profeta dei Tempi Nuovi*.

[46] I owe this interpretation of the episode to a sermon of Fr Cornelius Ernst OP. For another interpretation more favourable to the friars, see M.-H. Vicaire, *St Dominic and His Times*, trans. Kathleen Pond (London: Darton, Longman and Todd, 1964), 310–311, and *Early Dominicans: Selected Writings*, ed. Simon Tugwell (New York: Paulist Press, 1982), 20, 74 and n. 74.

[47] For a modern translation of this Rule see *St Francis of Assisi: his Life and Writings as Recorded by his Contemporaries*, trans. Leo Shirley-Price (London: A.R. Mowbray and Co., 1959), 204–226 (the quoted passage taken from Shirley-Price's introduction to his translation of the Rule, 205).

MS Cotton Claudius B.I.:
A Middle English Edition of
St Bridget of Sweden's *Liber Celestis*[1]

JOAN ISOBEL FRIEDMAN

The British Library possesses a precious illuminated manuscript containing a Middle English translation of the *Book of Revelations* by the great mystic and prophetess, Bridget of Sweden (c.1303–1373).[2] As the only illuminated copy in English to survive from the fifteenth century, this volume is of great interest art historically. In addition, it is very important textually, being one of the two known manuscripts from this period to contain the complete text of Books I to VII of the *Liber Celestis*.[3] The only

---

List of Manuscripts: see p. 113.

[1] *Liber Celestis* is an abbreviated form of the Latin title *Il Liber Celestis Revelationum* (or *Revelaciones*); in English, the text is referred to as the *Book of Revelations,* or *Revelations*. These titles will be used interchangeably throughout this essay.

[2] The most reliable sources for the biography of St Bridget of Sweden are found in the *Vita s. Birgittae* compiled by her two Swedish confessors and spiritual advisors, Petrus Olavi of Alvastra and Petrus of Skänninge, in *Scriptores rerum seucicarum*, III (Uppsala-Lund, 1876), 185–206, and in the *Acta et processus canonizaciones beatae Birgittae*, ed. Isak Collijn, SFSS ser. 2, Latinska Skrifter, I (Uppsala, 1924–31). See also I. Cecchetti, *Biblioteca Sanctorum*, III (Rome, 1963), 439–530, and F. Vernet, *Dictionnaire de spiritualité ascetique et mystique*, I (Paris, 1937), cols. 1934–1958.

[3] Together with the majority of fifteenth-century copies in English translation, MS Cotton Claudius B.I. belongs to a distinctive group of manuscripts whose texts are based on the first authoritative Latin edition of the *Revelations* which was published in Italy c.1377. Prepared by Alfonso Pecha de Vadaterra, one of St Bridget's confessors, the first edition, which is known as the *Liber Alfonsi*, contains only the Prologue of Master Matthias and Books I to VII of the *Revelations*. A revised and amplified version of the Alfonsine text was presented at the canonization proceedings in 1379. The text of this second redaction is found in two codices of the *Liber Celestis* illuminated in Naples between c.1378 and 1380, New York, Pierpont Morgan Library, MS 498, and Palermo, Biblioteca centrale della regione siciliana, MS IV.G.2. For a discussion of the so-called *Liber Alfonsi*, see *The Liber Celestis of St Bridget of Sweden*, ed. Roger Ellis, I, Text, EETS, os 291 (London: Oxford University Press, 1987), xii; for the second Alfonsine redaction, consult *Sancta Birgitta. Revelaciones Book IV*, ed. Hans Aili, SSFS ser. 2, Latinska skrifter VII: 4 (Stockholm, 1992), 43–47 and *passim*. A detailed study of the text tradition is provided by Aili, 'St.

91

other contemporary codex to have the entire text, MS Julius F.II, also belongs to the British Library. The latter is unillustrated.[4]

MS Cotton Claudius B.I. is distinguished for the beauty of its decoration in gold and vivid colours. With one exception, the opening page of each book of the *Liber Celestis* is embellished with either a large miniature, or an initial of elaborate foliate design accompanied by finely rendered marginal ornament which partially or fully surrounds the text. In this latter category, four exceptionally attractive pages serve to introduce Books II, IV, V, and VI of the *Revelations*. Two of the three framed miniatures appear at the beginning of Books III and VII. The third miniature is found at the head of Book I, chapter 31. As the sole illustration to appear anywhere other than on an opening page, its location is not consistent with the practice observed elsewhere in the decoration of the manuscript.

Due to the loss of a leaf, the first page of Book I of the *Revelations* is missing.[5] As the introductory page of an illuminated codex, it is natural to expect this leaf to be furnished with handsome ornament. In view of the fact that fine illuminations have long been prized as unique works of art, it is tempting to speculate that this lost leaf was excised sometime before the manuscript entered the British Library.[6] While this supposition may provide an explanation for the missing leaf, it does not account for the presence of the miniature in the midst of Book I.

Quite apart from their technical merit and visual appeal, the three framed miniatures in MS Cotton Claudius B.I. are particularly important because of their iconography. A discussion of these miniatures will consti-

Birgitta and the Text of the *Revelationes*: a Survey of Some Influences Traceable to Translators and Editors', *The Editing of Theological and Philosophical Texts from the Middle Ages*, ed. M. Asztalos (Stockholm, 1986), 75–91.

4 Written on paper, MS Julius F.II. is a fifteenth-century manuscript comprised of 254 pages and measuring 304.8 x 215.9mm. It contains Books I to VII of the *Revelations*, plus the Prologue to Book I which is missing from MS Cotton Claudius B.I., making it the more complete of the two copies. See W.P. Cumming, *The Revelations of St. Birgitta*, EETS 178 (London, 1929; rpt Millwood, NY, 1987), xvi, xx.

5 Roger Ellis specifically remarks on the loss of this leaf at the beginning of MS Cotton Claudius B.I.; as a result of this lacuna, the *Life of St Bridget* is left incomplete, and the first page of the text for Book I of the *Revelations* is also lacking. See Ellis, *Liber Celestis*, 5. For a complete list of missing pages in the manuscript, see n. 8 below.

6 The practice of mutilating manuscripts by cutting out individual pages or even disassembling entire volumes to obtain their illuminations was not uncommon. In a recent study of medieval manuscripts in the collection of the present-day Brigittine convent of Syon Abbey, James Hogg mentions the loss of two miniatures from a manuscript, which were 'presumably cut out on account of high quality illuminations'. Dated c.1424 and catalogued as MS 4, this volume contains the Hours of the Blessed Virgin and the Office for the Dead. See James Hogg, 'Brigittine Manuscripts Preserved at Syon Abbey', *Spiritualität Heute und Gestern* ll, *Analecta Cartusiana* 35:15 (1993), 230. I wish to thank Professor Ann Hutchison of the Pontifical Institute of Medieval Studies, Toronto, for bringing this article to my attention.

tute the primary focus of this paper, as an analysis of their style and iconography may help to establish a date for the manuscript, and may also yield information regarding the identity of the artist or workshop responsible for its decoration.

In view of its decorative programme, it is very surprising that MS Cotton Claudius B.I. has escaped the scrutiny of art historians for so long. To my knowledge, no thorough art historical investigation of this manuscript has hitherto been undertaken. Such is not the case, however, insofar as textual analysis is concerned. Since the early decades of the twentieth century, the manuscript has received the serious attention of specialists of Middle English literature. In 1929, W.P. Cumming examined the volume in conjunction with his publication of another Middle English translation of the *Book of Revelations* in the Garrett Collection of Princeton University Library.[7] His observations regarding the Cottonian codex are restricted to the text; there is absolutely no mention of the illuminations.[8]

In 1987, Roger Ellis published a critical edition of MS Cotton Claudius B.I.,[9] together with a short Life of St Bridget by Birger Gregersson, the Archbishop of Uppsala, that is appended to the manuscript.[10] Like Cumming, Ellis's primary concern is the text, and consequently no details regarding the codicology or the overall appearance of the manuscript have been included in his introductory remarks.[11] Nevertheless, attention is drawn to the manuscript's decoration by the fact that the opening page of Book II on fol. 69r, with its handsome foliate initial *Y* and beautiful border ornament, serves as a frontispiece for Ellis's book.[12] In addition, the three miniatures which appear on folios 33r, 116r, and 269r have also been reproduced: each illustration is located in proximity to the passage of text

---

[7] See n. 4 above.

[8] In his analysis of MS Cotton Claudius B.I., Cumming systematically lists the location of missing leaves. In addition, he notes that the manuscript contains many abbreviations and also omits lengthy sections or paragraphs from the Latin text, xvii, xx.

[9] See n. 3 above. Ellis claims that MS Cotton Claudius B.I. is 'the sole surviving copy . . . of an anonymous Middle English translation' of St Bridget of Sweden's *Liber Celestis* (ix).

[10] Written in 1376, Birger Gregersson based his *Life of St Bridget* on select passages from the Office he composed in the saint's honour. The Middle English translation of the Life appears on fols. 1r to 3v of MS Cotton Claudius B.I.; the text is incomplete due to the loss of a leaf in the manuscript. For a critical edition of the Office see C.-G. Undhagen, *Birger Gregerssons Birgitta Officium*, SFSS ser. 2, Lat. Skrift., VI (Uppsala, 1960). This biography differs from other extant *vitae* of the Swedish saint.

[11] Ellis, *Liber Celestis*, ix, proposes producing a second volume as a complement to the critical edition of the text now in print; in this future publication, the author intends to include a description of the manuscript. Presumably, the book's decoration will be discussed at this time.

[12] The foliate initial *Y* on fol. 69r introduces the opening lines of *Rev.* II:1: 'þe son saide to þe spouse . . .' In this initial, the letter *Y* has been substituted in place of the Middle English symbol þ. It was acceptable to employ these letters interchangeably; this same practice was also followed by one of the scribes of the Garrett manuscript. See Cumming, xxxix. A second use of the inital *Y* in place of þ occurs on the opening page to *Rev.* VI:1 (fol. 229r).

to which it belongs and is accompanied by a caption identifying its subject matter. While these four monochromatic facsimiles lack the gold and brilliant colours of the original illuminations, they nevertheless provide an indication of the quality of this very fine volume.[13]

Described as *Magnum volumen Revelationum Scq Brigittae Anglice*,[14] the manuscript measures 336.5 x 228mm and contains 281 parchment leaves.[15] Although the parchment has discoloured with age, the manuscript is in very good condition, with the exception of the first few pages which show repairs. Written throughout in brown ink in a neat fifteenth-century cursive hand, there are two columns of text with thirty-six lines to the page. The foliation has been slightly altered: the original numbering in ink at the upper right-hand corner of each recto page has been crossed out and replaced in pencil, with the result that fol. 2r has become fol. 1r and so on.[16] Chapter headings are rubricated. All paragraph headings are blue. Attractive blue calligraphic initials with delicate penwork flourishes in red ink appear at intervals throughout the manuscript, undoubtedly with the purpose of directing attention to especially important chapters of text; these initials vary in size and intricacy of design.

Few details regarding the patron, provenance and early history of MS Cotton Claudius B.I. are known. The catalogue of the Cottonian manuscripts at the British Library contains only a brief reference to this edition of the *Liber Celestis*.[17] F.R. Johnston has proposed a northern provenance for the manuscript. As a basis for his assertion, he noted the presence of northern forms in the Middle English translation,[18] and the fact that the manuscript had come from the library of Sir Henry Savile, whose collection was composed primarily of volumes originating in the north of England.[19]

Johnston also suggests that MS Claudius B.I. may earlier have been

---

[13] The framed miniature on fol. 33r of British Library, MS Cotton Claudius B.I. which illustrates *Rev.* I:31, appears as the frontispiece for this volume. Due to the fact that it has not been possible to include other illustrative material with this essay, readers are directed to the four reproductions furnished by Ellis, *Liber Celestis*. Full bibliographical references will be provided for all comparative material discussed in the following pages.

[14] This inscription is handwritten in brown ink at the top of the verso side of a blank leaf preceding the first page of text in the manuscript.

[15] These statistics are provided by Cumming, xx. [The manuscript's measurements are given as 13¼ x 9 inches.]

[16] For the sake of consistency, the folio numbers referred to in the following pages will coincide with those cited by Ellis, *Liber Celestis*.

[17] *A Catalogue of the Manuscripts in the Cottonian Library Deposited in the British Museum*, I (London, 1802), 191, contains a single paragraph regarding this manuscript, which reads as follows: 'Codex membran. in folio, contains 280 folios. The heavenly revelations unto blessed Bride, princess of Nerice in the realm of Swecie; with some miniature paintings. The first sheet, and some at the end, are wanting.'

[18] Cumming observed that the translation 'differs in both style and wording from other manuscripts and has many Northern forms (*kyrke, ilk, ane, wald, swylke*)' (xx).

[19] See J.P. Gilson, 'The Library of Sir Henry Savile of Banke', *TBS*, IX, 135ff, as cited by

in the possession of Lord Scrope of Masham, whose will refers to a copy of St Bridget's works.[20] It is likely that Scrope's interest in the writings of the Swedish saint came about through the influence of his kinsman, Sir Henry Fitzhugh, one of the individuals responsible for the introduction of the Brigittine Order into England.[21] Johnston's arguments deserve consideration, but much of his evidence is speculative. Consequently, further investigation must be undertaken to substantiate the claim that MS Claudius B.I. is the product of a northern workshop.

W.P. Cumming maintained that the first editions of the *Liber Celestis* reached England sometime between 1370 and 1373;[22] Ellis considers this too early, and argues for a date within thirty-five years of the saint's death.[23] It is conceivable, however, that copies of the Latin text had already arrived in England by 1379. Interest in the *Book of Revelations* was at its height at that time, undoubtedly stimulated by the attention surrounding the proceedings for Bridget's canonization currently in progress in Rome.[24] In a communication of January 15, 1378, addressed to the Archbishop of Uppsala, Alfonso Pecha de Vadaterra reported on its favourable reception in Spain, in the Kingdom of Sicily, and in Italy.[25] Subsequently, many ecclesiastics and members of the nobility acquired copies for their personal use: the Bishop of Worms obtained a copy for the German emperor, and the Franciscan, Peter of Aragon, a relative of the French king, carried a volume to France.[26] The queens of Spain and Cyprus were

---

F.R. Johnston, 'The English Cult of St Bridget of Sweden', *Analecta Bollandiana* 103 (1985), 80 n. 37.

[20] Johnston, 80 n. 38, who cites C.L. Kingsford, 'Two Forfeitures of the Year of Agincourt', *Archaeologia* (1918), 82. Scrope's will states that he had purchased the manuscript at Beverley (Yorkshire).

[21] For Henry Fitzhugh's contribution to the introduction of the Brigittines to England, see Johnston, 80, 89, and D. Knowles, *The Religious Orders in England. The End of the Middle Ages*, II (Cambridge: Cambridge University Press, 1955), 176–77.

[22] Cumming, xxix, and nn. 1, 2.

[23] Ellis, *Liber Celestis*, xii, and n. 3. St Bridget died in Rome on 23 July, 1373.

[24] The English cardinal, Adam Easton (d.1397), a staunch supporter of Bridget and a member of her spiritual family, was among those who testified on behalf of her canonization during the papal commission initiated by Urban VI in 1379. Due to the outbreak of the Great Schism, these proceedings were aborted. More than a decade later, in 1391, Bridget of Sweden was canonized by Boniface IX. For a contemporary report of the 1379 canonization proceedings, see *Laurentius Romanus*, ed. K. Karllson, *Lars Romares Beratelse om den Heiligi Birgittas Kanoniserung* (Stockholm, 1901), 1–15. For a brief discussion of Adam Easton, see Knowles, *The Religious Orders in England*, II, 56–58.

[25] A portion of the letter's contents was quoted by K.B. Westman, *Birgittastudier* (Uppsala, 1911), I, 21 n. 5, and are repeated by Carl Nordenfalk, 'St Bridget of Sweden as Represented in Illuminated Manuscripts', *De Artibus Opuscola XL, Essays in Honour of Erwin Panofsky*, ed. Millard Meiss, 2 vols. (New York, 1961), II, 379 n. 24.

[26] The edition of the *Revelations* which Peter of Aragon carried with him to France is likely identical with the volume which today belongs to the library of the Louvre in Paris; this manuscript, in turn, is considered the probable model for a miniature in a French translation of Book VIII of the *Liber Celestis* commissioned by Louis d'Orleans in 1397

among the recipients, as was Queen Giovanna I of Naples.[27] While the list contains no mention of England, at least one copy of the *Revelations* is known to have arrived in the country prior to the end of the century.[28]

In 1929, Cumming identified a total of seven copies of the *Liber Celestis* in Middle English translation.[29] Compared with the meagre quantity of extant manuscripts in English, the number of surviving copies in Latin is considerably larger.[30] Like their counterparts in English translation, however, many of the Latin copies in England contain only a selection of revelations, or consist merely of excerpts. The excessive length of the complete set of revelations, which total almost seven hundred, undoubtedly explains the dearth of volumes containing the entire text. The *Book of*

for presentation to his uncle, Jean de Berry, the following year. François Avril, 'Trois manuscrits napolitains des collections de Charles V et de Jean de Berry', *Bibliothèque de l'École des Chartes* CXXVII (July–December, 1969), 328, n. 1, maintains that the miniature in the French copy is related iconographically to its counterparts in two Neapolitan codices now in New York and Palermo. The manuscript from the library of the Duke de Berry is discussed by L. Delisle, *Le Cabinet des manuscrits de la Bibliothèque Imperiale. Étude sur la formation de ce depot*, 3 vols. (Paris, 1868–81), I: 101, and III: 182, no. 135. For the Louvre copy, see L. Delisle, *Recherches sur la librairie de Charles V* (Paris, 1907), II: 56, no. 320.

[27] The list of distinguished patrons, both lay and ecclesiastic, who had acquired copies of the *Book of Revelations* in 1379, was provided by Juan de Turrecremata (Torquemada), the eminent Dominican theologian (later a Cardinal) who defended the orthodoxy of St Bridget and her *Liber Celestis* at the Council of Basle in 1436. Turrecremata's report was based on a letter written some fifty years earlier by the Confessor General of the Brigittine Order, Magnus Petri. The document is quoted by Nordenfalk, 380, and n. 26. According to Johnston, 79 n. 29, a copy of the list compiled by Magnus Petri exists in a manuscript in the Chapter Library of Lincoln Cathedral, MS 114 (f. 16r).

[28] Oxford, Merton College, MS CCXV is written in an English hand and includes a biography of the saint by a different scribe. The manuscript is discussed by H.O. Coxe, *Cat. cod. Mss in Collegiis Aulisque Oxon.* (1825), I: 71, as cited by Johnston, 79 n. 30.

[29] In addition to MS Cotton Claudius B.I. and MS Cotton Julius F.II., the four other codices of the *Liber Celestis* in Middle English which Cumming examined in preparation for his publication of the so-called Garret manuscript, Princeton University Library, MS 1397, included Oxford, Bodleian Library, MS Rawlinson C.41, Lambeth Palace Library, MS 432, plus two others in the collection of the British Library, MS Harley 4800 and MS Arundel 197. All seven copies are said to differ significantly in size, content and literary merit and appear to be quite independent from one another. For observations concerning these manuscripts, see Cumming, xvi–xx.

[30] Cumming lists sixteen extant Latin manuscripts of the *Book of Revelations* in British collections, xx n. 2. Recent scholarship has increased our knowledge of the numbers of surviving copies in both Latin and Middle English. Cf. Roger Ellis, ' "Flores Ad Fabricandam . . . Coronam": an Investigation into the Uses of the Revelations of St. Bridget of Sweden in Fifteenth-Century England', *Medium Aevum* 51 (1982), 163–186; Domenico Pezzini, '*How Resoun Schal Be Keper of þe Soule*: Una Tradizione del Quattrocento Inglese Dalle Rivelazioni (VII, 5) di S. Brigida di Svezia', *Aevum* 60 (1986), 253–271; and *idem*, '*The Twelf Poyntes*: Versioni di un Tratto Brigidino (*Rev.* II,16) nel Quattrocento Inglese', *Aevum* 62 (1988), 286–301.

Revelations has frequently been criticized for its numerous repetitions and undue length.[31] Roger Ellis was not the first to recognize this fact when he described the book as 'a vast and sprawling collection of revelations . . . [which] repeat themselves to a fault on a fairly narrow range of topics'.[32] Indeed, the art historian, Carl Nordenfalk, went so far as to suggest that the revelations 'did not offer sufficient individuality to inspire artistic invention'.[33] Such a statement ignores the fact that St Bridget has been acclaimed as an author with imagination, poetic scope, and a lively sense of narrative, whose writings ensured her an honoured position in Swedish literature. Not only did her *Book of Revelations* serve as a major influence on the religious literature of the Late Middle Ages,[34] it was also destined to foster a wealth of artistic invention.

Seeking papal sanction for her Order, Bridget left her homeland for Rome in 1349. She never returned to Sweden, choosing to reside in Italy for the last twenty-three years of her life.[35] In her later years, she was a frequent guest at the court of Queen Giovanna I in Naples, and her cult became widespread in the Neapolitan capital and its environs. Indeed, the first devotional paintings of the Swedish prophetess appeared in that city in the years immediately following her death.[36] Some of the earliest and most enduring images of the Swedish saint are found in a group of illuminated manuscripts of the *Liber Celestis* executed in a Neapolitan scriptorium towards the end of the fourteenth century. Closely contemporary in date, these four codices have almost identical cycles of illustrations. Their importance to the history of art has been considerable, as their imagery was responsible for establishing an iconography for representations of St Bridget in miniature painting and in monumental art, both in Italy and in Northern Europe, which survived for centuries.

The most beautiful and most complete copy belongs to the Pierpont

---

[31] The text contains flaws and numerous repetitions, as well as some errors in dogma; in addition, it was not compiled chronologically. For a discussion of these problems, see The Benedictine Fathers of Paris, *Vie des Sts et des Bienheureux selon l'ordre du calendrier avec l'historique des fêtes*, vol. 10 (Paris, 1952), 241–42; cf. also, Aili, 'St Birgitta and the Text', 75–91.

[32] Ellis, 'Flores Ad Fabricandam', 163 and n. 4. Similar observations were made earlier by Cumming, xxi, and by A. Lindblom, 'Den heliga Birgittas uppenbarelser illustrerade i medeltidskonsten', *Ord och bild*, XXIV (1915), 514.

[33] Nordenfalk, 376.

[34] In the Introduction to the *Acta et processus*, Isak Collijn refers to Bridget as 'the greatest poetic genius of our [Swedish] Middle Ages' (i).

[35] Collijn, *Acta et processus*, 94.

[36] Collijn, *Acta et processus*, records the names of witnesses and the accounts of numerous miracles attributed to the intercession of Bridget as the result of prayers directed to devotional images displayed in Neapolitan churches of Sta Maria de Carmelo, S. Giorgio Maiore, S. Eligio, and S. Antonio de Vienna *extra muros* (166–173 and 233). None of these paintings are believed to be extant.

Morgan Library in New York.[37] Catalogued as Morgan MS 498,[38] the decoration of this luxurious manuscript includes two splendid full-page miniatures and twelve historiated initials.[39] The second manuscript, Palermo, Biblioteca centrale della regione siciliana, MS IV.G.2.,[40] though larger in scale and lacking full-page miniatures, is otherwise so closely related in style and iconography to the New York codex its ten historiated initials have been ascribed to the same anonymous master. Both volumes date c.1378–80.[41] A manuscript in Warsaw, Biblioteka Narodowa, MS 3310 (formerly Lat. Q.v.I.123.),[42] and a fragment from a severely burned

---

[37] Hans Aili considers MS 498 as 'undoubtedly the most beautiful of the surviving *Revelaciones* manuscripts'. See Aili, *Revelaciones Book IV*, 23. See also *Sancta Birgitta Revelaciones Liber I. Cum prologo Magistri Mathie*, ed. C.-G. Undhagen, SSFS ser. 2, Latinska skrifter VII:1 (Stockholm, 1978), 156–162; *Italian Manuscript Painting 1300–1550. Catalogue of an exhibition held at the Pierpont Morgan Library, 7 December 1984 to 17 February 1985*, Preface by C. Ryskamp, Introduction by W.M. Voekle (New York, 1984), cat. no. 17 (unpaged). A codicological report of the manuscript prepared by M. Harrsen in 1946 is available in typescript in the Morgan Library.

[38] Written in Latin on parchment and measuring 268 x 192mm, Morgan MS 498 has 414 leaves. In addition to the Prologue by Master Matthias, and Books I to VII of the *Revelations*, it contains the text of the *Epistola solitarii ad reges*, the *Liber coelestis imperatoris ad reges* (Book VIII), the *Sermo angelicus*, and the *Orationes divinitus revelatae*.

[39] F. Bologna, *I Pittori alla corte angioina di Napoli, 1266–1414* (Rome, 1969), 329, suggests that MS 498 was commissioned by Queen Giovanna I of Anjou. To date, neither the curators at the Morgan Library nor other specialists of Neapolitan illumination have accepted Bologna's attribution, and there is no inscription, coat-of-arms, or colophon to indicate either the original patron or the original owner. Two *Ex-Libris* inscriptions on fols. 301v and 414r state that the volume once belonged to the Olivetan monastery of S. Girolamo in Quarto near Genoa. Alfonso Pecha de Vadaterra retired to this monastery shortly before his death in 1389, and it is likely that the manuscript was among his personal belongings when he took up residency there. Just when the manuscript passed out of the possession of the monastery is not known. In 1884, it belonged to A. Firmin Didot. The Morgan Library purchased it from the firm of Leo S. Olschki in 1912.

[40] Formerly known as the Biblioteca Nazionale, the library in Palermo has been renamed as the Biblioteca centrale della regione siciliana. The copy of the *Revelations* in their collection, MS IV.G.2., is written in Latin on parchment and measures 375 x 260mm. In addition to the *Prologue*, Books I to VII of the *Revelations*, the *Epistola solitarii ad reges*, the *Liber coelestis imperatoris ad reges* (Book VIII), the *Sermo Angelicus*, and the *Orationes divinitus revelatae*, the manuscript also contains the text of the *Regula S. Salvatoris* which is absent from Morgan MS 498.

[41] Minor differences in the compositions and the marginal decoration can undoubtedly be attributed to the increased scale of this volume over that of MS 498. For details regarding the Palermo manuscript, see Nordenfalk, 378, and *passim*; Angela Daneu Lattanzi, *Il 'Liber Celestis Revelationum' di S. Brigida in un codice campano della seconda metà del secolo XIV* (Palermo, n.d. [1955]); *idem, I Manoscritti ed Incunaboli Miniati della Sicilia*, I, *Biblioteca Nazionale di Palermo* (Rome, 1965), no. 21, 62–4; and Undhagen, *Revelaciones Liber I*, 150–152. On the dating of the New York and Palermo manuscripts and their relationship with the text tradition of the *Liber Celestis*, see n. 3 above.

[42] Written in Latin on parchment, and measuring 265 x 180mm, the manuscript in Warsaw has been dated in the late 1370s. Its decoration includes one full-page miniature and six historiated initials. (The initial for Book IV has been excised.) The fact that this codex and the copy of the *Liber Celestis* in the Biblioteca Nazionale in Turin each contained a

manuscript in the Biblioteca Nazionale in Turin, MS J.III.23.,[43] make up
the original quartet.

Carl Nordenfalk was the first to bring these four volumes of the *Liber
Celestis*, as a group, to the attention of the English-speaking scholarly
community.[44] In his monograph of 1961, some manuscripts of later date
and diverse provenance whose iconography is clearly dependent upon one
or more of these Neapolitan prototypes are also identified.[45] Much more

full-page miniature as a frontispiece to *Rev.* V which is not present in Morgan MS 498, led
some scholars to conclude that they were based on a different prototype. On stylistic
grounds, however, it is evident that all three manuscripts are derived from the same source.
In his discussion of the Warsaw and Turin copies, Nordenfalk inadvertently confused the
two manuscripts. Consequently, his observations concerning the volume in Warsaw should
be applied to Turin, and vice versa. Formerly catalogued as MS Lat.Q.v.I.123, the volume
in the Biblioteka Narodowa now bears the shelf number MS 3310. It was believed to have
been lost during World War II, but has since been recovered. The manuscript is discussed
by Nordenfalk, I, 379. See the recent article by M. Lindgren, 'Ett återupptäckt Birgit-
tamanuskript' [A Rediscovered Bridget Manuscript], *ICO* [Nordic Review of Iconogra-
phy] 4 (1993), 1–15, with an English summary. Lindgren reproduces the six historiated
initials in colour. See also Jan Svanberg and Hans Aili, 'Två tidiga Birgittahandskrifter –
en återfunnenoch en brunnen' [Two early St Birgitta manuscripts – one of them lost and
recovered and the other partly burnt], *ICO* [Nordic Review of Iconography] 1 (1994),
28–40, with English summary and bibliography. My thanks to Dr Zuzana Sěbková-Thaller
for providing me with copies of these two publications.

[43] Until recently, the illuminations in the Turin codex were known only from written
records and the reproduction of a single full-page miniature which were made prior to
1904, when a fire in the Biblioteca Nazionale in Turin almost totally destroyed the book.
Nordenfalk's discussion of the manuscript was based on these early documents. Svanberg
and Aili examined the surviving fragments in 1993, and subsequently published a hitherto
unknown full-page illumination (fol. 278v) which accompanied the text for the *Regula
Salvatoris*. The manuscript was written in Latin on parchment and measures 318 x 228mm.
Dated after 1391, it is slightly later than the three other Neapolitan manuscripts, and its
illuminations are inferior in calibre, which suggests that they were executed by assistants.
See Nordenfalk, I, 378–379, and Svanberg and Aili, 'Två tidiga Birgittahandskrifter', as in
n. 42 above.

[44] Nordenfalk as in n. 25 above. Much of the earlier literature regarding the individual
manuscripts is cited in Nordenfalk's footnotes.

[45] The so-called 'Eriksberg Castle manuscript', Katrineholm, Ericsbergs slottbibliotek
[c.1415], was made available to Nordenfalk by Baron C. Bonde of Eriksberg, who gave
permission for its publication. Unknown prior to 1961, the manuscript is now in a private
collection in Sweden. It has been described as 'a North European variant of the International Style', and was possibly executed at Constance: the miniatures have stylistic
affinities with a fresco cycle in the Augustinerkirche in that city which dates from
1417–18. Though the style of the miniatures is 'Northern', their iconography is identical to
that in the Neapolitan codices. See Nordenfalk, 386–387; Undhagen, *Revelaciones Liber I*,
187–191; and Lindgren, *Bilden av Birgitta* (Höganäs: förlags AB Wiken, 1991), 15 and
passim. The second manuscript cited by Nordenfalk is now in Berlin, Staatsbibliothek der
Stiftung Preussischer Kulturbesitz, MS theol. Lat. fol. 33 [after 1460]. This edition is
believed to have come from the Brigittine Convent at Marienboem and was executed either
in Flanders or Germany. It is considered an 'extremely crude' copy of an Italian *Liber
Celestis* which was presented to Mary, Duchess of Cleves, by Friar Peter of Burgundy in

recently, Swedish scholars such as C.-G. Undhagen, Mereth Lindgren,[46] Tore Nyberg,[47] Jan Svanberg, and Hans Aili have added considerably to our knowledge of these manuscripts, expanding upon and clarifying issues addressed by Nordenfalk some thirty years previously.[48]

The decorative programme of Morgan MS 498 and its sister manuscripts is a consistent one, in which the ornament and the historiated initials are reserved for the opening page of each book of the *Revelations*, as well as for the first page of all ancillary texts, excluding the Warsaw manuscript which terminates following Book VII.[49] The two full-page miniatures in the New York copy serve as frontispieces to Books I and VIII: in each case, the historiated initials on the facing pages present an abbreviated version of the larger compositions, thus functioning as pendants. Since none of the Neapolitan copies are complete, the number of illuminations varies with individual manuscripts.

The scheme of decoration employed in MS Cotton Claudius B.I. generally adheres to the one observed in the Neapolitan codices: with a single exception, the illuminations are reserved exclusively for the first pages of individual books of the *Revelations*, chapter headings are rubricated, and attractive calligraphic initials are employed throughout. Aside from these similarities, the Cottonian manuscript differs in several respects from its Italian counterparts. First of all, there are no full-page miniatures. In place of historiated initials, MS B.I. contains three framed miniatures, two of

1387. A discussion of the manuscript is found in Nordenfalk, 384–85; Undhagen, 170–174; and Aili, *Revelaciones Book IV*, 19–21.

[46] Lindgren, *Bilden av Birgitta, passim*, discusses aspects of the miniatures in the Neapolitan manuscripts and their later derivatives, and includes some colour reproductions. There is a bibliography and a summary of the text in English, 167–178. For her study of the Neapolitan manuscript in Warsaw, see n. 42 above.

[47] Tore Nyborg, 'Birgittahandskriften i Waszawa', *ICO* [Nordic Review of Iconography] 2 (1994), 33–35.

[48] *Roster från svensk medeltid. Latinska texter i original och oversatting*, ed. Hans Aili, Olle Ferm and Helmer Gustavson (Stockholm and Goteborg: 1990), includes a discussion of Morgan MS 498 by art historian Jan Svanberg, 123–124, with full-page colour reproductions of the miniatures on fols. 4v, 5r, and 343v. In 1994, Svanberg and Aili collaborated on an article regarding the loss and rediscovery of the manuscript in Warsaw, Biblioteka Narodowa, MS 3310 (formerly MS Lat. Q.v.I.123), and a surviving fragment from the severely burned codex in Turin, Biblioteca Nazionale, MS J.III.23. See Jan Svanberg and Hans Aili, 'Två tidiga Birgittahandskrifter', as in n. 42 above. These scholars are currently preparing a much larger study encompassing the art history, codicology, and philology of the Neapolitan manuscripts: *Imagines S. Birgittae. The Neapolitan Iconographic Tradition in Brigittine Manuscripts* (forthcoming).

[49] In the textual tradition of the *Liber Celestis*, the manuscript in Warsaw, Biblioteca Narodowa, MS 3310, belongs to the first edition, or *Liber Alfonsi*, a fact which distinguishes it from the other Neapolitan codices, in spite of the iconographic similarities of their miniatures. New York, Morgan MS 498 and Palermo, MS IV.G.2, are among a small number of manuscripts containing the second Alfonsine redaction. The differences in the two editions are discussed briefly in n. 3 above.

which are located on the introductory pages of Books III and VII. Notably, the latter are juxtaposed with opening pages for Books II, IV, V, and VI whose decoration is comprised solely of marginal ornament and large foliate initials. The opening page of *Rev.* III on fol. 116r represents a further anomaly, being the only leaf in the manuscript to include both a miniature and marginal ornament. Such variation in the embellishment of pages marking the major divisions of a manuscript departs from the more conventional approach and constitutes one of the most unusual features of this volume.

As the following analysis will reveal, both the miniatures and the ornament in the Cottonian manuscript exhibit stylistic characteristics which link them indubitably with trends in English illumination of the late- fourteenth and early-fifteenth centuries. Furthermore, the iconography also appears to be distinctively English, as all three miniatures are quite independent of influences from either the Neapolitan manuscripts, or from other nearly-contemporary codices of the *Liber Celestis* illuminated on the Continent.

The framed miniature which illustrates *Rev.* I: 31 is located in the lower right text column of fol. 33r, immediately following five lines of rubrics.[50] Extending for a full nine lines of text and occupying the entire width of the column, the miniature is almost square in format. A simple blue frame with delicate penwork flourishes at the corners surrounds the narrative scene on three sides, while the base line of the composition serves as the lower border. Below the miniature, a large blue initial T with fine red filigree ornament introduces the opening passage of text: 'The spouse sawe þe whene of heuen . . .'[51] In this chapter, Bridget describes a radiant vision of the Blessed Virgin, Queen of Heaven, arrayed in costly garments and wearing a golden crown ornamented with seven lilies and seven precious gems.[52] John the Baptist appears and explains the significance of these symbols to the saint.

---

[50] A reproduction of the miniature on fol. 33r is reproduced in Ellis, *Liber Celestis*, opposite 55. The rubrics immediately preceding the miniature read: 'Capitulum xxxi. Howe þe spouse sawe oure ladi coroned and araied and howe Saint John declare[s] hir vision.'

[51] Calligraphic initials with penwork flourishes have been a characteristic of English manuscript decoration from the mid-fourteenth century. See *The Glory of the Page: Medieval and Renaissance Illuminated Manuscripts from Glasgow University Library. Catalogue of an exhibition organized for the Art Gallery of Ontario, 16 October 1987 – 3 January 1988*, Introduction and Catalogue by Nigel Thorp (London: Harvey Millar Ltd, 1987), cat. 40, 93. Evidence that this style of initial continued in popularity well into the fifteenth century is provided by the examples found in the Chichele Breviary, Lambeth Palace Library, MS 69. Fol. 4r is reproduced by O.E. Saunders, *English Illumination*, 2 vols. (Paris: Pantheon Casa Editrice, 1928), II, plate 122.

[52] The Latin text of *Rev.* I, 5: 8 describes the Virgin Mary as 'angelorum gloria et regina' [the glory and the queen of the angels]. The wording differs somewhat in the Middle English translation of MS Cotton Claudius B.I., where the passage reads 'þou art þe ioi of aungels and of all saintes . . .'

Bare shouldered and wearing a long blue cloak, the Baptist is portrayed on the left and slightly to the rear of the kneeling Bridget, who occupies the central position in the composition; in a gesture of reassurance, he places his hand on her shoulder. The Swedish saint is clad in the white wimple and the black robe of a widow:[53] the folds of her garment open to display a soft grey lining. With her hands clasped in prayer, she gazes with rapt attention towards the Virgin, who stands opposite her on the right. Wearing a golden crown and holding a large sceptre, the Virgin Mary is splendidly attired in a blue, ermine-lined cape over a crimson gown embellished with gold. Acknowledging the suppliant saint, she reaches out and gently touches Bridget with her free hand. Portrayed in close proximity to one another, the three figures are aligned directly on the picture plane where they occupy a narrow strip of grass dotted with small white flowers. A delicately diapered background comprised of a gold foliate design on a red ground has been substituted for a landscape, with the result that all sense of spatial recession is completely negated.[54]

The flesh tones have been skilfully modelled and facial features are rendered with sensitivity; indeed, there is a genuine sense of psychological interaction between the protagonists, a quality which is reinforced by the intimate gestures that link the three figures. Together, these elements combine to create a strong composition with considerable emotional appeal. The Virgin, the Baptist, and St Bridget have been given identical gold haloes outlined in black: those belonging to the Virgin and the Baptist extend beyond the miniature field, as does a small piece of the latter's robe, which intrudes into the frame on the extreme lower left. This

[53] St Bridget founded the Order of the Most Holy Saviour [SS. Salvatoris], also known as the Brigittine Order; confirmation of the Order was conferred by Pope Urban VI in 1378, five years after the saint's death in 1373. Bridget was never professed, but because she is associated so closely with the Order, she is sometimes depicted in the habit of a Brigittine nun. In the three miniatures in MS Cotton Claudius B.I. the representation of the saint in widow's attire is correct and conforms with the iconographic model traditionally established for her depiction. For a full discussion of the Order and the conditions surrounding its foundation, see *Sancta Birgitta. Opera minora I. Regula Salvatoris*, ed. Sten Eklund, SSFS ser. 2, Latinska skrifter VIII:1 (Stockholm: Almquist & Wiksell International, 1975), esp. 21, 22, and n. 16.

[54] Although they vary in design, gold-tooled diaper patterns of the kind employed as backgrounds for the miniatures on fols. 33r and 116r in MS Cotton Claudius B.I. have a long tradition in manuscript illumination both in England and on the Continent. An English example closely contemporary in date to the Cottonian codex is provided by the *Psalter and Hours of John, Duke of Bedford*, London, British Library, MS Additional 42131. The historiated initial introducing Psalm 80 on fol. 151v is reproduced by Richard Marks and Nigel Morgan, *The Golden Age of English Manuscript Painting 1200–1500* (New York: George Braziller Inc., 1981), plate 34 B. The illumination, which has been attributed to Herman Scheerre, depicts the marriage of King David to Saul's daughter Mical (I Samuel 18.27), and is probably a visual allusion to the nuptials of Henry V to Catherine of Valois on 2 June 1420. The reference to this historical event provides an important *terminus post quem* in dating the manuscript. The gold-tooled diaper background in this representation is very close to those in the *Liber Celestis*.

compositional trait, which occurs in an even more pronounced fashion in the illumination on fol. 269r, seems to be one of the distinguishing features of this artist's style, together with the tendency to delineate drapery with ample, curvilinear folds.

The iconography of the miniature on fol. 33r accords so faithfully with the text, it is obvious that it was created specifically to illustrate *Rev.* I: 31. Whether its design originated with MS Cotton Claudius B.I., or whether it was copied from a now lost exemplar, must remain an open question. I am unaware of any other copies of the *Liber Celestis* which contain an illustration for this particular chapter. Consequently, the miniature on fol. 33r may very well be a unique image.

The opening page for *Rev.* III in MS Cotton Claudius B.I. is the most sumptuous of the entire manuscript: an elaborate decorative border completely surrounds the two text columns on fol. 116r. This beautiful page is further enhanced by the presence of a large framed miniature at the top of the left text column,[55] followed by rubrics, and a fine decorative initial *I* [*esu Criste . . .*] which introduces the text of *Rev.* III:1. The gold ground and the rich colours employed in the foliate design of this initial closely parallel those found in the letter *Y* on fol. 69r. Similarly, many of the details in the border ornament correspond very closely with the decorative borders on fols. 69r, 148r, 211r, and 229r.

Like the illustration for *Rev.* I: 31, the miniature on fol. 116r is also enclosed within a simple frame. Rectangular in format, it occupies the entire width of the column and extends in length for a full fifteen lines of text. It is the largest of the three miniatures in MS B.I. The composition is limited to Bridget, on the right, who is seated upon a large, throne-like chair surmounted by a canopy, and a bishop, wearing liturgical dress and holding a crosier, who stands on the left facing the saint with his right hand raised in a gesture of blessing. Wearing a black robe and a white wimple, Bridget is holding an open book on her lap. A plain gold halo rimmed with black encircles her head.

A comparison of this miniature with an historiated initial *I* on fol. 93r from the Neapolitan codex, Morgan MS 498, reveals how little correspondence there is in their iconography, despite the fact that each serves as an illustration for *Rev.* III:1.[56] The only elements which the two compositions have in common, the figures of the saint and the bishop, are determined by the rubrics.[57] Otherwise, the activities of the individuals in the respective scenes differ appreciably.

---

55 The miniature on fol. 116r, together with a detail of the border ornament in the left margin, has been reproduced by Ellis, *Liber Celestis*, opposite 195.

56 The historiated initial on the opening page of *Rev.* III in the Morgan manuscript, MS 498 [fol. 93r] is reproduced in monochrome by Nordenfalk, 124, fig. 13, and in colour by Lindgren, *Bilden av Birgitta*, 50, fig. 34.

57 The rubrics commence: 'Capitulum primum. Wordes of informacion and monicion saide to a bishope . . .' and conclude: 'And howe in all he sall exercise a bishopes office'.

In the Cottonian manuscript, Bridget is portrayed as a *femme des lettres*, seated at a desk and writing in a book, an iconographic motif with which she is closely identified:[58] this imagery not only alludes to the saint's literary accomplishments, but also directs attention to the *Liber Celestis*, considered one of the major works of religious literature produced during the late Middle Ages.[59] It is the erect, authoritative figure of the bishop clad in rich ecclesiastical attire, however, who dominates this composition.

By contrast, his counterpart in the Neapolitan illumination has been cast in a subordinate role, and Bridget has been given greater prominence, due both to her increased scale and to her actions. Standing on the right, the saint receives the *Liber Celestis* from Christ, who appears in a mandorla on the upper left; she then consigns the book to a bishop in cope and mitre who stands opposite her on the left. In lieu of a full halo, her head is encircled with golden rays, an indication that she has not yet been canonized.[60] While no attempt at true portraiture was intended, the prelate depicted in this historiated initial may represent Alfonso Pecha de Vadaterra, the former Bishop of Jaén, a devoted disciple who served the saint both as a confessor and amanuensis. Towards the end of her life, she entrusted Alfonso with her literary remains, and likewise charged him with the responsibility of preparing an authoritative edition of the *Liber Celestis* in Latin.[61]

In spite of the disparity in their iconography, the two illuminations do share a number of stylistic traits: in both representations, compositional elements have been reduced to a minimum, and the protagonists are situated upon a shallow stage in the immediate foreground. In the Cottonian miniature, spatial recession has been minimized by the use of a diaper pattern identical to that employed as a background in the illustration on fol. 33r. A similar negation of space occurs in the historiated initial from

The Middle English translation of the rubrics for *Rev.* III:1 in MS Cotton Claudius B.I. is very close to the original Latin.

[58] Representations of Bridget writing down her revelations recur frequently in a variety of media, including manuscript illumination, woodcuts, textiles, frescoes, altarpieces, and sculpture. Depictions where she appears accompanied by an angel are generally associated with the *Sermo Angelicus*: the latter consists of liturgical readings composed by the saint for daily use by the members of her Order. One of the earliest representations of this subject appears in the New York manuscript, MS 498. The historiated initial on fol. 392r depicts the saint seated in her cell, one hand resting on an open book, while a nimbed angel stands at her side dictating. Above the two figures, rays of golden light issue from a tiny mandorla containing the head of Christ. This illumination is reproduced in monochrome by Nordenfalk, 125, fig. 25, and in colour by Lindgren, *Bilden av Birgitta*, 87, fig. 83.

[59] See n. 34 above.

[60] This visual evidence is one of the factors considered in dating the New York, Palermo and Warsaw manuscripts to the decade or so prior to her canonization by Boniface IX on 7 October 1391.

[61] For Alfonso Pecha da Vadaterra's contribution to the compilation and editing of the *Liber Celestis*, see n. 3, above.

the Morgan manuscript, where a simple gold ground provides a neutral, indeterminate foil for the figures.

One of the best-known of all St Bridget's revelations is represented in the miniature on the opening page to Book VII of the *Liber Celestis*.[62] During a pilgrimage to the Holy Land in 1372, just a year prior to her death, Bridget visited Bethlehem. Her devotions at the site of the holy birth precipitated a vision of the Nativity.[63] Her vivid account of the birth of Christ was responsible for establishing an entirely new iconography for representations of the Nativity throughout the late-fourteenth and fifteenth centuries, particularly in Italy, Spain, Germany and the Netherlands.[64] Indeed, depictions of the 'Nativity according to St Bridget of Sweden' made their appearance in monumental painting in Italy even before the appearance of the authoritative edition of the *Liber Celestis*.[65]

Due to a plentiful use of gold, the illustration on fol. 269r is the richest in appearance of the three miniatures in MS Cotton Claudius B.I.[66] Even the frame enclosing this composition is considerably more refined than its

---

[62] The placement of this miniature on the opening page of Book VII (fol. 269r) is not inappropriate, as the rubrics read: 'Capitulum primum. How þe spouse þoght in Rome of þe birth of Criste, and how þe modir spake to hir'; there is a further reference to the birth of Christ in the text of Chapter I. In the Cottonian manuscript, the full text of the vision of the Nativity is actually found in *Rev*. VII: 22 (fols. 278r–278v). This placement differs from the Latin editions of the *Liber Celestis*, where the vision is recorded in *Rev*. VII: 21. See *Den heliga Birgittas Revelaciones Bok VII*, ed. Birger Bergh, SSFS. ser. 2, Latinska skrifter VII:7 (Uppsala: Almquist & Wiksell, 1967), 187–190.

[63] Collijn, *Acta et processus*, 270.

[64] The earliest example in Northern European art occurs in an illumination on fol. 4v in the *Très Belles Heures de Notre Dame* [the Turin-Milan Hours], Turin, Museo Civico, which dates between 1385 and 1390. Nevertheless, it remains an isolated example in French and Franco-Flemish painting, which shunned motifs considered either exotic or overtly emotional; conversely, it was just such motifs which received an enthusiastic reception in the provincial Netherlandish schools, and it was here that the new iconography of the Nativity influenced by the revelation of St Bridget was fully developed. See Erwin Panofsky, *Early Netherlandish Painting. Its Origins and Character*, 2 vols. (Cambridge, Mass.: Harvard University Press, 1953; rpt Icon Editions, New York: Harper & Row, 1971), I, 46 n. 3, and 125–126. The miniature is reproduced in II, plate 15, fig. 37.

[65] The earliest known Italian example, an altarpiece now in the Vatican Pinacoteca in Rome [Inventory no. 137 (172)], was executed by Niccolò di Tommaso, a Florentine artist who was active in Naples during the early 1370s. Measuring 43.5 x 53.8cm, the small panel painting was executed soon after 1372. For a discussion of the altarpiece, see Wolfgang Fritz Volbach, *Il Trecento. Firenze e Siena. Catalogo della Pinacoteca Vaticana*, II (Città del Vaticana, 1987), 25–26 and fig. 42. An altarpiece in the Museo Civico in Pisa represents St Bridget's vision of the Nativity with even greater detail than the Vatican panel. Originally from the monastery of S. Domenico in Pisa, the painting has been attributed to Bernardo Falconi and has been dated between the end of the fourteenth and the beginning of the fifteenth century. E. Carli, *Il Museo di Pisa* (Pisa, 1974), reproduces the altarpiece, plate XIX. The panel in Pisa is also reproduced by Panofsky, *Early Netherlandish Painting*, II, plate 15, fig. 38. For the influence of St Bridget's vision of the Nativity on the visual arts, see H. Cornell, *The Iconography of the Nativity of Christ* (Uppsala: Universitets Arsskrift, 1924).

[66] The miniature on fol. 269r is reproduced by Ellis, *Liber Celestis*, opposite 470.

counterparts on fols. 33r and 116r; in place of simple strips of colour, this frame consists of alternating bands of red and blue, with a gold square at each corner.[67] Delicate penwork flourishes embellish the outer edges of the frame. Almost square in format, the miniature is situated at the bottom of the left text column, where it extends the length of twelve lines of script. While the page contains no border ornament, this lack is amply compensated by the large quantity of rubrics, plus the addition of a large calligraphic initial *I* in the lower right text column.

The Virgin Mary is portrayed on the left, kneeling in adoration before her newborn son;[68] symmetrically balancing the figure of the Madonna, the Swedish saint kneels opposite her on the right, her hands clasped in prayer. In deference to the text, the infant Christ lies on the ground between them, his naked form surrounded by a mandorla from which golden rays emanate like tongues of flame.[69] Immediately to the rear of the child, an ox and an ass peer from behind a manger; rather than a simple wooden trough, however, the manger resembles an ornate stone sarcophagus. In this particular context, it must surely be interpreted as an allusion to Christ's future Passion.[70] The interior setting, with its tesselated floor of alternating tiles in terracotta and beige, also constitutes a decided

[67] This type of decorative frame is found frequently in English and French illuminations, and enjoyed prolonged usage. Similar frames to the one employed for the miniature on fol. 269r in MS Claudius B.I. are found in a manuscript from East Anglia of c.1300, Oxford, Bodleian Library, MS Douce 79, fols. 2v and 3r. For reproductions of these miniatures, see the exhibition catalogue *Art and the Courts, France and England from 1259 to 1328*, ed. Peter Brieger and Philippe Verdier (Ottawa: The National Gallery of Canada, 1972), cat. no. 30, plate 45.

[68] The position of the Blessed Virgin in the miniature is a direct response to the text of *Rev.* VII: 22:

> And when þe maiden felide þat sho had born hir childe, sho bowed doune
> hir heed and held vp hir handes and wirship[d] þe childe, and saide to
> him: 'Welcom mi God, mi lord, and mi son!'

Erwin Panofsky observes that the new Nativity type with the kneeling Virgin suggests an 'adoration' rather than the traditional 'nursery' type of Nativity with Mary reclining in bed. The *Meditationes Vitae Christi* by Pseudo-Bonaventure [identified as Johannes de Caulibus of San Gimignano] is considered the source for the first precise description of the Virgin kneeling in adoration before her new-born son. See E. Panofsky, *Early Netherlandish Painting*, I, 46 and n. 3.

[69] A flame-like mandorla which closely resembles the one depicted in the miniature on fol. 269r is found in an altar frontlet which was embroidered at the Brigittine motherhouse at Vadstena for Linköping Cathedral, c.1400. A detail of the embroidery is reproduced by Lindgren, *Bilden av Birgitta*, 100, fig. 93. An altarpiece of the *Nativity* executed in Lübeck, c.1420–30, whose iconography is based on the vision of St Bridget, also replicates the gilded mandorla in the Cottonian miniature. I am not aware of a publication which reproduces this painting.

[70] On page 261 of the Sherborne Missal, a manuscript in the collection of the Duke of Northumberland, Alnwick Castle, an historiated initial R portrays the Resurrected Christ emerging from a sarcophagus whose design is similar to the one employed for the manger in the Nativity scene in MS Claudius B.I. Dated between c.1400 and 1406, the

departure from both the biblical account (Luke 2.7) and the description provided by Bridget, as it reflects a much more luxurious environment than the humble grotto in Bethlehem, the traditional site of the birth of Christ.[71]

In a manner which corresponds well with her portrayal in the miniature on fol. 33r, the Virgin Mary is once again regally attired in a red gown trimmed with ermine; a voluminous, blue ermine-lined cloak, which she has removed, billows about her feet in an agitated manner. A white turban covers her head, partly obscuring her long blond hair. Bridget is depicted in her habitual white wimple and black robe; the grey lining of her garment is identical with the one in which she is shown in the illustration for *Rev.* I:31. Both the Virgin and the saint have haloes of tooled gold. Flesh tones have been delicately modelled and facial features have been subtly delineated. Care has been taken to differentiate between the youthful Madonna, who reverently contemplates the child, and the aged saint, whose attention is focused upon his Virgin Mother.

Like the miniature on fol. 33r, the illumination on fol. 269r also succeeds in conveying a sense of the psychological interplay between the personages in this scene. In spite of its intimacy and aesthetic appeal, however, the iconography departs substantially from the text of *Rev.* VII: 22. For example, the richness of the apparel worn by the Blessed Virgin is in sharp contrast to the description given in Bridget's account. According to the vision, Mary was bare-headed and clad in a simple white garment. Her cloak and shoes, which she had removed prior to the birth, lay on the ground beside her, together with rolls of linen cloth she had prepared to swaddle the infant. Before withdrawing from the scene, St Joseph had placed a lighted candle in the grotto to dispel the gloom. Following the birth, which was without pain,[72] the supernatural light radiating from the divine child completely eclipsed the material light of the flame.[73] In the Cottonian miniature, the candle is lacking, an omission which decreases the spiritual dimension of the composition.

In contrast with the earlier miniatures, where the protagonists have been aligned in the immediate foreground, the figures in this

---

Missal was illuminated by John Siferwas and assistants. The full-page miniature on page 261 is reproduced by Marks and Morgan, *The Golden Age of English Manuscript Painting*, 94, plate 28.

[71] The pattern used for the tesselated floor is similar to one employed in a representation of the *Annunciation* on fol. 12r in the Psalter and Hours of Henry Beauchamp, Earl of Warwick. Dated between 1439 and 1446, this manuscript is now in the Pierpont Morgan Library, New York, MS M. 893. The miniature, which adheres to the canons of the International Gothic style, is reproduced in colour by Marks and Morgan, *The Golden Age of English Manuscript Painting*, 114, plate 38.

[72] Regarding the painless birth, see Louis Réau, *Iconographie de l'art chrétien* (Paris: Presse Universitaires de France, 1955–59), vol. II, 218–219.

[73] The text reads in part:

And þare com so grete a light and brightnes þat it passed þe brightenes of representation are set back from the picture plane. Significantly, the ample folds of drapery from the garments of the two holy women extend beyond the miniature field and overlap the frame. By situating his subjects in front of the frame, the artist has given them greater prominence, and has also succeeded in conveying a sense of limited depth. In spite of this illusion, one tends to read the composition vertically as a result of the tipped-up perspective of the tiled floor. In addition, although the gold background enhances the preciosity of the scene, it also contributes to the negation of space. Notably, this gold ground, with its intricate tooled design, is quite different from the diaper patterns employed for the miniatures on fols. 33r and 116r.[74]

It is indeed surprising that there is no equivalent to this representation of the Nativity in any of the Neapolitan manuscripts or their later derivatives. The historiated initial *C* which appears on the introductory page of *Rev.* VII in Morgan MS 498 (fol. 304v),[75] depicts St Bridget kneeling in prayer with her eyes raised towards the vision of the Virgin in a mandorla borne by four angels. This allegorical image provides absolutely no indication of the textual contents of Book VII.[76]

The fact that the iconography of the miniature representing the 'Vision of the Nativity' in MS Cotton Claudius B.I. does not conform with the Middle English text of *Rev.* VII: 22 suggests one of two possibilities: either the artist chose to copy from an existing model, in which case he had a rich store of available imagery at his disposal,[77] or he created an

---

þe son, and þe lightnes of þe candill þat Joseph sett on þe wall might nozt be sene.

Erwin Panofsky maintains that a description of the supernatural light suffusing the grotto following the birth of Christ is found in the Apocrypha (Pseudo Matthew, XIII; Arabic Infancy Gospels, III). The motif of a supernatural light extinguishing a natural light source may originate from the account of the birth of Dionysus by Philostratus (*Imagines*, I:14). See Panofsky, *Early Netherlandish Painting*, 126, n. 3. For the symbolic interpretation of the candle, see M. Meiss, 'Light as Form and Symbol in some Fifteenth-Century Paintings', *Art Bulletin* XXVII (1945), 176, n. 2.

[74] Similar tooled-gold grounds are found in the *Liber Regalis* of c.1382, London, Westminster Abbey, MS 38. See *The Coronation of a King and Queen*, fol. 20r, which is reproduced by Marks and Morgan, *The Golden Age of English Manuscript Painting*, 87, plate 24.

[75] The Latin text of *Rev.* VII:1 begins: 'Cum esset in roma . . .'

[76] The historiated initial on fol. 304v of Morgan MS 498 is reproduced by Nordenfalk, II, 125, fig. 21.

[77] In addition to panel paintings and frescoes, illuminated manuscripts such as Bibles and Books of Hours invariably contained representations of the Nativity. Embroidery, too, was a popular medium for the illustration of Christological imagery, and proved to be an important vehicle for the depiction of themes from the *Book of Revelations*, particularly in Northern Europe and Scandinavia. For example, an altarcloth embroidered for the monastery church at Vadstena during the first half of the fifteenth century contains a representation of the Nativity according to the vision of St Bridget. Aili *et al.*, *Roster från svensk meteltid*, reproduce a detail with the Annunciation and the Nativity (156). The entire

original composition. If he adopted the second option, the liberties taken with the interpretation of the text may well have been made deliberately as an accommodation to the overall design of the manuscript, whose luxurious appearance undoubtedly reflects the taste of an aristocratic patron.

Indeed, the Cottonian manuscript exhibits many characteristics which relate it to the elegant, courtly style known as International Gothic. Introduced to England during the last decades of the fourteenth century, this style achieved its greatest popularity during the early fifteenth century. The unknown artist responsible for the miniatures in MS Claudius B.I. adheres to the canon of the International Gothic style in his predilection for intricate patterns and textures, which are enhanced with glowing colours and a plentiful use of gold. Spatial illusion is minimized through the placement of the protagonists in close proximity to the frontal plane, and the use of decorative diaper patterns or gold as a ground in lieu of landscape or architecture. Individual figures are well-proportioned and delineated with refinement and grace. In addition, compositions are enlivened by the inclusion of minute details, such as the tiny flowers which carpet the ground in fol. 33r, the fringe which decorates the canopy above Bridget's head on fol. 116r, and the hand-written notations in the book she is holding in the same miniature.

Significantly, there are compositional elements in MS Cotton Claudius B.I. which reveal a remarkable resemblance to the ornament and the miniatures in a manuscript in the Bodleian Library, Oxford, MS Bodley 264. Dated to the beginning of the fifteenth century, the illustrations for Marco Polo's *Li Livres du Graunt Caam* are considered among the most outstanding representatives of the International Gothic style in the field of English book production.[78] The thirty-eight miniatures were executed by Johannes, in collaboration with members of his workshop. This artist is recognized as one of the most accomplished of the period.[79]

---

altarcloth is reproduced by Mereth Lindgren, 'De heliga ankorna', *Kunsthistorisk tidskrift* I (1990), 61.

[78] The decoration of MS Bodley 264 was the result of two different campaigns. Following the arrival of the book in England c.1400, *Li Livres du Graunt Caam* was added to an already existing volume of *Li Romans du Boin Roi Alexandre* which had been written in Northern France more than a half-century earlier and illuminated by a Flemish artist, Jehans de Grise, in 1344. For details concerning the history and decoration of the manuscript, consult Marks and Morgan, *The Golden Age of English Manuscript Painting*, 109, and plate 35, which reproduces the full-page miniature on fol. 2v in colour. This beautiful illumination, which is comprised of four narrative scenes from the *Romance of Alexander*, is believed to be a replacement to the original frontispiece. Its execution is attributed to an assistant of the artist responsible for the design and execution of the miniatures for the *Graunt Caam*.

[79] The artist identified himself with the following inscription painted on the hem of the Graunt Caam's robe: 'Johannes me fecit'. His contribution to the International Gothic style in English book illumination is discussed by Margaret Rickert, *Painting in Britain: the Middle Ages* (Harmondsworth: Penguin, 1954), 180–181 and n. 62; see also Marks and Morgan, *The Golden Age of English Manuscript Painting*, 26–27.

For purposes of comparison with the Cottonian manuscript, a particularly good example is provided by the illumination on fol. 220r of the Oxford codex.[80] In the episode portrayed, the Great Caam is shown receiving a group of travellers at his court. Seated on the left, wearing an imposing crown and a flowing, ermine-lined robe, the emperor graciously accepts a book offered to him by a bearded visitor and two companions who kneel respectfully in front of his throne. A group of richly clad nobles and courtiers are crowded together immediately behind the main protagonists. Care has been taken to differentiate individuals by means of physiognomy, hair style, and dress. Skin tones are delicately modelled, and the expressions and gestures are rendered in a lively and convincing manner. Costly fabrics embroidered with gold thread, or adorned with jewels and fur, give the costumes a sumptuous appearance. The ample draperies fall in gentle, undulating folds, occasionally exposing the underlining of the garments. The scene takes place within a shallow chamber whose floor is composed of minute tiles; an ornate diaper pattern, which serves as a backdrop, effectively eliminates all sense of spatial depth.

Admittedly, the miniatures which illustrate the *Graunt Caam* in MS Bodley 264 are more complex in composition and more lavish in treatment than those in MS Claudius B.I. Nevertheless, it is apparent that the imagery in the two manuscripts shares many of the same characteristics. The similarities in style are not limited solely to the miniatures, but extend to the ornament as well. Like their counterparts in the Cottonian manuscript, the *Graunt Caam* miniatures are framed. Rectangular in shape, the illustration on fol. 220r occupies the entire width of the left text column. A large decorated initial *Q* appears immediately below the miniature. Despite the difference in shape and scale, there is an astonishing similarity in the foliate design of the initial in the Oxford codex and the decorated initial *Y* on fols. 69r and 229r in MS Claudius B.I.[81] In both manuscripts, a gold ground provides a luminous background to the painted foliate forms of the initials.

Vivid shades of red, pink, blue and green, heightened with white, are employed for the Cottonian initial on fol. 69r; this same palette has been used consistently for the decorated initials on fols. 116r, 148r, 211r, and 229r.[82]

[80] Fol. 202r from MS Bodley 264 is reproduced by Eric G. Millar, *La miniature anglaise du XIVe et du XVe siècles*, trans. from the English by Jean Buhot (Paris and Brussels: G. van Oest, 1928), plate 87a. [The original English version of this text is entitled *English Illuminated Manuscripts of the XIVth and XVth Centuries* (Paris, 1926).]

[81] This correspondence becomes even more obvious when the initial *Y* in MS Claudius B.I. is inverted and compared with the upright initial *Q* in MS Bodley 264.

[82] The colours employed for the decorated initials in MS Claudius B.I. conform with those found in many contemporary English manuscripts: the most common colours are combinations of pink, blue, orange and green, heightened with white and yellow. See, for example, the decorated page on fol. 7r, in Glasgow University Library, MS Hunter 268 (U.5.8), a Book of Hours which is dated to the mid-fifteenth century. The illuminated leaf is reproduced by Thorp, *The Glory of the Page*, cat. 37, colour plate 11.

These colours harmonize well with the more delicate hues of blue, mauve, green and gold found in the leaf and spraywork decoration which embellish the upper, lower, and right margins.[83] The elaborate frame bar in gold and brown which extends the full length of the left margin is decorated with intertwining acanthus leaves, floral sprays and barred quatrefoils: these elements are part of the repertory of motifs which are a distinguishing feature of the ornament in English illumination during the late fourteenth and early fifteenth centuries. In very costly and luxurious codices such as *Li Livres du Graunt Caam*, the *Bible of Richard II*,[84] the *Chichele Breviary*,[85] and the *Hours of Elizabeth the Queen*,[86] the ornament tends to be heavier and considerably more ornate than that found in MS Cotton Claudius B.I.

In this preliminary investigation of the manuscript, there are many questions which presently remain unanswered: the patron and the provenance of the book are unknown, and the artist's identity remains a mystery. The unusual decorative scheme employed for pages marking major divisions in book, and the random insertion of a miniature in the midst of *Rev*. I, also demand further explanation. Nevertheless, the uniqueness and importance of this manuscript is indisputable. As the only illuminated copy of the *Liber Celestis* in a Middle English translation to survive from the fifteenth century, its art historical and textual value is inestimable.

The beauty of its decoration and its substantial size suggest that MS Cotton Claudius B.I. was commissioned for a wealthy patron. The elegance and refinement of its illuminations are closely allied to the International Gothic style. This courtly style, which dominated the visual arts in England during the early decades of the fifteenth century, was eminently suited to the tastes of an aristocratic collector. While it is not possible to establish a precise date, the stylistic evidence indicates that the manuscript was illuminated during the first decades of the fifteenth century. This corroborates the date of c.1410–1420 proposed by Roger Ellis,

---

[83] Leaf and spraywork ornament of almost identical design is found in a copy of *The Mirrour of the Blessed Lyf of Jesu Christ*, a manuscript of c.1430–1440 which is now in Glasgow University Library, MS General 1130. The decorated page on fol. 142r is reproduced by Thorp, *The Glory of the Page*, cat. 33, 85.

[84] British Library, Royal MS I E. IX is dated to the end of the fourteenth century. An example of the lavish border ornament in this manuscript appears on fol. 230r. See the reproduction in Millar, *La miniature anglaise*, II, plate 74.

[85] Lambeth Palace Library, MS 69, is dated to the early fifteenth century. On fol. 4v of this manuscript, the ornament appears in the division between the two text columns and extends across the full width of the upper and lower margins. A identical placement is employed for the ornament on the opening page of *Rev*. VI on fol. 229r of MS Cotton Claudius B.I. A large foliate initial *Y* in the right text column dominates the page. In its design and colour, this initial corresponds very closely with its counterpart fol. 69r of the *Liber Celestis*. However, the location of the ornament on fol. 229r sets it apart from the other decorated leaves in the book where the ornament is confined to the outer margins.

[86] London, British Library, MS Additional 50001, which is dated between c.1420 and

who maintains that the Middle English translation is contemporary with the execution of the manuscript.[87]

Iconographically, the three miniatures in the Cottonian manuscript present an interesting study in contrasts. The illustration on fol. 33r accords so faithfully with the text of *Rev*. I: 31 that it may have been created expressly for this manuscript. In the case of the miniature on fol. 269r, however, the representation of the 'Vision of the Nativity' deviates so markedly from the account provided by St Bridget in *Rev*. VII: 22, that much of the original substance of the vision has been lost. The only miniature in the Cottonian manuscript whose iconography bears any similarity to its counterparts in the Neapolitan codices is the one on fol. 116r. In this case the resemblance in their compositions is due to a dependence on the rubric preceding *Rev*. III:1. Indeed, the iconography of the illuminations in MS Cotton Claudius B.I. appears to be completely free of the influence of the late fourteenth-century manuscripts from Naples, as well as other closely contemporary editions of the *Liber Celestis* produced on the Continent. Significantly, the attributes which are most frequently identified with the representation of St Bridget in European and Scandinavian art, such as the pilgrim's staff, the crown, the burning candle, and the angel standing beside the saint dictating her visions, are absent from the miniatures in MS Claudius B.I.[88] On the basis of this evidence, it is safe to conclude that the manuscript's distinctive iconography is English in origin.

F.R. Johnston has observed that the cult of St Bridget in England was primarily a literary one based on her writings.[89] The fact that surviving artistic evidence is limited almost exclusively to books lends particular weight to this argument. Among the corpus of extant manuscripts of the *Liber Celestis* in England, in Latin and in English translation, MS Cotton Claudius B.I. holds a pre-eminent position. Beyond its intrinsic artistic and philological value, it is a testament to the respect and devotion accorded the Swedish mystic and prophetess in fifteenth-century England.

1430. An example of the elaborate border ornament in this manuscript is found on fol. 22r. Reproduced in Saunders, *English Illumination*, II, plate 125.

[87] Ellis, *Liber Celestis*, ix.

[88] In representations of Bridget of Sweden, the pilgrim's staff refers to her role as patroness of pilgrims, and the crown alludes to her noble birth. The candle is a reference to her asceticism: in commemoration of Christ's Passion, she reputedly had the wax of a burning candle drip onto her naked flesh each Friday, as a constant reminder of Christ's suffering. The angel who appears standing beside her as she writes down her visions is associated with the Office Bridget composed for her Order, often referred to as the *Sermo Angelicus* (see n. 58 above).

[89] Johnston, 89, 93.

List of Manuscripts

Alnwick Castle, Collection of the Duke of Northumberland [The Sherborne Missal]

Berlin, Staatsbibliothek der Stiftung Preussischer Kulturbesitz, MS theol. Lat., fol. 33

Cambridge, Corpus Christi College, MS 61

Glasgow University Library, MS Hunter 268 (U.5.8)

Glasgow University Library, MS General 1130

Katrineholm, Ericsbergs slottsbibliothek (Library of Ericsberg Castle)

Lincoln, Cathedral Chapter Library, MS 114

London, British Library, MS Cotton Claudius B.I.

London, British Library, MS Cotton Julius F.II.

London, British Library, MS Harley 4800

London, British Library, MS Arundel 197

London, British Library, MS Additional 42131

London, British Library, MS Additional 50001

London, British Library, MS Additional 22285

London, British Library, MS Royal I.E.IX

London, Lambeth Palace Library, MS 432

London, Lambeth Palace Library, MS 69

London, Lambeth Palace Library, MS 233

London, Westminster Abbey, MS 38

New York, Pierpont Morgan Library, MS 498

New York, Pierpont Morgan Library, MS 893

New York, Public Library, MS Spencer 26

Oxford, Bodleian Library, MS Rawlinson C.41

Oxford, Bodleian Library, MS Douce 79

Oxford, Bodleian Library, MS Bodley 264

Oxford, Merton College, MS CCXV

Palermo, Biblioteca centrale della regione siciliana, MS IV.G.2

Syon Abbey, MS 4

Turin, Biblioteca Nazionale, MS J.III.23

Turin, Museo Civico [Turin-Milan Hours]

Warsaw, Biblioteka Narodowa, MS 3310 (formerly Lat.Q.v.I.123)

Holy Women and their Confessors or Confessors and their Holy Women? Margery Kempe and Continental Tradition

JANETTE DILLON

The Book of Margery Kempe begins and ends with the relationship between woman and confessor. Book I, chapter 1 opens with the woman in imminent danger of death following childbirth, and 'in ful wyl to be schreuyn of alle hir lyfe-tym as ner as sche cowde', including a particular sin long concealed. Her confessor, however, is 'a lytyl to hastye' and begins 'scharply to vndyrnemyn hir' before she has fully confessed, thus preventing confession of her particular sin. It is the combination of 'hys scharp repreuyng' and her fear of damnation that, the book tells us, is to blame for the derangement of her mind that then ensues.[1] The last chapter, Book 2, chapter 10, concerns Kempe's return from Danzig (Gdansk),[2] where she has spent six weeks with her daughter-in-law without the permission of her confessor. The book ends where it began, with 'ful scharp wordys' from her confessor, 'for sche was hys obediencer & had takyn vp-on hir swech a jurne wyth-owten hys wetyng' (247: 24–6).

This relationship between woman and confessor is central not only to *The Book of Margery Kempe*, but to the whole tradition of Continental female piety in the late Middle Ages. It is through this particular lens, therefore, that this paper will seek to examine the influence of the lives of Continental holy women on *The Book of Margery Kempe*. In so doing, I

---

[1]   *The Book of Margery Kempe*, ed. Sanford Brown Meech and Hope Emily Allen, EETS, OS 212 (1940), 7: 13–20. Further references to this edition are given in brackets following quotations. References to prefatory material cite page number only; references to the text cite page and line; references to Allen's notes cite page number first, followed by page/line reference to the text. More general references to *The Book of Margery Kempe* are given by chapter number, for ease of access to any edition.
[2]   There is an argument for consistency of practice in the rendering of foreign names, but an attempt at consistent anglicisation would produce anomalies in the case of names that have no English form, while consistent use of the native form occasionally courts perverse unfamiliarity. I have therefore chosen to sacrifice consistency to familiarity, and regularly render names in the form most current in English secondary literature.

also wish to underline the central importance of the work done in this area by Hope Emily Allen. Scholars working on relations between Margery Kempe and Continental holy women owe a major debt to Allen, and it is one that needs to be more explicitly acknowledged. Even where references in my work and that of others go back to primary sources, such as the *Acta Sanctorum*, Allen has almost always been there first, as her notes to the Meech and Allen edition of *The Book of Margery Kempe* indicate. Acknowledgements to later scholars can also misleadingly efface Allen from the picture, since although the particular point or quotation may be rightly referred to the later source, that source is also frequently grounded, sometimes at several removes, in Allen's work.

It was Allen who first drew attention to 'an accumulation of coincident commonplaces' between Kempe's work and that of European female mystics, and highlighted the significance of the fact that 'the commonplaces in question are not those of Middle English mysticism' (lv). This influence, in Allen's view, did not necessarily go back to any reading of Continental women's writing by Kempe or her confessor, but might have come as a result of the placing of Lynn on trade and pilgrim routes and the international status of the Dominican order to which Kempe's first principal confessor belonged (liii).[3] Lynn was the main port for travel between Sweden and England and as such was an obvious location for awareness of the developing Brigittine order. From before the order's arrival in England, however, the cult of St Bridget had been fostered in East Anglia by Cardinal Easton, who worked actively for Bridget's canonisation and maintained contact with Norwich Priory, where he had been a monk

---

[3] Other scholars have looked further at the possible reading done by Kempe and her confessors and have developed Allen's suggestions concerning the place of Lynn and its East Anglian context. For material that develops Allen's work in this paragraph I am particularly indebted to Julia Bolton Holloway, 'Bride, Margery, Julian, and Alice: Bridget of Sweden's Textual Community in Medieval England', *Margery Kempe: a Book of Essays*, ed. Sandra J. McEntire (New York and London: Garland, 1992), 203–21. See also Clarissa W. Atkinson, *Mystic and Pilgrim: The Book and the World of Margery Kempe* (Ithaca and London: Cornell University Press, 1983), ch. 6; Alexandra Barratt, 'Margery Kempe and the King's Daughter of Hungary', McEntire, 189–201; Susan Dickman, 'Margery Kempe and the Continental Tradition of the Pious Woman', *The Medieval Mystical Tradition*, ed. Marion Glasscoe (Cambridge: D.S. Brewer, 1984); John A. Erskine, 'Margery Kempe and Her Models: the Role of the Authorial Voice', *Mystics Quarterly* 15 (1989), 75–85; Gail McMurray Gibson, *The Theater of Devotion: East Anglian Drama and Society in the Late Middle Ages* (Chicago and London: University of Chicago Press, 1989), chs. 2 and 3; Lynn Staley Johnson, 'The Trope of the Scribe and the Question of Literary Authority in the Works of Julian of Norwich and Margery Kempe', *Speculum* 66 (1991), 820–38; Karma Lochrie, *Margery Kempe and Translations of the Flesh* (Philadelphia: University of Pennsylvania Press, 1991); Ute Stargardt, 'The Influence of Dorothea von Montau on the Mysticism of Margery Kempe' (Ph.D. diss., University of Tennessee, 1981); and 'The Beguines of Belgium, the Dominican Nuns of Germany, and Margery Kempe', *The Popular Literature of Medieval England*, ed. Thomas J. Heffernan (Knoxville: University of Tennessee Press, 1985), 277–313.

(Allen, 280: 47/26). Alan of Lynn, the Carmelite doctor of divinity who was so close to Margery Kempe, also worked on Bridget's revelations. The Brigittine order's ties with England were fostered by the marriage of Philippa, the sister of Henry V, to the King of Sweden, Norway and Denmark in 1406.[4] At the wedding Henry Fitzhugh donated Upperhall near Cambridge to the Brigittines, and Brigittine brothers were also sent to found another monastery in East Anglia in 1407. When the Brigittines arrived to found Syon Abbey in 1415, given to them by Henry V, they arrived at the port of Lynn. Kempe later took pains to visit Syon herself (see further Allen, 349: 245/31).

Lynn also had close ties with Danzig through the Hanseatic league, and Kempe visited her daughter-in-law's home there towards the end of her life. Through the Danzig connection Kempe may have learned of the life of Blessed Dorothea of Montau (d.1394), who had lived there from her marriage until the time she was enclosed as an anchorite. There must have been people still alive in Danzig who remembered Dorothea or her confessors (both d.1417), and Dorothea's cell at Marienwerder may have come to Kempe's attention while she was there by virtue of the fact that it was occupied by another recluse. Similarly the campaign of the Teutonic Knights for Dorothea's canonisation may well have made her a talking point during Kempe's stay. Danzig, as a frequent port on the route between Rome and Sweden, had also been a temporary resting-place for the relics of St Bridget (Allen, 258: 4/4, 343: 231/25–26, 344: 232/27, 280: 47/26).

We know from the text that at the very least Kempe was familiar with the life of St Bridget, and that the priest who wrote the book of Kempe's life had read lives of Marie d'Oignies and Elizabeth of Hungary and had been persuaded by his reading to accept Kempe's tears as a gift from God (ch. 62; cf. ch. 68). All of these lives were available in Middle English translations, as were materials concerning the lives of Catherine of Siena, Elizabeth of Spalbeck, Christina Mirabilis and Mechtild of Hackeborn, and various of their writings.[5] The text also makes clear that Kempe's pilgrimages and journeys were directed to places especially associated with some of the Continental women saints whose influence on her seems greatest, and that she specifically sought out, for example, St Bridget's maidservant in Rome (ch. 39).[6] Examples of other holy women may have

---

[4] Philippa was later buried in the Brigittine habit.
[5] Allen discusses available texts in more detail in her Prefatory Note, liii–lxviii. Dating is not certain enough for us to know how many of these texts were available in Middle English before the writing down of Kempe's text in 1436. Kempe's learned confessors would have been able to read them in Latin anyway. The relevance of such a number of Middle English translations is not to prove anything about what Kempe or her confessors had access to, but to suggest a flourishing interest in England in the lives and works of Continental holy women, together with an attempt to make these texts available to a non-Latinate audience, which might include nuns and laywomen.
[6] Holloway discusses this visit in more detail, 208–9. (See, however, Roger Ellis's caveat

come to her notice on her travels, adding to those she already knew about. In Rome, for example, she would be likely to have heard about Catherine of Siena, evidence for whose canonisation was being collected in Venice from 1411–16 (Kempe was in Rome during the winter of 1413–14), and perhaps also about Blessed Dorothea, whose miraculous pilgrimage to Rome in 1390 might still have been a topic of conversation among pilgrims (Allen, 300: 84/10).

Julia Bolton Holloway has suggested that Margery Kempe consciously modelled her life on the life of St Bridget and that both *The Book of Margery Kempe* and the *Revelations* of Julian of Norwich are created in the image of Bridget's *Revelations*, hence working together to construct 'a powerful woman's textual community, fostered by the men who were their spiritual advisors and who were willing to be their amanuenses'.[7] Although Julian of Norwich was the only woman in fourteenth-century England to have written a book of revelations, there seems to me no good case for seeing her as part of this community, nor does Holloway offer any evidence for it beyond the binding together of Julian's Short Text and Bridget's *Revelations* in one manuscript.[8] Nevertheless, the idea of a women's textual community is suggestive in terms of Kempe's relations with Continental tradition, since her pilgrimages, her reading and the various parallels between her spirituality and that of Continental holy women (documented by Allen) may well indicate a desire to participate in and extend just such an international network.

Before Holloway, Allen had already called attention to the role of confessors in assuring the status of the women under their control within this holy community. She notes that the Continental women whose influence is visible in *The Book of Margery Kempe* themselves 'had most enthusiastic confessors' and argues that

> the theory of foreign influence helps to explain why [Kempe's] obviously cultivated and conscientious confessors allowed her to continue in a type of mysticism which at many points would almost certainly have been condemned by the Middle English mystical writers whom we know to have been read in their world. (lv)

No mystic, as she points out, could have maintained his or her course without clerical support, and Kempe's learned clerical supporters may

---

concerning Holloway's identification of the maid Kempe spoke to as Catherine of Flanders in his review of the McEntire collection in *Mystics Quarterly* 19 (1993), 184. Ellis directs attention to Allen's more detailed and cautious commentary, 304: 95/11.) Holloway makes the further point that Kempe's scribe began to write the revised version of her book on St Bridget's Day, 23 July 1436 (203; see Kempe, 6: 21–4).

[7] Holloway, 215.

[8] Holloway, 211. Ellis (184) is also sceptical of Holloway's attempt to read Julian of Norwich in this context of male-fostered female piety.

have been 'swayed in their judgement of her by knowledge of the distinguished support given abroad to feminine writers' (lv).

Certain clerics became noted for their skills in supporting such women.
Alfonso de Jaén, spiritual advisor and confessor to St Bridget at the end of
her life, was also at different times advisor to St Catherine of Siena, St
Katherine of Sweden and Blessed Clare Gambacorti.[9] More generally, the
Dominicans, as an order, had built a reputation for their support of holy
women. They supervised many beguine communities and were also spiritual advisors to the famous nuns of Helfta.[10] Allen notes that a specific
revelation to Catherine of Siena on the subject of women's power to
answer clerics 'would have encouraged Dominican confessors in an indul-
gent attitude to women visionaries' (264: 17/19; cf. Kempe's own text at
this point, 17: 19). Kempe's Dominican confessor was no doubt well
aware of the activities of his Continental predecessors in supporting
women mystics.

The confessor occupied a very special place in the lives of these
women. Kempe mourns the death of the Dominican anchorite as the loss
of 'þe most special and synguler comforte þat euyr I had in erde, for he
euyr louyd me for thy lofe & wold neuyr forsakyn me for nowt þat any
man cowd do er seye' (168: 32–5). His death meant that this special place
had to be ceded to another confessor, Master Robert Spryngolde, parish
priest of St Margaret's. Kempe asks for this second confessor as her
companion in heaven, rather than her husband, father or children, and
prays that he should be rewarded in heaven for half of her tears and half of
her good works (chs. 8, 88).

The central importance of the confessor to the holy woman was no
random development. The sacrament of penance had become more important in church doctrine since the famous 1215 decree *Omnis utriusque
sexus,* requiring annual confession, and manuals for confessors on the
proper conduct of confession proliferated during the thirteenth and fourteenth centuries.[11] The growing emphasis on the importance of confession
from the early thirteenth century onwards coincided with the development
of the beguines, extraregular groups of religious women, independent of

[9] Eric Colledge, '*Epistola solitarii ad reges*: Alphonse of Pecha as Organizer of Birgittine
and Urbanist Propaganda', *Mediaeval Studies* 18 (1956), 41.

[10] Ernest W. McDonnell, *The Beguines and Beghards in Medieval Culture* (1954; rpt New
York: Octagon Books, 1969), 191–204, 341–61, 402–5. Allen notes that Thomas Netter,
Provincial of the English Carmelites from 1414, was well-known for his support of holy
women, but made a firm distinction between anchoresses and unattached women like
Kempe, whom he saw as a threat to the orthodox church (Allen, 270: 27/31, 328: 168/5,
329: 170/7). The Dominicans too preferred the holy women they supervised to be attached
to the Dominican order in the regular way (see 120 below).

[11] See Thomas N. Tentler, *Sin and Confession on the Eve of the Reformation* (Princeton,
N.J.: Princeton University Press, 1977) and 'The Summa for Confessors as an Instrument
of Social Control', *The Pursuit of Holiness in Late Medieval and Renaissance Religion*, ed.
Charles Trinkaus and Heiko A. Oberman (Leiden: Brill, 1974), 103–26.

any monastic institution. Thomas Tentler (note 11 above) has argued for confession as a form of social control, insofar as it encourages penitents to internalise the values of the church and to regulate their own behaviour through a sense of shame. In the case of beguines and other unattached holy women, confessors occupied a very explicit controlling role, since they were the church's only mechanism for supervision. It is likely that confessors to such women specifically encouraged frequent confession as a way of keeping an eye on the orthodoxy of their spiritual development.[12] The Dominicans, who were made responsible for most of these women's communities, clearly felt more at ease supervising women who had taken vows that brought them under the full control of the order, and they frequently nurtured the transformation of beguinages into Dominican convents.[13]

The Clementine decree, *Cum de quibusdam mulieribus* (1311), shows the fear and hostility of the orthodox church towards these independent female communities, and its discomfort with any religious grouping which did not come under the aegis of its established religious orders.[14] It also indicates the pressure on confessors to such groups to prove that the women under their guidance were both exceptional (in terms of their spiritual gifts and their entitlement to live in extraregular communities) and orthodox (in terms of church doctrine). It is notable therefore that holy women do not flourish in total isolation. They are dependent on the authorisation of trusted men. *Mulieres religiosae*, as these women were first known, are licensed, in both senses, by *viri probi*.[15] They are both dominated and liberated, living under the spiritual direction of authorised agents of the established church, yet set free to live lives of unorthodox independence by those very directors.

The role of the confessor, as Tentler shows, is inherently paradoxical in other ways too. He must both discipline and console, just as the penitent must feel both sorrow and joy in confession. *The Book of Margery Kempe* clearly demonstrates this paradox and the difficulty of holding discipline and consolation in balance. Kempe remarks on the apparently unconditional love and support of the Dominican anchorite and the harshness of

---

[12] See Caroline Walker Bynum, *Jesus as Mother: Studies in the Spirituality of the High Middle Ages* (Berkeley, Los Angeles and London: University of California Press, 1982), 256.

[13] McDonnell, 191–204. See further John B. Freed, 'Urban Development and the "Cura Monialium" in Thirteenth-Century Germany', *Viator* 3 (1972), 311–27 on the implications of the geographical location concerning Dominican activity in either supporting beguines or establishing nunneries.

[14] The decree is quoted in full in McDonnell, 524.

[15] The terms come from a document of 1233, recording a donation of land for the use of these women (McDonnell, 205). The *viri probi* are noted as advisers to the *mulieres religiosae*, providing them with the basis of a rule.

other confessors.[16] When she complains to the anchorite of the sharpness of the confessor who has heard her confession during the anchorite's absence, he suggests that God has as it were solved a paradox for confessors in this instance by separating the two functions of discipline and consolation between two different confessors. As the anchorite expresses it:

> God for ȝowr meryte hath ordeynd hym to be ȝowr scorge . . . & God hath ordeyned me to be ȝowr norych & ȝowr comfort. Beth ȝe lowe & meke & thanke God boþe of on & of oþer. (44: 30–45: 2)

There is a danger, of course, that the confessor who does not discipline sufficiently may provoke inordinate love to himself. As God tells Kempe, concerning Robert Spryngolde:

> þu xalt blissyn me wyth-owtyn ende þat euyr I ȝaf þe so trewe a gostly fader, for, þow he hath be scharp to þe sum-tyme, it hath ben gretly to thy profyte, for þu woldist ellys an had to gret affeccyon to hys persone.
> (216: 33–217: 3)

The dependence of women visionaries on orthodox male clerics for their authority to speak can produce an obsessive devotion to confession. Kempe is not unusual in her need to be shriven sometimes two or three times in one day (12: 23). St Bridget and Blessed Dorothea, as Allen notes, also confessed several times a day, and this within a culture where confession was normally relatively infrequent.[17] (Although Bridget herself confessed several times daily, she prescribed confession only three times a year for Brigittine nuns.[18]) The confessions of these holy women could be extremely long as well as inordinately frequent. Kempe, having failed to

---

[16] I argue in a piece forthcoming in *Leeds Studies in English* N.S. 27 that all the sharp confessors after the first are probably the same man, Master Robert Spryngolde.

[17] Frequent confession or communion (which was normally preceded by confession) is a regular feature of the lives of holy women. Margaret of Cortona, Ida of Louvain, Flora of Beaulieu, Christina Mirabilis, Catherine of Siena and Catherine of Sweden are noted for it (see further Allen, 263: 17/10; Bynum, 'Women Mystics and Eucharistic Devotion in the Thirteenth Century', *Women's Studies* 11 (1984), 179–214 and *Holy Feast, Holy Fast: The Religious Significance of Food to Medieval Women* (Berkeley: University of California Press, 1987); Richard Kieckhefer, *Unquiet Souls* (Chicago and London: University of Chicago Press, 1984), 124–31). Lutgard of Aywières was once deprived of frequent communion as a penance (Brenda M. Bolton, '*Vitae Matrum*: A Further Aspect of the *Frauenfrage*', *Medieval Women*, ed. Derek Baker (Oxford: Blackwell, 1978), 267), and Raymond of Capua notes the fact that St Catherine got on better with him than with her previous confessors because of his willingness to satisfy her desire for frequent communion 'notwithstanding the objections raised by those who wanted to deprive her of Holy Communion' (*The Life of St Catherine of Siena*, trans. George Lamb (London: Harvill Press, 1960), 284).

[18] Johannes Jørgensen, *Saint Bridget of Sweden*, trans. Ingeborg Lund, 2 vols. (London, New York and Toronto: Longmans Green, 1954), vol. I: 180.

make a complete confession at the beginning of the book, describes four occasions thereafter on which she confesses her whole life to different confessors (chs. 17, 27, 33, 69). Catherine of Siena regularly made such general confessions of all her sins,[19] and Dorothea of Montau always confessed her whole life after a revelation instructing her to do this even if her confessors objected (Allen, 261: 13/18).

Jean Gerson, a member of the commission appointed to consider the canonisation of Bridget of Sweden, is one voice of objection. He is insistent that, if the visionary is a woman, she must be questioned about how she converses with her confessors and spiritual directors:

> si collocutionibus intendit continuis, sub obtentu nunc crebrae confessionis, nunc prolixae narrationis visionum suarum, nunc alterius cujuslibet confabulationis. Expertis credite, praesertim Augustino ac domino Bonaventurae; vix est altera pestis vel efficacior ad nocendum, vel insanabilior.[20]

> [whether she draws out endless conversations, under the pretext now of frequent confession, now of a lengthy account of her visions, now of whatever conversation she chooses. Trust the experts, especially Augustine and St Bonaventure; there is scarcely any more killing or incurable disease than this.]

Gerson is not the only one to resent this obsessional devotion to confession, and occasionally the controlling power of confession is emphasised through its withdrawal. The *Revelations* of St Elizabeth describe her spiritual distress over a period of three years when 'she myght not haue her confessour as ofte as she wolde be confessyd', until God takes pity on her and sends St John to be her confessor, 'commaundynge that soo ofte as she wolde be shryuen, he sholde besely here hir and assoyle her by his auctoryte'.[21] Allen (299: 81/4) notes other examples indicating the growth of a tradition whereby St John hears the confessions of holy women deprived of an earthly confessor, a tradition which Kempe treats in some detail in describing his appearance to her when she is refused confession

---

[19] Raymond of Capua, 37.

[20] *De Probatione*, 11; *Oeuvres Complètes*, ed. Mgr Glorieux, 9 vols. (Paris: Desclée: 1960–73), vol. IX: 184. (Translations are mine except where otherwise indicated by the placing of note numbers *after* translated text.) This partly explains the tendency of female saints' lives to concentrate on the wonderful capacity of the saint for prolonged periods of silence. Raymond of Capua records Catherine of Siena's three-year period of total silence (except for confession) (71), and the Middle English version of the life of Marie d'Oignies similarly notes Marie's love of silence, commenting: 'Here-by shewiþ how grete is þe vice of eloquacite and iangelynge, syþen þat silens & stilnesse is so plesaunde to oure lorde' (C. Horstmann, ed., 'Prosalegenden: Die legenden des ms. Douce, 114', *Anglia*, 8 (1885), 148).

[21] Cited in Barratt 196–7 and noted by Allen, 299: 81/4. Barratt argues that the St Elizabeth of these *Revelations* is Elizabeth of Toess, daughter of King Andreas III of Hungary, and not Elizabeth of Thuringia, daughter of King Andreas II of Hungary. Clerical suspicion of immoderate devotion to confession should be compared with the attitudes towards frequent communion cited in n. 17 above.

by the Hospital of St Thomas of Canterbury in Rome (ch. 32). It would seem that supernatural powers of patience were sometimes called for in hearing the confessions of female visionaries.

The quasi-divine authority of the confessor is signalled by the fact that the woman is often directed to him through divine revelation. God instructs Kempe to

> gon to þe ankyr at þe Frer Prechowrys, & shew hym my preuyteys & my cownselys whech I schewe to þe, and werk aftyr hys cownsel, for my spyrit xal speke in hym to þe, (17: 31–4)

and Allen notes that Bridget, Dorothea and Blessed Angela of Foligno were also directed to their confessors by divine instruction (264: 17/31, 275: 38/1). St Bridget, when first directed to Master Matthias, Canon of Linköping, is so dubious about whether the voice that instructs her is a delusion that she at once goes to confession and takes communion. She has to hear the voice three times before she accepts its direction as authoritative.[22]

The direction to a particularly learned confessor is also widely shared. Master Matthias and Canon John of Marienwerder (Dorothea's confessor) were two of the most learned scholars of their time, and Kempe's tendency to seek out bachelors of theology and doctors of divinity is conspicuous. Naturally enough, if female visionaries were dependent on their confessors to protect them from charges of heresy and perhaps promote them as saints, then the more respected the confessor, the more secure the position of the woman whom he approved. Tentler expresses some doubt about how seriously the confessional manuals intend their direction that penitents should 'examine the intellectual credentials of their confessors'.[23] But in the specific case of holy women, whose position was so dangerous, it can be no accident that they are so frequently attached to high-ranking intellectuals. The pope had almost as much interest as the women in question in making sure that they were spoken for by reliable and educated men whose views would be taken seriously; and contemporaries were reminded of the ultimate penalty paid by women whose confessors provided inadequate authentication by the burning of Joan of Arc in 1431.[24]

Part of the role of these confessors was to undertake responsibility for the authenticity of their penitents' visions. They were therefore in the position of having both to test and to testify. 'Discretio spirituum', the ability to 'discern spirits', or recognise truly divine inspiration as opposed to delusion or deception, was recognised as problematic. Gerson wrote a famous treatise on the subject, *De Probatione Spirituum (On Proving*

---

[22] Jørgensen, vol. I: 137.

[23] Tentler, *Sin and Confession*, 124.

[24] Allen notes that Joan of Arc was not attached to a confessor in whom she had full confidence (265: 18/7).

Spirits, written 1415), and also warned elsewhere against the particular difficulty of establishing true inspiration in the case of women. All women's teachings, he argued, should be treated with scepticism, because women are explicitly forbidden to teach. And in answering the question why they are forbidden, he responded that it is 'because they are easily seduced, and determined seducers; and because it is not proved that they are witnesses to (*cognitrices*) divine grace'.[25] As Eric Colledge comments,

> The very passion with which such writers as Henry of Langenstein and John Gerson inveigh against those whom they suspect of fraud is a measure of the credence which they, in common with all medieval men, were bound to give to seers and visionaries who could pass the tests.[26]

Ironically, much of Gerson's *De Probatione*, an implicit attack on St Bridget, rearranges material from the *Epistola Solitarii* of Alfonso de Jaén, which was written specifically to defend the case for Bridget's sanctity against allegations that her revelations were from the devil.[27]

The Book of Margery Kempe gives full expression both to the mystic's need to obtain clerical support and to the weight of this responsibility on the confessor's soul.[28] Although Kempe frequently refuses to speak of her visions to the laity, she seeks out high-ranking clerics for their validation:

> Thys creatur schewyd hyr maner of leuyng to many a worthy clerke, to worsheful doctorys of divinitye, boþe religiows men & oþer of seculer abyte, & þei seyden þat God wrowt gret grace wyth hir & bodyn sche xuld not ben aferde, – þer was no disseyte in her maner of leuyng. (43: 21–5)

Above all, her Dominican confessor volunteers to be responsible for the authenticity of her claim to divine grace when others speak evil of her:

> Neuyr-þe-lesse þe ankyr of þe Frer Prechowrys in Lenn, whech was princi-pal gostly fadyr to þis creatur as is wretyn be-forn, toke it on charge of hys sowle þat hir felyngys wer good & sekyr & þat þer was no disseyt in hem.
> (43: 35–44: 3)

The book is full of examples of clerics seeking to test Kempe and

---

[25] This quotation from *De Examinatione Doctrinarum* is cited in translation by Edmund Colledge and James Walsh, ed., *A Book of Showings to the Anchoress Julian of Norwich*, 2 vols. (Toronto: Pontifical Institute of Mediaeval Studies, 1978), vol. I: 151.

[26] Colledge, 49.

[27] Colledge, 40, 44–6; Arne Jönsson, *Alfonso de Jaén: His Life and Works with Critical Editions of the Epistola Solitarii, the Informaciones and the Epistola Serui Christi* (Lund: Lund University Press, 1989), 29–30.

[28] Gerson also makes reference to the burden of responsibility carried by spiritual directors of holy women. Very few, he says, can discern whether thoughts and feelings are sent from God, a good angel, an evil angel, or the human spirit itself; and there is danger for the spiritual director in approval and reproval alike (*De Prob.*, 5, 12; *Oeuvres*, vol. IX: 179, 184).

Kempe in turn seeking clerical testimony. Alan of Lynn is convinced of the presence of the holy spirit in Margery Kempe when she is unhurt after a rafter and a stone fall on to her head and her back from the top of the church vault. The text describes how he carries out his testing by questioning Kempe, weighing the stone and getting the rafter out of the fire (where it has been put to burn) in order to inspect it (ch. 9). Her other confessor at Lynn, Master Robert Spryngolde, seeks her advice during the fire that strikes the parish church of St Margaret's, asking her whether to carry the sacrament towards the fire or not. She replies that he should take it towards the fire, since the Lord has told her all will be well. Immediately following her prayers and tears a snowstorm arises to quench the fire. For Master Robert, already convinced of her holiness, this is miraculous proof (ch. 67).[29]

It was in the interests of both holy women and the church to establish the orthodoxy of women who claimed special grace. Catherine of Siena was questioned by the provincial chapter of the Dominican order; Angela of Foligno's writings were approved by Cardinal James Colonna and eight Franciscan theologians; Alfonso de Jaén draws attention to how Bridget's *Revelations* show that she was taught to distinguish between true revelations and the devil's deceptions and to the fact that she was closely examined by authoritative representatives of the church ('prelatos ac viros spirituales et magistros in theologia').[30] The need to obtain such testimonials and even to incorporate them in the manuscript of the saint's revelations demonstrates their importance to a medieval audience.[31] The greatest testimony a cleric could offer to a female visionary was of course his decision to document her life or her visions in writing. Nearly all the revelations of Continental holy women were written down for them by their confessors, and many confessors, besides acting as scribes for the revelations, also wrote *vitae* or letters testifying to the women's holiness and took an active part in promoting their canonisation. It is not surprising, then, that confessors occupy a special position in these texts. As writers of the texts, they necessarily present the woman's life from a particular point of view, a point of view which does not fail to enhance their own status. As Richard Kieckhefer argues:

> It should be a truism that when we study the saints of the fourteenth or any
> other century what we are in fact studying are not the saints themselves but

---

29 There are many more references to such testing. See also chs. 15, 18, 24, 33, 34, 41, 75. 83. Twice the text repeats the formula that Kempe regularly spoke with many worthy and well-educated clerics and that they testified that there was no deception or delusion in her feelings (26: 21–7, 43: 21–5).

30 Jönsson, 153.

31 The 'Approbation' that precedes Angela's book can be easily consulted in the recent edition of her *Complete Works*, trans. Paul Lachance (New York and Mahwah: Paulist Press, 1993), 123. The testimonial obtained for Gertrude by the nuns of Helfta became similarly incorporated into the manuscript (Bynum, *Jesus as Mother*, 179–80).

the documents that claim to inform us about them. To be precise, we should not say that Peter of Luxembourg confessed his sins several times daily but that the sources represent him as so doing. . . The central question is not why the saints were as they appear in the sources; they may or may not in fact have been so. The fruitful question is why their biographers represented them as they did – why they recognized certain traits and not others as integral to sanctity.[32]

Thomas Heffernan's more recent work on medieval saints and their biographers examines this question further and shows how the tendency to represent saints' lives as a set of repeatable motifs stems from an impetus to produce in the reader a recognition of God's universal truth working itself out in the lives of particular individuals. The churchmen who author these lives do so from a position of conviction and are concerned less with arbitrary facts particular to the specific life in question than with the need to strengthen the audience in its faith. Revelations and lives mediated through confessor-scribes predictably tend to make confession central to the female visionary experience and to highlight the woman's relationship with the confessor as the only one of any significant depth or closeness; and this tendency reflects what Heffernan calls the 'cumulative hermeneutic' produced by parallels between successive saints' lives alongside the more obvious personal investment of the authors in such a focus.[33]

Yet it would be taking scepticism too far to see this evidence, contaminated though it is, as having no bearing at all on actual relations between woman and confessor beyond the text. Interdependence between them necessarily constructs the text in addition to being constructed by it. Woman and confessor/scribe are bound together by the secrecy and exclusiveness of their spiritual relationship as well as by their common project. The confessor is the recipient of the secrets of the confessional and also of the secrets of revelation which cannot be told to unworthy auditors. As Kempe tells the Mayor of Leicester:

> ʒe xal not wetyn of my mowth why I go in white clothys; ʒe arn not worthy to wetyn it. But, ser, I wil tellyn it to þes worthy clerkys wyth good wil be þe maner of confessyon. Avyse hem ʒyf þei wyl telle it ʒow. (116: 15–17)

The exclusiveness of the relationship encourages a closeness which is expressed in the imagery of the family, even though it is presented as closer than any actual family relationship. The group of confessor(s) and attendants that comes together around a saint is commonly referred to as a 'family', and the saint herself is commonly addressed as 'mother'. Kempe's text too constructs her as a mother on occasion: twice, clerics are

---

[32] Kieckhefer, 3–4.
[33] Thomas J. Heffernan, *Sacred Biography: Saints and their Biographers in the Middle Ages* (New York and Oxford: Oxford University Press, 1988). The phrase is cited from 121.

described as caring for her as they would for their mothers (64: 13–15, 83: 28–30).[34]

Sometimes the language of family affection seems to be pressing towards a degree of closeness beyond acceptable limits; Gerson recognised one of the dangers of protracted confession as its tendency to produce an 'insatiable itch' ('insatiabilem . . . pruriginem') to see, to talk and also to touch.[35] The correspondence between Margaret Ebner and Heinrich von Nördlingen or between Christine of Stommeln and Peter of Dacia, for example (Allen, 306: 100/23), is highly intense in its expression of affection. For Peter, Christine is his 'filia spiritualis et amica singularis, a seculo relictae', while Christine speaks of a love for Peter so great that she fears temptation.[36] Jacques de Vitry carries Marie d'Oignies's finger around with him in a reliquary after her death; Margaret of Ypres is inconsolable during the absence of her confessor, Siger of Lille, and Christ himself has to appear to comfort her.[37] Tears run down the cheeks of both Margery Kempe and her confessor in Rome as she leaves for England (100: 21–5), and when she sees Alan of Lynn again after a long embargo on their meeting, she cannot speak for weeping and joy. He too is presented as moved, for he gives her a pair of knives 'in tokyn þat he wolde standyn wyth hir in Goddys cawse, as he had don be-forn-tyme' (170: 24–6).[38] The language of women's revelations often suggests sublimated sexual desire, but we must remember that such language is usually the product of collaboration between the female speaker and the male scribe. Bynum notes that 'nuptial language is often most elaborate in *male*

---

[34] The text, in its description of spiritual relations with the Godhead, is also, of course, rooted in what Sarah Beckwith calls 'Holy Family Romance' (subsection title in Beckwith's chapter on Kempe in her book *Christ's Body: Identity, Culture and Society in Late Medieval Writings* (London and New York: Routledge, 1993)).

[35] *De Prob.*, 11; *Oeuvres*, vol. IX: 184.

[36] McDonnell, 347; John Coakley, 'Friars as Confidants of Holy Women in Medieval Dominican Hagiography', *Images of Sainthood in Medieval Europe*, ed. Renate Blumenfeld-Kosinski and Timea Szell (Ithaca and London: Cornell University Press, 1991), 232. Coakley's discussion of the relationship between Peter and Christine is part of a wider analysis of the strong personal ties existing between several friar/holy woman pairs, and the 'needy fascination' (232) that characterises the male experience of the female in these instances.

[37] Brenda M. Bolton, 'Mulieres Sanctae', *Sanctity and Secularity: the Church and the World*, ed. Derek Baker, Studies in Church History 10 (Oxford: Blackwell, 1973), 82; Bynum, 'Women Mystics', 184. Bynum specifically suggests that Margaret found in her confessor a substitute for her ex-lover, and perhaps also for her dead father and uncle. Coakley notes the acknowledgement in Thomas de Cantimpré's *Vita Margarete de Ypris* that their intimacy attracted disapproving attention from their superiors ('Friars as Confidants', 227).

[38] Alan of Lynn is of course not her confessor, but seems to stand in the analogous role of spiritual director, which may or may not include hearing confession. He comforts and encourages her and testifies to the truth of her visions.

biographers, who may have had their own reasons for describing women they admired and loved in erotic metaphors'.[39]

Gerson was not alone in seeing the dangers of confessing holy women, who, if threatening to the celibate cleric by virtue of their gender, were even more threatening than other women precisely because of their devotion to confession. Writers of confession manuals, while arguing the need for completeness in the good confession, were anxious to limit excesses: too much brooding on sins could be detrimental to both penitent and confessor.[40] (Too much intimacy as a result is an unstated, though obvious risk.) A sequence of statutes in the Dominican provinces of Rome and Provence issued repeated warnings against hearing the confessions of women, especially nuns and beguines; and although the Dominicans nurtured so many female mystics, they were unwilling from the start to take on the supervision of these women.[41]

Danger lay not only in the development of excessively close relations between confessors and holy women penitents, but in the threat such women offered to the authority of the confessor. Women who spoke with the voice of God, especially from outside the walls of a convent, challenged the authority of the clerical establishment even as they sought it. Though they needed the support of respected confessors and the orthodox church, their authority to speak, if it was established as divinely inspired, superseded the very authority that validated it. The church could not claim to be above God. The woman, even as she bowed to the church on earth, was in fact speaking from a position of higher authority that bypassed the church's mediation. The image of the spiritual woman as mother to her followers reverses the classic father/child model of the confessional relationship and demands reverence flowing from man to woman rather than from woman to man. Relations between holy women and their confessors threaten to overturn the classic power relations of the confessional: where the theology of confession appoints the confessor as God's representative and mediator of his grace, the woman's claim to direct revelation puts *her* in the role of divine representative.[42]

---

[39] 'Women Mystics', 192.

[40] Tentler, *Sin and Confession*, 113–15.

[41] Jo Ann McNamara, '*De Quibusdam Mulieribus*: Reading Women's History from Hostile Sources', *Medieval Women and the Sources of Medieval History*, ed. Joel T. Rosenthal (Athens and London: University of Georgia Press, 1990), 237–8; McDonnell, 189–91.

[42] John Coakley discusses the issue of role reversal in 'Friars as Confidants' and 'Gender and the Authority of Friars: The Significance of Holy Women for Thirteenth-Century Franciscans and Dominicans', *Church History* 60 (1991), 445–60. In the latter article, with its specifically thirteenth-century focus, Coakley argues that, although there was a risk that the holy woman's authority might compromise that of the friar, 'it was a danger that remained muted' (456); friars' encounters with holy women, he concludes, 'left their authority undiminished' (459). In 'Friars as Confidants', which extends its analysis into the fourteenth century, Coakley argues that 'what changes over time in these men's experience

Gerson, as we have seen (122 above), focuses the problem of gender very clearly: women's teachings must be considered highly suspect by virtue of the fact that they are forbidden to teach. Yet spiritual women are found breaking not only this prohibition, but also the prohibitions against preaching and hearing confession. Nuns, abbesses and mistresses of beguinages can all be found preaching, while the mystics of Helfta counselled not only the nuns but also both clergy and laity who came to them from outside.[43] Though they had no power to give absolution, their actions adopted a pseudo-clerical role without the sacraments. On occasion they appear to have been more successful in this role than their male superiors. Gertrude the Great was able to offer comfort to a sinner who had failed to find it from his confessor, while Bridget received a revelation instructing her confessor on how to be a better confessor.[44] Bridget's revelation concerning the monk on the ladder has also been interpreted as an indictment of the spiritual pride of her former confessor Master Matthias.[45] As Bynum suggests, female mysticism seems to have offered a substitute for the clerical status which women were denied.[46]

Although the devotion of female mystics to confession and the eucharist seems at one level to reinforce the exclusive power of the male cleric to celebrate the sacraments, this devotion is undercut by incidents which suggest the woman's dominance over her confessor. Thus, although Jacques de Vitry was confessor to Marie d'Oignies, and hence in possession of the knowledge of her sins, it is she who has a vision of *his* sins on the point of death.[47] Undoubtedly her visionary access to his soul takes spiritual precedence over his merely practical access to hers. The relationship between Marie d'Oignies and Jacques de Vitry offers an interesting model for further examination of the question of who really has the controlling role between confessor and female visionary. De Vitry moved from Paris to Oignies in order to become linked with Marie's work and it was she who asked him to return to Paris to be ordained before returning to

---

of the women concerns the question of the relation of that power to be a locus of the divine to their own authority as priests' (242). While the broad outline of Coakley's assessment is surely right, I find the conclusion that male authority was left 'undiminished' even in the early period a strange one, given Coakley's own evidence of the pressures on it. Such pressures, I would argue, *could* not leave male clerical authority intact. Its functioning may have remained superficially unaltered, but its status, the way it was conceived and understood by both parties, could not fail to change.

43 McDonnell, 343–4; Bynum, *Jesus as Mother*, 15–16, 181, 247–62.

44 Bynum, *Jesus as Mother*, 222; Jørgensen, 47–8.

45 Bridget Morris, 'The Monk-on-the-Ladder in Book V of St Birgitta's *Revelaciones*', *Kyrkohistorisk årsskrift* (1982), 95–107. There is a version of this revelation in the Middle English translation of *The Liber Celestis of St Bridget of Sweden*, ed. Roger Ellis, vol. I, EETS 291 (1987), 366ff.

46 *Jesus as Mother*, 185.

47 *Acta Sanctorum*, ed. Johannes Bollandus, Godefridus Henschenius *et al.* (rpt Brussels 1965–70) (hereafter *AASS*), June, vol. 4: 663.

dedicate himself to her community. By his own account, he was merely her instrument, his preaching inspired by her prayers. After her death he wore her relics round his neck. In return for her inspiration he offered her and her extraregular community spiritual guardianship and eased their relations with the pope.[48] McDonnell notes that other beguines who did not themselves violate the prohibition against preaching influenced the development of male Dominican sermons;[49] and Margery Kempe too seems aware of the tradition whereby the male preacher becomes a mouthpiece for female inspiration. In Chapter 89 she wishes that Alan of Lynn would preach an outstanding sermon and Christ tells her that it shall be so. She then reports this to her confessor and two other priests she trusts, and immediately regrets doing so, in case the wonderful sermon does not materialise. As so often, *The Book of Margery Kempe* gives expression to what is hidden from view in the texts of other female mystics.

It was the expected role of holy women not only to inspire but to criticise the clergy. Other religious women besides Marie d'Oignies were given power to see the sins of priests: Margaret of Cortona and Ida of Louvain had miraculous ability to see unworthiness, especially unchastity, in priests celebrating the eucharist.[50] Clare Gambacorti specifically turned confession against priests by pretending to go to confession in order to chastise sinful priests;[51] and other holy women did not hesitate to chastise their confessors if they found them wanting. Margery Kempe is unusual in complaining of the sharpness of her confessor (44: 18–24);[52] more commonly holy women complain that confessors are not sharp enough. And confessors note in turn the tendency of these women to lambast themselves for sins that would seem trivial to others. A Middle English version of the life of St Bridget notes that 'her confessoure wald sometime say þat Bride had one token of grete grace, for sho charged als mikill a litill þinge als oþir comon men charged one grete þinge'.[53] Raymond of Capua describes how, when he tried to moderate Catherine of Siena's weeping over what seemed to him a very mild sin, 'she raised her eyes and her voice to God and exclaimed, "Oh, Lord God, what kind of a spiritual father is this

---

[48] *AASS*, June, vol. 4: 667, 654–5, 674; see McDonnell, 20–27, 121.

[49] McDonnell, 344.

[50] Bynum, 'Women Mystics', 194. St Catherine tells the pope that the stench of the sins committed at the papal court in Rome reaches her in Siena (Raymond of Capua, 138–9), and Raymond cites several instances of her ability to see that individuals are in a state of unconfessed sin even before they speak.

[51] *AASS*, April, vol. 2: 511; Kieckhefer, 45.

[52] This confessor is, however, not her regular confessor, but filling in for the Dominican anchorite in his absence. Also, the sharpness Kempe describes is specifically his refusal to take her spiritual feelings seriously, and to treat them as 'tryfelys & japys'. Allen notes the comparison here with Continental women whose early revelations were not taken seriously (280: 44/3).

[53] Ellis, *Liber Celestis*, 1. Cf. the Middle English version of the life of Marie d'Oignies, ed. Horstmann, 138–9.

you have given me, who finds excuses for my sins!" '.[54] St Bridget, confronted with a confessor who was also too consolatory, declared that such confessors 'are nothing but deceivers – they look like innocent sheep, but in reality they are foxes!'[55]

These specific relations between confessors and holy women highlight the confessor's problem of finding a balance between discipline and consolation in an unusual way by comparison with more routine confession. Where commonly the confessor must balance his sense of the need to correct the sinner with the sinner's need for consolation, here the confessor must balance his impulse to console the penitent with the penitent's longing for harsher correction. Often the confessors of these women attempted to moderate the most extreme of the penances their holy penitents inflicted upon themselves, but in return they were likely to be chastised for their laxity. And this kind of relationship was liable to reduce the confessor's sense of control, his feeling that having the keys of knowledge and absolution placed him above the penitent. Instead he was likely to feel belittled by the penitent's questioning of his fulfilment of that role.

Margery Kempe's book brings this tension between her power and that of the church into very direct focus. Throughout the book, alongside her devotion to her confessors and others who believe in her, runs open hostility to those who doubt her. Humility is quite absent from assertions such as these statements from God:

> I schal ȝeue þe grace j-now to answer euery clerke in þe loue of God.
> (17: 19–20)

> Ther is no clerk can spekyn a-ȝens þe lyfe whech I teche þe, &, ȝyf he do, he is not Goddys clerk; he is þe Deuelys clerk. (158: 12–14)

Those who presume to test her are likely to have to respond to her testing of them. A priest who tries to sow doubt in her German confessor's mind and goads him to test her obedience, is answered with a clever reply proving her moral superiority (chs. 33–4).[56] When she encounters a monk who tells her he will not believe in her unless she tells him his sins, she not only specifies them as sins of lechery and covetousness, but is able to assure him of his salvation if he confesses and reforms (ch. 12). She even usurps her confessor's role so far as to take responsibility for his soul, just

---

[54] Raymond of Capua, 38. Coakley's discussion of this incident is pertinent, however: though Catherine seems to have the last word on the subject, Raymond uses it as a starting point for his own discussion of Catherine's spiritual state, a discussion that aims to demonstrate his own wisdom in the role of spiritual director ('Friars as Confidants', 236).
[55] Cited in Jørgensen, vol. II: 251. The confessor in question on this occasion was not Bridget's own, but confessor to the Duke of Antioch.
[56] The writer of the gloss that declares this cleric 'a proud prist' and Kempe's reply 'a meke hanswer' is in no doubt as to who is the spiritual victor in this encounter.

as he does for hers. In God's words again (necessary to authorise this kind of power-reversal):

> Sum-tyme, dowtyr, I make þe to haue gret sorwe for þi gostly fadyrs synnys in special þat he xulde haue as ful forʒeuenes of hys synnys as þu woldist haue of thyn. And, sumtyme whan þu receyuyst þe precyows Sacrament, I make þe to prey for thy gostly fadyr on þis wyse: þat as many men & women myth be turnyd be hys prechyng as þu woldist þat wer turnyd be þe teerys of thyn eyne. (212: 22–9)

The direct parallel between the power of Kempe's tears and her confessor's preaching posits spiritual equality between them, while the fact that God explains this to Kempe puts her in the superior position.

The slipperiness of power relations between holy women and their confessors produces predictable anxiety around the question of obedience. Obedience was and is central to the good confession. The penitent, as well as being under an obligation to make a full, unadorned and sorrowful confession, had to be prepared to submit utterly to the direction of the confessor. Obedience holds the climactic place in this mnemonic giving the sixteen conditions of a good confession:

> Sit simplex, humilis, confessio, pura, fidelis,
> Atque frequens, nuda, discreta, libens, verecunda,
> Integra, secreta, lachrimabilis, accelerata,
> Fortis, et accusans, et sit parere parata.

> [Let the confession be simple, humble, pure, faithful,
> And frequent, unadorned, discreet, willing, ashamed,
> Whole, secret, tearful, prompt,
> Strong, and reproachful, and showing readiness to obey.][57]

It may be that obedience is placed last because it is chronologically the last aspect of confession, yet nevertheless its prominence in the mnemonic would be likely to imprint itself on the memory of the penitent. (The rhythmic repetition and chiming sound of the Latin phrase, 'parere parata', makes it the most memorable element in the Latin version.)

Holy women's texts generally place great emphasis on obedience, though this may be linked to the special difficulties it presented for them. Why, after all, should a woman who believed God spoke directly to her follow her confessor's will rather than God's? St Bridget's *Revelations* speak at length of obedience, and try to resolve the problem of owing obedience to two masters by making God insist on obedience to the earthly master:

---

[57] Tentler, *Sin and Confession*, 106–7.

Ideo plus placuit michi, quod obedisti magistro tuo contra velle tuum, quam si secuta fuisses tuam voluntatem contra preceptum eius.[58]

[I have been so much more pleased, that you have obeyed your director against your will, than if you had followed your will against his command.

As Bridget Morris argues, it is precisely the forcefulness of St Bridget's statements concerning obedience that suggests her difficulty in submitting.[59] The excessive submissiveness of some of her behaviour similarly reinforces a sense of doubt around this issue of the will: she is said not even to have directed her glance at anyone without her confessor's permission.[60]

The question of will was crucial to establishing the true presence of the holy spirit in visionary women. Alfonso de Jaén was following the church fathers (and Gerson followed Alfonso) in insisting that the visionary should be questioned most precisely on this issue of submission of the will:

1 Dicunt sancti patres et doctores Ecclesie, quod persona visiones videns debet tali modo examinari,
2 an scilicet sit persona spiritualis vel an sit mundana et secularis,
3 an eciam viuit sub disciplina et obediencia speciali, continua, spirituali alicuius senioris, discreti, virtuosi et maturi, catholici et experti patris spiritualis vel an in proprio arbitrio et voluntate.[61]

[1 The holy fathers and doctors of the church say that a person seeing visions should be examined in this way,
2 namely, whether this is a spiritual person or a worldly and secular one,
3 also whether he/she lives under discipline and particular, continuous, spiritual obedience to a spiritual father superior to him/her, discriminating, virtuous and of mature years, orthodox and expert, or according to his/her own will and desire.]

Obedience is the first issue about which the visionary must be questioned, and the questions go on to refine the issue: does the visionary submit his/her visions and temptations to the examination and judgement of the spiritual director or exalt himself/herself on account of the visions? Is his/her faith and obedience true or suspect? A direct revelation from God is an inherent challenge to the role of the church and a natural temptation

---

[58] Cited in Morris, 101.

[59] Morris, 102. Morris argues that Bridget found particular difficulty with *this* confessor, Master Matthias (the one, as Morris suggests, whom she later attacks through the vision of the monk on the ladder).

[60] Jørgensen, 138. For more direct expression of Bridget's feeling of failing in obedience see Revelation VI. 43 in *Liber Celestis*, ed. Ellis, 434.

[61] Jönsson, 123; cf. Gerson, *De Prob.*, 7, 10; *Oeuvres*, vol. IX: 180, 183.

to the visionary to disregard the church in giving priority to the revelation. Hence the church's need to examine obedience so strictly.

Disobedience to the confessor or the rules of the church is correspondingly very significant, and rarely appears in texts authored either by the confessor or by the collaborating female visionary and male scribe. It is normally part of the confessor-scribe's agenda to show that the holy woman was never disobedient to her confessor.[62] Gertrude the Great of Helfta documents a notable instance of disobedience: she describes how she encouraged her sister-nuns, in the absence of their confessor, to go to communion unconfessed, assuring them that they had God's own warrant, as directly communicated to Gertrude, for the forgiveness of their sins.[63] Gertrude's text, however, is unusual in having been written down by Gertrude herself, and thus remaining free of the constraints of most other women's texts. Mechtild of Hackeborn, Gertrude's contemporary at Helfta, describes a similar act of disobedience in quite different terms. When Christ tells her to take communion without confessing he is insistent on the need to confess later. For Mechtild, as Bynum writes, disobedience is 'the paradigmatic sin'.[64] It is thought that Gertrude wrote down Mechtild's revelations, but although in that case there would have been no male clerical involvement in the actual act of writing, the very 'publicity' of involving another person may have contributed to the production of more orthodox revelations. It is known that Mechtild kept her revelations a secret even from the other nuns for many years.

The Book of Margery Kempe embraces disobedience more frequently and openly than any other female revelations. We have already seen that Kempe disregards her confessor in order to go to Danzig with her daughter-in-law, but manages to turn this disobedience into an obedience to the higher master, who obligingly bids her to 'gon in my name, Ihesu, for I am a-bouyn thy gostly fadyr & I xal excusyn þe' (227: 4–6). Even where she is obedient to her confessors, her obedience is structured around negotiated disobedience. In the matter of white clothes, for example, the instruction comes directly from God (ch. 15) and her confessors have to be manipulated to endorse the instruction. As she tells the clerics in Leicester, she puts the command to wear white clothes into the mouths of her confessors, and they are then frightened to disobey it:

And so haue I tolde my gostly faderys. And þerfor þei han chargyd me þat I

---

[62] Coakley, citing Raymond of Capua's defence of St Catherine's deathbed assertion that she could not remember a single instance of disobedience to any of her superiors, discusses the necessity that compels a text dedicated to promoting the canonisation of its subject to present that subject as fully embracing sacerdotal authority ('Friars as Confidants', 234–8). Raymond's care in documenting an instance of Catherine's wish to disobey is discussed in note 66 below.

[63] Gertrude, *Legatus*, Bk. 4, ch. 7; cited in Bynum, *Jesus as Mother*, 204–5.

[64] Bynum, *Jesus as Mother*, 223.

xulde gon thus, for þei dar not don a-geyn my felyngys for dred of God, and, ȝyf þei durste, þei wolde ful gladlych. (116: 25–8)[65]

The text here conveys the full reversal of the power-relations of the confessional threatened by the status of the holy woman. Obedience, as constructed by Kempe's revelations, is a matter of negotiated agreement between Kempe and Christ to which confessors are mere adjuncts. The agreement, in Christ's words, is that 'ȝyf þu wilt be buxom to my wyl, I schal be buxom to thy wil' (158: 4–5).

Again, on the question of fasting, Christ steps in to license the woman's superiority over her confessors. The hierarchy of wills here is revealing:

Now, dowtyr, I wyl þat þu ete flesch a-ȝen as þu wer won to don, & þat þu be buxom & bonowr to my wil & to my byddyng & leue thyn owyn wyl and bydde thy gostly fadyrs þat þei latyn þe don aftyr my wyl. (161: 25–7)

It is God's will that Kempe's will should be subject to his, but the form that subjection takes is that Kempe is to instruct her confessors, and they are to obey. Her seasoned confessors, presumably used to this kind of instruction, know better than to argue:

Whan hir gostly faderys knew þe wyl of God, þei chargyd hir be vertu of obediens to etyn flesch mete as sche had don many ȝerys be-forn.

(162: 7–9)

Though they charge her by the obedience she owes to them, there is no doubt as to who initiates the command. Nor does the power-play stop there. Next Our Lady appears to Kempe, ordering her to go to her confessor and tell him that she is to be discharged of the vow to fast one day a week. Again her confessor, 'seyng be þe eye of discresyon it was expedient to be do' (162: 18–19), orders her as he is ordered to do. The 'discresyon' that informs the confessor's decision here is very far from the *discretio spirituum* that is supposed to sit in judgement over the authority of holy women.[66]

---

[65] Cf. ch. 37, where she is again 'comawndyd' by God to go to her German confessor '& byddyn hym ȝeuyn hir leue to weryn a-geyn hir white clothys . . . &, whan sche teld hym þe wyl of owr Lord, he durst not onys sey nay' (91: 35–92: 3).

[66] Raymond of Capua recounts an incident in the life of St Catherine which parallels Kempe's experience here in reverse. St Catherine wishes to refuse all food except the sacrament, while her confessor (one who preceded Raymond himself), insists that she must eat every day. Raymond narrates her achievement of disobedience in terms which carefully underline the correctness of her desire for obedience. 'Being a true daughter of obedience', he writes, 'she did her best to obey, but this so exhausted her that she seemed almost on the brink of death'. At this point she reasons with her confessor that since he would forbid her do anything that would result in her suicide, he must therefore forbid her to eat. Like Kempe's confessor, he defers to the holy spirit that prompts the saint's actions (152–3).

Difficulties in relations between holy women and their confessors were emphasised where the confessor was also the scribe to the woman's revelations, since, although his willingness to write testified to his belief in her inspiration, and his authority to testify gave him power over his protégé, nevertheless his role as receiver rather than originator of holy text put him at the woman's bidding. As with instances of female disobedience, the scribe's control over the written word made it unlikely that much evidence of such difficulties would be written down, but some is occasionally expressed. Blessed Angela of Foligno's dissatisfaction with her confessor's attempts to give expression to her visions is made unusually explicit. She frequently finds his written account of her dictation faulty and can be harsh in her criticism: 'You have written what is bland, inferior, and amounts to nothing; but concerning what is precious in what my soul feels you have written nothing.' Fra Arnaldo tells us that he thinks of himself as 'a sieve or sifter which does not retain the precious and refined flour but only the most coarse'. Sometimes he even takes the trouble to confess beforehand in order to be more receptive to the grace that allows her dictation to seem 'orderly' to him.[67] Less directly critical, but still suggestive of some recognition of scribal inadequacy, are Bridget's dealings with her various confessor-scribes, and her decision to leave Alfonso de Jaén in control of producing a final text of her revelations (see below). Peter of Alvastra's initial resistance to becoming Bridget's scribe is expressed by him in terms of self-doubt and humility, but may in fact suggest that potential scribes were aware of the difficulties inherent in the role and reluctant to take it on. Peter is knocked to the ground by a miraculous blow which paralyses him until he asks God's forgiveness and agrees to obey his command.[68]

Kempe's book makes much more explicit the unwillingness of scribes to write it. Unusually, as Sarah Beckwith has pointed out, it 'contains an account of its own difficult genesis',[69] and portrays the feelings of fear, shame and guilt that beset the priest who finally does take on the task (Proem). Predictably, these difficulties are resolved by miraculous events, such as the second scribe's sudden ability to read the writing of the first, and the sudden restoration of his deteriorating eyesight (Proem). The

---

[67] Angela of Foligno, 137–8. Angela's description of how she herself receives the Word from Christ suggests that she conceives of this communication as beyond the mediation of language: her text makes Christ describe the Word as wishing to be incarnated for her. The Word is said not to reach her through her senses, but to pass through her whole body, touching and embracing her whole being. See further Lochrie's discussion, 44–5, in the wider context of her analysis of the relation of the female mystic to language (chapter 1, 'The Body as Text').

[68] Jørgensen, 141–3.

[69] 'A Very Material Mysticism: The Medieval Mysticism of Margery Kempe', *Medieval Literature: Criticism, Ideology and History*, ed. David Aers (Brighton: Harvester, 1986), 37.

prohibitions of the church against women's preaching or teaching made a woman's text of divine revelation highly suspect, just as the woman herself was. The text therefore had to authorise itself via the explicit expression of divine approval. *The Book of Margery Kempe* tells us that when the book was first being written the time taken up by the writing took away the time available for prayer, and that Kempe feared God's displeasure on that account. The Lord's authorisation of her writing in response to her fear is unreserved:

> Drede þe not, dowtyr, for as many bedys as þu woldist seyin I accepte hem as þow þu seydist hem, & þi stody þat þu stodiist for to do writyn þe grace þat I haue schewyd to þe plesith me ryght meche & he þat writith boþe. For, þow ʒe wer in þe chirche & wept bothyn to-gedyr as sor as euyr þu dedist, ʒet xulde ʒe not plesyn me mor þan ʒe don wyth ʒowr writyng, for dowtyr, be þis boke many a man xal be turnyd to me & beleuyn þerin. (216: 12–20)

Both Kempe and her scribe are approved as pleasing to God, and their writing is specifically affirmed as part of God's purpose. As Allen points out in a note to this passage, female revelations routinely incorporate either an explicit order from God to write or divine approval of the act of writing (340: 216/18).[70] Such authorisation is directly comparable with incorporating the testimonials of the church on earth (cf. Angela and Gertrude, n. 31 above) and may be read as an attempt to deflect the potential scepticism of the orthodox church.

The alliance of female visionary and male confessor was more resistant to scepticism than either could have been in isolation. Together, especially given the usually outstanding credentials of the confessor, they combined the validation of the church on earth with the authority of divine revelation. The woman has the vision, but it is the scribe who is responsible for helping her to express it in a form which will not incur charges of heresy. The scribe, more than anyone else, has to be certain that the visions are within the bounds of orthodoxy, since his own safety and reputation are bound up with the woman's. This is one reason why the confessor is the most natural candidate for scribe. Though we may not be able to prove that Kempe's scribe was also her confessor, we are told that her scribe took great pains to ask her questions and test her feelings, and that without such questioning he would not have gladly written the book. Kempe, in her turn, has to respond because she is 'compellyd' by fear that he will not fulfil his part as scribe (ch. 24; 55: 17).[71] It is instances like these which

---

70 Allen specifically cites Dorothea and Bridget.
71 The scribe also offers his own testimony to Kempe's holiness in chapter 75 when he describes her help in restoring to sanity a woman who has 'gone mad' following childbirth as 'a ryth gret myrakyl, for he þat wrot þis boke had neuyr be-for þat tyme sey man ne woman, as hym thowt, so fer owt of hir-self as þis woman was ne so euyl to rewlyn ne to gouernyn' (178: 37–179: 2).

focus attention on the complexity of the question: who speaks in the text?[72] The book may describe the process of composition as broadly one of dictation, but it may well be the scribe's initiative that requires the process of testing to be made explicit.

Evidence from the writing of other holy women makes it clear that the scribe often took a far more active role than Fra Arnaldo was allowed. As well as usually translating the vernacular language of dictation into Latin, the scribe was sometimes 'supernaturally directed to polish the narrative' (Allen, 259: 6/7, writing of the work of Blessed Dorothea).[73] Bridget's Rule for the nuns of Vadstena was deemed unsatisfactory by the pope, whose disapproval may have stimulated the first of the three revelations which inspired Bridget to give her books to Alfonso de Jaén to improve on. The pope's stated reason for disapproving of the Rule was the inadequacy of the Swedish scribes' Latin, but this may well have been fronting for a deeper anxiety about the work's orthodoxy. The second of Bridget's revelations on the subject portrays Christ openly stressing the need for Alfonso to guard the catholic sense of his spirit ('catholicum sensum spiritus mei'), as well as to clarify obscure passages.[74]

Censorship may seem a cynical term to use in this context, but it undoubtedly plays a crucial part in explaining the process of revision and rearrangement that so often characterises this kind of writing. Allen notes what she calls 'a curious incident' in relation to the Blessed Dorothea: Dorothea's confessor complains that her revelation about the timing of Christ's wounding by the lance is unscriptural, and Dorothea responds by having a counter-revelation (338: 208/3). What is curious here, of course, is less the fact of revision than the frankness with which it is documented. Despite the relative absence of such incidents from the texts of women's revelations, John of Marienwerder cannot have been the only scribe who suggested alterations, or himself rewrote, for the sake of orthodoxy. However great the love and respect of the confessor for the holy woman under

---

[72] I ask the question here in very literal terms, with primary reference to the collaboration of woman and scribe (the occasional Latin insertions and the orthodoxy of Kempe's replies on trial are other obvious locations that raise doubt). I discuss this question more fully in 'The Making of Desire in *The Book of Margery Kempe*', *Leeds Studies in English* N.S. 26 (1995), 114–44. As Sarah Beckwith and Karma Lochrie have both argued in their recent books (*Christ's Body*, *Margery Kempe and Translations of the Flesh*), the question of who speaks is also fundamental in a much wider sense to any 'mystical' utterance.

[73] Cf. the freedom of Bridget's confessors to 'colour stylistically' her revelations (the phrase is cited from Carl-Gustaf Undhagen in Jönsson, 29).

[74] Cited in Jönsson, 27. For further discussion of the difficulty of distinguishing Bridget's voice in her *Revelations*, see Bridget Morris, 'Labyrinths of the Urtext', *Heliga Birgitta –budskapet och förebilden*, Proceedings of the Symposium in Vadstena 3–7 October 1991, ed. Alf Härdelin and Mereth Lindgren (Kungl. Vitterhets Historie och Antikvitets Akademiens Konferenser 28), 23–33. Morris looks closely at the *Revelaciones Extravagantes*, excluded from the central canon of Bridget's *Revelations*, and suggests the openness with which some of them admit to the editorial licence given to confessors as a possible reason for their exclusion from the canon.

his obedience, his duty as spiritual director included an obligation to the church whose representative he was as well as to the woman in his care. The text was produced in conditions of competing fear and love: the confessor/scribe loved the woman and the church and stood in awe of both. In writing the text he had to try to resolve any conflict there might be between the two.

Fear and love are the paradoxical foundation of the confessional relationship, linked to Tentler's two functions of discipline and control. What is specific to relations between holy women and their confessors is the reciprocity of that fear and love. Where customarily the confessor is the recipient of his penitent's fear and love, in the case of holy women these same responses are also demanded of him. Kempe's love and fear of Robert Spryngolde, the sharp confessor whom she wishes to have with her in heaven, are matched by her prayer that her confessors should also love and fear her: 'Lord, make my gostly fadirs for to dredyn þe in me & for to louyn þe in me' (249: 31–2). The careful phrasing which selects 'þe in me' rather than 'me' may itself represent an instance of scribal editing. Whether the phrase is Kempe's or the scribe's, its tokenism is revealed by the events recorded in the narrative.

It is the strength and reciprocity of these ties of mutual affection, obedience and control that produces the writing which in turn testifies to both the sanctity of the woman and the holy calling of her confessor. The confessor, in promoting the canonisation of the visionary woman who confesses her revelations as well as her sins to him, promotes his own reputation at the same time, for in fostering the cult of her sanctity he ensures recognition for the status of his authority as her staunchest supporter.[75] If the mutuality of that relationship is not working properly, recognition of sanctity cannot follow. Only the confessor can transform signs of eccentricity into marks of sanctity.[76] Without the right confessor the woman is liable to be identified as a freak, a heretic or a madwoman. And if the woman's claim to holiness fails to attain recognition, there is no corresponding enhancement of the confessor's status.

It would seem that the death of the anchorite deprived Margery Kempe of the confessor who, as Allen says, 'marked her for sanctity' (275: 37/25). Robert Spryngolde, her principal confessor following the death of the anchorite, clearly has doubts about Kempe's sanctity, doubts powerful enough to be articulated in the text that might otherwise have functioned as a testimonial to that sanctity. He scarcely dares speak to her after Alan of Lynn is warned by his Provincial to have no further contact with her

---

[75] Raymond of Capua, for example, was elected Master General of the Dominicans two weeks after Catherine's death. Coakley discusses his skilful self-inclusion in the book of her life, comparing it to 'the way that psychotherapists' interaction with patients becomes the stuff of therapeutic insight' ('Friars as Confidants', 235).
[76] Kieckhefer, 31.

(168: 38), and he is still uselessly trying to exert his control over her in the face of her divinely ordained disobedience at the end of the book.

In the end it is this disobedience, together with the text's surprising explicitness concerning this same disobedience, that differentiates *The Book of Margery Kempe* from the texts of other holy women's revelations and debars Margery Kempe from fully becoming a 'holy woman'. We have seen that obedience was a problem for female saints, and that their questioning of male authority also posed a problem for the male clerical elite that presumed to assess their sanctity. We have seen too that negotiated disobedience is not peculiar to the case of Margery Kempe. The difference is that Kempe's text confronts it as a problem.

Where Mechtild's scribe tells of disobedience, the text is hedged round by the secrecy of its telling and by qualifications that both authorise the special circumstances of the disobedience and set it in relation to a subsequent reaffirmation of obedience (134 above). When Raymond of Capua tells of the disobedience of St Catherine he encloses his account within the bounds of similarly emphatic insistence on St Catherine's love of obedience, the extremity of her circumstances and the referring of the whole incident to the authority of the holy spirit (n. 66). In Kempe's text, however, disobedience is more frequent and more explicitly recognised for what it is. It is characteristic of this book's difference from the books of Continental holy women that it ends with an act of supreme and prolonged disobedience, named and highlighted as such. Kempe's confessor is unwilling to let her go even as far as Ipswich with her daughter-in-law, and when she first conceives of the idea of going all the way to Danzig with her Kempe reminds the Lord that she does not have her confessor's permission: 'I may not do thus wyth-owtyn hys wil & hys consentyng' (227: 2–3). Even as she sets sail, she prays the hermit who has accompanied her thus far to excuse her to her confessor when he gets home. The insistence that God's command overrules the confessor's cannot negate the effect of this recurrent underlining of disobedience. Her return home follows the same pattern of emphasis. A brief reference to the honour the journey has brought to God and her soul gives way to a final paragraph recounting her need to humble herself before the anger of her confessor. For all that *The Book of Margery Kempe* tries to show that this is a woman obedient to a higher authority than that of her confessor, its concern with the earthly disobedience that this entails is finally more dominant. It is the 'scharp wordys' that are left ringing in our ears.

Ecstatic Reading and Missionary Mysticism: *The Orcherd of Syon*

DENISE L. DESPRES

Catherine of Siena's ecstatic utterances underscore a 'missionary mysticism', a 'mysticism of apostolate', that integrated the contemplative path to the 'cell' of self-knowledge, as Catherine called it, with the active life.[1] With insuperable energy and an unyielding will, she embraced the mendicant ideal of the mixed life, whereas other holy women, such as St Clare of Assisi, reluctantly compromised with authority. Like Francis, Catherine interpreted the apostolic ideal literally, and her imitation of Christ (*imitatio Christi*) resulted in stigmata signalling her radical identification with Christ's suffering flesh. Even excepting Catherine's political influence and engagement in conciliar politics, and her sanctity as a stigmatic, Catherine's visible success in joining the active with the contemplative paths distinguished her in an age of extraordinary women like Delphine of Puimichel, Clare of Montefalco, St Bridget of Sweden, and Dorothy of Montau.[2]

The Church hierarchy recognized the troubling sanctity of these female visionaries and prophets who led a mixed life, evidenced by a shift of power between these women and their male sponsors, who assumed the role of disciples to female instructors in the fourteenth century.[3] For a brief time, prelates like Raymond of Capua witnessed in a strikingly intimate

---

[1] For biographical information on Catherine of Siena, see Suzanne Noffke, OP, *Catherine of Siena: The Dialogue* (New York: Paulist Press, 1980), 3–7; and Valerie M. Lagorio, 'The Medieval Continental Women Mystics: An Introduction', *An Introduction to the Medieval Mystics of Europe*, ed. Paul E. Szarmach (Albany: UP, 1984), 184–193. A selective bibliography may be found in Ray C. Petry, *Late Medieval Mysticism* (Philadelphia: Westminster P, 1957), 265. I borrow these terms from Petry's introduction: 'It is obvious from the *Dialogue*, Chapter 64, for example, that Catherine's is a missionary mysticism, a mysticism of apostolate. The false incompatability of the active and the contemplative life is certainly no postulate of hers' (265).

[2] For a discussion of conciliar politics, women visionaries, and *probatio*, see Eric Colledge, 'Epistola solitarii ad reges: Alphonse of Pecha as Organizer of Birgittine and Urbanist Propaganda', *Mediaeval Studies* XVIII (1956), 19–49.

[3] See John Coakley, 'Friars as Confidants of Holy Women in Medieval Dominican

manner the ecstatic experiences of women uttering and thus authoring God's will in vernacular, proverbial language.[4] Such relationships necessarily became problematic, however, when religious crises forced the issue of the balance between the priest's sacerdotal power and the saint's charismatic power (Coakley 246). Although Catherine's colloquies always reinforced orthodox Church doctrine, her ecstatic experiences were verified through radical charity in the world. Catherine's *Dialogue* insists that spiritual comfort derived from contemplation and visions, and even strict adherence to prayers, are worthless unless the devout soul transforms this comfort of self into active service of her neighbors. Undoubtedly, Catherine assumed a sacerdotal role in her pursuit of this ideal, as is best illustrated in her moving account of the execution of Niccolo Tuldo.[5]

Key to Catherine's own exploration of *probatio*, clearly set forth in her discussion of visions in the *Dialogue*, is a definition of charity informed by her own experiences as a Dominican Mantellate.[6] Catherine's vocation required her to emerge from contemplation at the very moments when charity required active participation in the world: at executions, burials, the sick-bed, in the homes of the poor and desperate. Spiritual consolation assumes many forms, but it necessarily fuels the spirit's ardor for Christ through service:

> These people find all their pleasure in seeking their own spiritual consolation – so much so that often they see their neighbors in spiritual or temporal need and refuse to help them. Under the pretense of virtue they say, 'It would make me lose my spiritual peace and quiet, and I would not be able to say my Hours at the proper time.' Then if they do not enjoy consolation they think they have offended me. But they are deceived by their own spiritual pleasure, and they offend me more by not coming to the help of their neighbors' need than if they had abandoned all their consolations. For I have ordained every exercise of vocal and mental prayer to bring souls to perfect love for me and their neighbors, and to keep them in this love . . . When their charity for their neighbors is diminished, so is my love for them.

Hagiography', *Images of Sainthood in Medieval Europe*, ed. Renate Blumenfeld Kosinksi and Timea Szell (Ithaca: Cornell UP, 1991), 222–46.

[4] Other relationships explored by John Coakley are those of Sebastian of Perugia and Columba of Rieti, Francis Silvestri of Ferrara and Osanna of Mantua, Margaret of Ypres and Siger of Lille, Peter of Dacia and Christine of Stommeln, and Conrad of Castillerio and Benvenuta Boiani. This discussion is particularly pertinent as it explores these relationships in a Dominican context.

[5] Reproduced in Elizabeth A. Petroff, *Medieval Women's Visionary Literature* (Oxford: UP, 1986), 273–275.

[6] I am borrowing the definition Eric Colledge provides in his discussion of St Bridget's revelations: 'On such occasions as these Bridget was being subjected to *probatio*, to tests designed to show whether she was divinely inspired or seduced by the devil, tests corresponding to doctrines and techniques about which a considerable literature, based upon quotations from the fathers, had grown' (40). For Catherine, acts of charity were a self-imposed test of spiritual, and thus visionary, rectitude.

And when my love is diminished, so is consolation . . . In other words, those who are willing to lose their own consolation for their neighbors' welfare receive and gain me and their neighbors, if they help and serve them lovingly. (130–131)[7]

Christ's instructions to Catherine on ghostly visions and spiritual delectation are explicit: without the trial of charity, defined in mendicant terms, one cannot know whether or not ghostly visitations are divine or diabolical. Furthermore, it is incumbent upon the visionary to tell others of Christ in an apostolic fashion. Such telling need not be instruction – a usurpation of priestly privilege – but may be the active life of charity. *The Orcherd of Syon* clearly translates this distinction:

> In þat same charite also sche takeþ part, and maketh strong her wille by grace and goodnesse of þe holy goost for to wilne to suffre peyne for my loue, and to go out in myn name of her hous to enfoorme her neiȝboris vertuously in knowynge of truþe. I sey not þat sche schulde go out of þe hous of her owne knowleche, but I saye þat þo vertues schulden goon out of þe hous of þe soule, þe which wer[e] conceyued by affeccioun of her owne comfort, and to make hem encreesse and growe in tyme of nede to help and sauacioun of her neiȝboris. (162: 20–28)

Christ's instructions to Catherine undoubtedly made practical sense in an Italian context; the period 1200–1540 was 'the era of the Italian saint, more specifically the northern Italian urban saint'.[8] Although the lay-piety influenced by mendicants challenged sacerdotal power, both local and papal authorities found mendicant devotion tolerable and useful, particularly in the fight against heresy. Democratization of the laity was a threat to the Church's hierarchy and potentially dangerous, but lay confraternities and tertiaries proved useful in attracting women, particularly, from the appeal of heresy. St Dominic even embraced the salvation of heretical women as a special Dominican mission.[9]

Catherine's particular sanctity, her supernatural power, her charitable activity, temporal power, and evangelical activity (Weinstein and Bell's categories), exemplified Italian sanctity. In assessing the influence of *The Orcherd of Syon* upon early fifteenth-century English devotion, however, we need to remember that English sanctity was practically polar in many respects to Italian sanctity, and this was particularly true of fifteenth-century English sanctity. Weinstein and Bell note the linked 'popular piety

---

[7] References from Catherine's *Dialogue* in modern English may be found in Susan Noffke, OP. Middle English passages are from *The Orcherd of Syon*, ed. Phyllis Hodgson and Gabriel M. Liegey (Oxford: EETS 258, 1966).

[8] See Donald Weinstein and Rudolph M. Bell, *Saints and Society: the Two Worlds of Christendom 1000–1700* (Chicago: UP, 1982), 167–8.

[9] See Michael Goodich, 'The Contours of Female Piety in Late Medieval Hagiography', *Church History* 50 (1981), 20–32.

and civic patriotism' of late medieval Italian cults; 'communal protectors', these Italian saints expiated the sins of their community, devoted their lives to the sick and the poor, and increasingly were women and lay folk of humble origins. Like Catherine, 'those who . . . steeled their wills through spiritual discipline became counselors to sinners in need of moral direction and consolation, to civic leaders torn between private virtue and the demands of political action, to peacemakers seeking an end to constant warfare' (Weinstein and Bell, 176–177). In contrast to supernatural activity, penitential asceticism, and charitable work, the distinguishing marks of Italian sanctity, martyrdom was the chief criterion for English sanctity from the early Middle Ages through the Reformation, when Thomas More and John Fisher continued in the steps of Thomas Becket and Edward the Confessor (Weinstein and Bell, 187). In fifteenth-century England, the mendicant-influenced piety of the previous century gave way among the literate to the extension of monastic devotions privileging the contemplative life and redefining the active life as exemplary piety rather than evangelical charity, particularly among the wealthy, literate laity.

There are thus two central issues pertinent to the translation of Catherine's *Dialogue* into English religious culture: (1) the fact that her visionary authority and apostolic spirituality confront priestly prerogatives, a deeply sensitive issue given the Lollard movement of the fourteenth and fifteenth centuries; and (2) the fact that her spirituality, which elicited fervent active discipleship and imitation in Italy, would be foreign to and problematic for English imitation, given England's fifteenth-century religious traditions. Much discussion has taken place in recent years of the influence of Continental devotionalism upon English sanctity, particularly by way of textual transmission. But we need to remember that books were read differently, or even heard differently, in the Middle Ages, depending upon cultural, class, gender, and educational variables. Despite the deep influence a Franciscan work like the *Meditationes Vitae Christi* had on private prayer life in fourteenth-century England, for example, it did not produce an army of Franciscan tertiaries when adapted by Carthusians for a fifteenth-century English lay audience. Rather, it was purposeful in enabling English clergy to meet the spiritual needs of laypeople by providing parascriptural meditations without fear of inculcating heresy.

Catherine's *Dialogue* was ecstatically dictated in a particular cultural context that was not duplicated when the work was translated for or received by the nuns of Syon and other wealthy patrons. So how did the nuns of Syon read *The Orcherd of Syon*? And who else read them who would, in fact, be able to serve the world as a testimony to divine revelation, according to Catherine's mendicant interpretation of the active life, as no strictly enclosed nun could? Did they read them meditatively, pondering them as doctrine during the period of Collacion at the end of day?[10]

---

[10] See Ann M. Hutchison, 'Devotional Reading in the Monastary and in the Late Medieval

Or did they read them as ecstatic utterance, experiencing vicariously mystical vision to inspire their own mystical experiences? Lee Patterson has noted that recovering the act of interpretation requires complex interpretive maneuvering on our part; our paradigms of devotional literacy cannot 'assume that the habits of one group of readers can simply be extended across the cultural field as a whole'. [11]

I would like to consider the influence and reception of *The Orcherd of Syon* from the few details we know about its translation, transmission, manuscript ownership, and Carthusian/Brigittine religious context. My real concern, however, is with the purpose of reading mystical texts, and whether or not reading could produce an imitative mysticism – in Catherine's case requiring apostolic action. In the end, I hope to show how the cultural and religious contexts of reception can actually limit or subvert the influence of a particular strain of mysticism, for Catherine's brand of mystical activism, shared by Margery Kempe and Elizabeth Barton, was transformed, defused one might say, for a spiritual 'elite' beyond suspicion of heresy in fifteenth-century England.[12] When women outside of this elite demonstrated her mystical activism and dared to write about or narrate their experiences, they inevitably suffered persecution.

Although Catherine's mystical colloquies were transcribed largely in the autumn of 1378, the two earliest manuscripts of *Il Dialogo* translated into Middle English as *The Orcherd of Syon* are dated to the first half of the fifteenth century (BL MS Harley 3432 and Cambridge, St John's College MS 75); a third is from the second half of the fifteenth century (New York Public Library MS Morgan M 162), and Wynkyn de Worde produced an edition in 1519.[13] The incipit to BL MS Harley 3432 is addressed to 'Religyous moder & deuoute sustren, clepid & chosen bisily

---

Household', *De Cella in Seculum*, ed. Michael G. Sargent (Cambridge: D.S. Brewer, 1989), 223. Hutchison refers to the period before Compline described in the section of 'The Sonday Seruyce' in *The Myroure of oure Ladye*, as *collacion*. During this time, the nuns at Syon were to read 'some spiritual matter for ghostly edification, to help to gather together the scatterings of the mind from all outward things'.

[11] Lee Patterson, *Negotiating the Past: the Historical Understanding of Medieval Literature* (Madison, WI: UP, 1987), 116.

[12] See André Vauchez, *The Laity in the Middle Ages, Religious Beliefs and Devotional Practices*, ed. Daniel E. Bornstein, trans. Margery J. Schneider (Notre Dame: UP, 1993). Vauchez claims, 'Far from being popular, late medieval mystical sanctity was, on the contrary, highly elitist. It reached for the summits and was comfortable there. It flourished in small circles of devout people, groups of "friends of God" where clergy and laity enamored of perfection came to seek the "spiritual consolations" that their parish or convent communites were unable to offer' (234). I would agree that the English Carthusian and Brigittine context of late medieval contemplative prayer constitutes such a circle; however, most fourteenth-century English mystics, with the exception of Hilton, wrote *outside* of this circle.

[13] See Sister Mary Denise RSM, 'The Orcherd of Syon: an Introduction', *Traditio* cxiv (1958), 269–93; and Alexandra Barratt, *Women's Writing in Middle English* (London: Longman, 1992), 95–107.

to laboure at the hous of Syon', by an anonymous cleric, most likely Carthusian, who names his assistant 'Dane (Dom) James'. We know, then, that although de Worde produced an edition for well-to-do lay patrons, *The Orcherd* was originally received in England by the Brigittines. Whatever its later dissemination, *The Orcherd* was originally, to use Vincent Gillespie's term, 'a devotional thoroughbred'.[14] Thus it was necessarily adapted for women in an enclosed religious life; the translator recognized this, of course, and provides an appropriate meditative context through 'allegorization' which indeed reinterprets and compromises, to some degree, Catherine's apostolic mysticism.[15] Whereas Catherine notes the duty of religious to say the Hours and exercise both vocal and mental prayer, she defines a third kind of prayer:

> I seyde þee also what is comowne preyer, for I seyde it was prayer of good wille; þat is, excercise of charitable bisynesse boþe in þee & in þi neiȝbore, þe which schulde be do wiþ a good wille. (151: 23–25)

Catherine no doubt envisioned her apostolic service and even her political intervention as 'common' prayer, an active laboring in the Vineyards of Christ that resulted from the contemplative life. The translator, however, was bound by another ideal of service and an implicitly narrower, intercessory definition of prayer. In his Prologue, he incorporates Catherine's imagery of the Vineyard of the soul and of Holy Church, but he transforms this allegory into a distinctly monastic image of an enclosed garden. The fruit and herbs are doctrine upon which to chew, or meditate, thereby enriching spiritual labor, as opposed to the tilling of one's neighbor's fields described by Catherine in her exposition of the Vineyard.[16] His instructions in the Prologue to 'taste of sich fruyt and herbis resonably aftir ȝoure affeccioun, & what ȝou likep best, aftirward chewe it wel & ete þereof for heelþe of ȝoure soule' places the text firmly in a mnemonic tradition of monastic reading (*lectio*) and composition (1: 27–29). Such meditative reading was 'ethical in its nature, or "tropological" (turning the text onto and into one's self) . . . tropology and anagogy are the activities of digestive meditation and constitute the ethical activity of making one's reading one's own'. [17]

---

[14] Vincent Gillespie, 'Vernacular Books of Religion', *Book Production and Publishing in Britain 1375–1475*, ed. Derek Pearsall and Jeremy Griffiths (Cambridge: UP, 1989), 331.

[15] Gillespie notes that 'The release of a text by a medieval author did not necessarily mark the end of his involvement with it. Equally, once released, a text might be developed and changed beyond the author's control, without indication of non-authorial intervention in any one copy. Furthermore, regardless of the original intention of the authors (or compilers), or of later editors, the manuscripts of most religious texts are likely to suggest a range of identifiably different uses to which each was put' (324).

[16] See also *The Orcherd* (66: 18–26).

[17] Mary Carruthers, *The Book of Memory: a Study of Memory in Medieval Culture* (Cambridge: UP, 1990), 165.

The translator clarifies the relationship between such reading and intercessory prayer in his Apologia, the 'Prolog' to *The Orcherd*: 'Grete leborer
was I neuer, bodili ne gostli. I had neuer grete strengþe my3tli to laboure
wiþ spade ne wiþ schouel. Þerfore now, deuoute sustern, helpeþ me wiþ
preiers' (16: 15–20). He defines his labor specifically in 'þis gostli
orchard' and commends the nuns' 'gostly lernynge and confortable rec-
reacioun' (17: 3).

The importance of books and reading at Syon has been amply demonstrated, but we need to recall that such meditative reading and rumination
often resulted in composition; at Collacion – the meditative period of
reading that took place before Compline on Sundays – the nuns were to
'gather to gyther the scaterynges of the mynde from all oute warde
thynges'.[18] This gathering is necessarily a part of monastic *lectio*, one of
the 'complementary activities of reading and composition, collection and
recollection' (Carruthers 166). It is striking, however, that despite reading
works like *The Orcherd* or Bridget's *Revelations*, presumably sometimes
three or four times, no nun of Syon produced visionary, devotional, or
speculative responses – a surprise among such highly educated women
well versed in the hermeneutics of monastic reading and writing. Furthermore, there is a conspicuous absence of evidence of manuscript production in the great women's religious houses in England. Ian Doyle puzzles:

> Although there was a low standard of literacy in many nunneries, we know
> of members of the bigger and richer ones owning a good many books, both
> for prayer and for reading, in French and English, besides for worship in
> Latin, and there is no reason why some anonymous manuscripts from the
> better-educated houses – such as Syon, Barking, Dartford, Shaftsbury,
> Denny, and so on – should not have been written, decorated and bound by
> them.[19]

Neither is there a record, to my knowledge, of any mystical or paramystical activity at Syon or any other women's house with access to the mystical writings of roughly contemporary Continental women writers.[20] In
other words, despite the wealth, education, and privilege of these women,
we have nothing like the spiritual, visionary, and intellectual movement of
Helfta, marked not only by the production of mystical writings but also by

---

[18] See Hutchison (223). On the importance of books at Syon, see Mary Carpenter Erler,
'Syon Abbey's Care for Books: its Sacristan Account Roles 1506/7–1535/6', *Scriptorium*
39 (1985), 293–307; and J.T. Rhodes, 'Religious Instruction at Syon in the Early Sixteenth
Century', *Studies in St Birgitta and the Brigittine Order*, vol. 2, *Analecta Cartusiana* 35:19
(1993), 151–69.
[19] A.I. Doyle, 'Book Production by Monastic Orders in England (c.1375–1530): Assessing the Evidence', *Medieval Book Production, Assessing the Evidence: Proceedings of the
Second Conference of the Seminar in the History of the Book to 1550*, Oxford, July 1988,
ed. Linda L. Brownrigg (Los Altos Hills, Ca.: Anderson Lovelace, 1990), 15.
[20] This issue is thoroughly discussed by Nicholas Watson in 'The Composition of Julian
of Norwich's Revelation of Love', *Speculum* 68.3 (1993), 637–83.

participation in book production. Oddly, we must turn to isolated figures outside of traditional monastic textual communities to find textual evidence of this kind of sensory mystical activity in fifteenth-century England, with the exception perhaps of the Carthusians Nicholas Love and Richard Methley.[21]

In fifteenth-century England, the Carthusians were largely responsible for transmitting Continental mysticism to a 'discrete section of the lay community'; thus their spiritual influence can hardly be 'over-estimated'.[22] At the same time that Lollardy, with its offer of spiritual independence and self-direction, was appealing to members of the laity, the Carthusians were introducing the same kind of 'privilege' normally associated with the contemplative life to a spiritual aristocracy. We must not confuse, however, the Carthusian response to the council of Oxford's prohibition of vernacular scripture (1408) with their careful dissemination and sponsorship of Continental mystical writings. The Carthusians provided the laity with an orthodox Gospel harmony in Nicholas Love's translation of the *Meditationes Vitae Christi*, but Love specifies that this work presents the Church's spiritual children with the milk of light doctrine, 'not with sadde mete of grete clergie and of hi3e contemplation' (Hogg, 21). Even the wide dissemination of this work, however, is hardly paradigmatic; the *PseudoBonaventure* had long been in circulation in England and read out loud, as is evidenced by the *Meditations on the Supper of Our Lord*. Love's translation is a rather conservative measure to counter heresy. Furthermore, the Carthusians did not control the manuscript production of this work (Gillespie, 322–4). When we turn to a specifically visionary work, such as Marguerite Porete's *The Mirror of Simple Souls* or *The Cloud*, the Carthusians 'exercised some control over . . . dissemination', whether or not the author warned against wide distribution, as is the case in *The Cloud* (Gillespie, 422). Carthusian authors and translators were sensitive to the authorized spiritual needs of their audiences. Richard Methley, for example, composed his treatises describing his own experiences of *amor sensibilis*, *Scola amoris languidi*, *Dormitorium dilecti dilecti*, and *Refectorium salutis* (1484–1487) to instruct his brother monks in sensory mystical experience, acknowledging that such experience could be painful and disruptive to the solitary. The Carthusians were discriminating in selecting works for dissemination to a select lay audience, taking care, as in the case of *A Ladder of Foure Ronges*, to modify or adapt the text for devotional, as opposed to contemplative purposes.[23]

---

[21] See Karma Lochrie, *Margery Kempe and Translations of the Flesh* (Philadelphia: U of Penn. P, 1991), 211–20; James Hogg, *Mount Grace Charterhouse and Late Medieval English Spirituality, Analecta Cartusiana* 82.3 (1980), 7–8.

[22] Hilary M. Carey, 'Devout Literate Laypeople and the Pursuit of the Mixed Life in Later Medieval England', *The Journal of Religious History* XIV (1987), 371.

[23] See George R. Keiser, ' "Noght how lang a man lifs, bot how wele": the Laity and the Ladder of Perfection', *De Cella in Seculum*, 145–59; and S.S. Hussey, 'The Audience for

When we consider Margaret Deanesly's claim that 'the Life of St Catherine of Siena' (sometimes confused with *The Dialogue*) was among the most popular devotional works bequeathed in the fourteenth and fifteenth century, we need to exercise caution.[24] Undoubtedly there was an increased circulation of mystical works like *The Dialogue* in the fifteenth century, thanks in part to Carthusian influence; but these complex networks of circulation, often involving families who had members in a religious house, do not necessarily indicate widespread influence.[25] As Hilary Carey has pointed out, exceptional wealth and high birth were characteristics of Carthusian lay patrons (377). Cecily, Duchess of York, and mother of Edward IV, was among the Carthusian patrons whose religious devotions were, in part, in imitation of Continental ecstatic women, such as Catherine of Siena (Carey, 377–78). As is clear from the examples of Alianore Roos, Cecily of York, and Elizabeth Sywardby, all patrons of Carthusian houses and readers of Continental mystical female works, such reading, while it may have inspired devotional emulation in terms of chastity, spiritual tears, contemplative prayer, did not necessarily inspire the kind of *imitatio* that transformed exclusive, private lives into missionary or even visionary lives. Although their reading apparently had a profound effect on their prayer lives, these women are typical of the spiritual elite of the fifteenth-century in that such reading 'regulated' and 'extended' private prayer, as opposed to transformed prayer into action, apostolic or visionary (Carey, 380). In gathering their gentlewomen for reading and prayer in imitation of religious communal life, women sufficiently privileged to own devotional manuscripts formed 'textual communities'.[26] Cecily of York, for example, instructed that she be read writings of St Bridget, Mechthild of Hackeborn, or Catherine of Siena during dinner, and this would form the conversation later during supper with those present.[27] In other words, they adhered much to the formulation of reading and devotion outlined in the Prologue to *The Orcherd of Syon*. Nuns and devout gentlewomen undoubtedly inhabited the same closely supervised textual communities and their books circulated accordingly. Thus, dame Mald Wade, prioress of Swyne, gave a religious anthology

---

the Middle English Mystics', *De Cella in Seculum*, 109–22. Hussey identifies the audience for these common profit books not as would-be mystics, but as recluses, devout and financially successful London merchants, nuns who would read the books communally, and rich and devout women like Lady Margaret Beaufort.

[24] Margaret Deanesly, 'Vernacular Books in England in the Fourteenth and Fifteenth Centuries', *Modern Language Review* 15 (1920), 349–58.

[25] See Gillespie's example of the Dominican house at Dartford and the Essex nunnery at Barking (330).

[26] See Brian Stock's discussion of textual communities in *The Implications of Literacy: Written Language and Models of Interpretation in the Eleventh and Twelfth Centuries* (Princeton: UP, 1983), 88–92.

[27] Felicity Riddy, 'Women Talking about the Things of God', *Women and Literature in Britain 1150–1500*, ed. Carol M. Meale (Cambridge: UP, 1993), 110.

including writings of Catherine of Siena to dame Joan Hyltoft, a nun of Nun Cotham, prior to 1482 (Riddy, 108).[28] Lady Margaret Beaufort willed to her granddaughter Brigitte the life of St Catherine of Siena (Riddy, 122, n. 41). When Sister Elizabeth Stryckland, a nun at Syon and original owner of one of three *Orcherd* copies, died in 1540, her treasured book became the property of Richard Assheton, executor of her will, who gave the book to his wife. The book then became the possession of Katherine Sacheverell (Driver, 231–32).

There is also some visual evidence of Syon's sponsoring of Catherine of Siena; for example, a painted screen at Horsham St Faith's in Norfolk (1528), paid for by wealthy parishoners, features St Catherine of Siena and St Bridget in two panels. Eamon Duffy admits that 'their presence is difficult to account for except through the contact of the donors with Syon or at least the literature emanating from there'.[29] As proof of this, Duffy notes that the image of St Catherine holding her burning heart is 'directly copied from a woodcut used in a number of Brigittine tracts, including one published by Wynkyn de Worde in 1520, the *Dyetary of Ghostly Helthe*' (86).

One of the most interesting visual testaments to Catherine's selective influence is in Cambridge Fitzwilliam MS 48, an Hours of the Virgin called the *Carew-Poyntz Hours*. Like the Bohun manuscripts, owned by the powerful Eleanor and Mary Bohun, the *Carew-Poynzt Hours* is a compendium of prominent devotional themes and iconography. Three successive artists illustrated the manuscript between c.1350–60, the end of the fourteenth, and the end of the fifteenth century.[30] Naturally, devotional trends and shifts influenced the programs of illustration, often reflecting competing interests. On folio 84r, for example, a picture of St George conquering the dragon while an adoring woman watches has been painted over a drawing of the Stigmatization of St Francis. Given the great influence of Franciscan devotion in the fourteenth century, one suspects this selection of the fifteenth-century illustrator reflects the fashionable tastes of his powerful female patron. Similarly, on folio 85v, a stunning image of an elongated, graceful Catherine of Siena has been painted over another figure. Standing before a lectern with a book, her palms upward and open, Catherine gazes up to a seraphic image who signifies her rapture and stigmata. Below, in the *bas de page*, St Catherine kneels prostrate before

---

28 For an intriguing example of the links forged between families and religious communities (Syon) see Mary Carpenter Erler's essay on the Fettyplace sisters, 'The Books and Lives of Three Tudor Women', *Privileging Gender in Early Modern England*, Sixteenth Century Essays and Studies XXIII (1993), 5–17.

29 Eamon Duffy, *The Stripping of the Altars: Traditional Religion in England c.1400–1580* (New Haven: Yale UP, 1992), 86.

30 The manuscript is discussed in detail by Lucy Freeman Sandler in *Gothic Manuscripts, 1285–1385*, 2 vols., *A Survey of Manuscripts Illuminated in the British Islands*, vol. 5 (London: Harvey Miller, 1986), 143–5.

an altar. Sandler links the artist's program with the canonization of Catherine in 1461, speculating that the artist worked around the middle of the fifteenth century. This would suggest a patron who participated in the spiritually elite circle of women influenced by the Carthusians or Brigittines, women like Margaret, Lady Hungerford, whose retreat to Syon after the 1470 Lincolnshire Rebellion influenced the iconography of the chapel she built shortly thereafter.[31] While the *Carew-Poyntz Hours* does not identify the original patron, a late fourteenth-century owner is most likely depicted on folio 86r, adoring the Virgin; the book eventually found its way into the possession of Elizabeth Poyntz in the late fifteenth century.

The images of Catherine of Siena on folio 85v are telling. They specifically link Catherine with enclosure and the contemplative life. Thus she is depicted as a visionary in the confines of enclosure. Her experience of the stigmata is visually connected to her speculative contemplation, inspired by reading. It is impossible to say what the book is on the lectern, but given the conventions of author portraits in the fourteenth and fifteenth century, it is not unlikely that the book is her divinely inspired *Dialogue*, and that the proximity of the vision and the book is deliberate. Authors/dreamers are frequently shown sitting, head in hand, before a book while they gaze upon the image that is projected by the imagination.[32] Appropriately, then, Catherine is not shown writing; she is depicted like the page upon which the divine words, like the stigmata themselves, are imprinted. [33]

The Carew-Poyntz Hours illuminations undoubtedly celebrate the mystical, ecstatic, and specifically visionary nature of Catherine's spirituality, but the image projects restraint and isolation. Visionary activity is not depicted as the communal affair which we know it to have been in Catherine's case, two or sometimes even three secretaries witnessing and recording her ecstatic utterance. Such activity is here private: Catherine inhabits the space of an anchoress, even though the Middle English translator remarks in his Prologue that Catherine's rapture was witnessed by 'hir clerkis & alle hir disciplis' (2: 3). In an illustration from Wynkyn de Worde's 1519 *The Orchard of Syon*, Catherine is shown seated at meditation, a book open before her, receiving the stigmata, a town landscape far

---

[31] M.A. Hicks, 'The Piety of Margaret, Lady Hungerford (d.1478)', *Journal of English History* 38.1 (1987), 19–38.

[32] Medieval author portraits are discussed extensively in David Hult, *Self-Fulfilling Prophecies: Readership and Authority in the First Roman de la Rose* (Cambridge; UP, 1986), 74–93.

[33] For an interesting image of female authorship, see the illustration of St Bridget writing down her visions in *The Pype or Tonne of the Lyfe of Perfection*, reproduced in Martha W. Driver, 'Pictures in Print: Late fifteenth- and Early sixteenth-Century English Religious Books for Lay Readers', *De Cella In Seculum*, 229–44 (plate 23). See 241–44 for a discussion of the influences of Syon upon these images and the iconography shared by Bridget and Catherine.

in the distance (Driver, Plate 20). The frontispiece and endpiece to this volume, in contrast, depict Catherine seated and gazing ahead, book open in her lap, burning heart in hand, with her community of sisters about her (Driver, Plates 21 and 22).

When we consider both the images of Catherine and owners of her *vita* or the *Dialogue* in fifteenth-century England, we begin to perceive the improbability of imitative 'ecstatic' reading – the kind of imitation that certainly took place in the visionary communities we know of on the Continent in the thirteenth and fourteenth centuries.

The 'visionaries' or mystics we know of in fourteenth- and fifteenth-century England, Richard Rolle, Julian of Norwich, Margery Kempe – perhaps even Langland – are primarily problematic figures who negotiate or challenge the strictures of mystical or visionary activity in a religious climate suspicious of religious anomaly or self-promotion. Other visionaries certainly existed, as is clear from the case of Richard Methley, whose visionary or mystical experience was probably inspired by the reading of mystical texts like Marguerite Porete's *The Mirror of Simple Souls* and *The Book of Margery Kempe*. But Richard Methley's status as a Carthusian, his life in a contemplative order, no doubt placated those who thought his visionary experience suspect or threatening. Similarly, Julian of Norwich, as Nicholas Watson has recently argued, incorporated strategies in her *Revelation of Love* deliberately countering any suspicion of heresy that might arise as the consequence of her writing. Watson concludes that 'English enthusiasm for Continental women writers did not have as liberating an effect on their insular counterparts as we might expect' (657). Julian's response to visionary experience is, at first, disbelieving, in keeping with the treatment of visions in contemporary English works of spiritual guidance for women (Watson, 651). Furthermore, her isolation, as Watson points out, distinguishes her from her Continental counterparts, and she makes much of the singular nature of her experiences and her long, lonely efforts to comprehend them. This isolation and construction of a private, self-examining voice, as opposed to the public and prophetic voice of Catherine, Elizabeth Barton and Margery Kempe, no doubt gave Julian credibility as part of the traditional hierarchy of visionaries.[34]

In addition to 'vigorous public activity', extreme penitence, in the form of fasting, physical discipline, and keeping vigil – all conducive to visionary or paramystical activity – characterizes the late-medieval archetype of female sanctity (Weinstein and Bell, 38). Catherine of Siena began these practices after her first vision of Christ at the age of six and she was unusual in making such rigorous penitence a communal affair. By the age

---

[34] Sarah Beckwith examines the problematic nature of Margery Kempe's mystical utterance in 'Problems of Authority in Late Medieval English Mysticism: Language, Agency, and Authority in *The Book of Margery Kempe*', *Exemplaria* 4.1. (1992), 171–99.

of seven, according to Raymond of Capua, she gathered other girls of her age 'to discipline themselves together with her' and pray (Weinstein and Bell, 38). In exploring Catherine's inedia, Caroline Bynum notes that, just as Catherine felt vindicated in her noneating by Agnes of Montepulciano's ability to survive on vegetables, so she urged others to survive on the eucharist instead of ordinary food. Among her vast correspondence are letters to laywomen arguing for Christ's blood and body as the only really nourishing food.[35] Thus, if her biographer felt that Catherine's self-abnegation was a mark of extraordinary sanctity, Catherine herself incorporated this practice into a general spiritual program that included members of the laity (Bynum, 166). The evidence for English reception, in contrast, diverts us from the fact that *The Dialogue* directs its comments on vocal and mental prayer, holy tears, the ability to discern real from false visions, to a general audience without making the traditional hierarchical distinctions so evident in Middle English contemplative treatises like Walter Hilton's. Catherine's colloquies, rather, set up a distinctly inclusive taxonomy. Love can be perfect or imperfect; souls can be worldly or unworldly, ignorant or self-knowing: in the end, as the Christ of her colloquy claims, 'al maner goostly exercise, be it vocale or mentale, was ordeyned of me, þe which a soule schulde vse for to come to perfecioun and to þe charite of his neiȝbore' (156: 13–15). Like other reforming women visionaries, Catherine is not above criticizing the clergy, but her condemnation of them in her discussion of mystical union is centered upon their pride: they mistakenly believe that they alone merit illumination:

> And þerfore vnkunnynge proude clerkis ben blynde in þat liȝt for pryde, and þe cloude of her owne loue couereþ, and bynymeþ away þat liȝt fro hem. Wherfore þei vndirstonde rapir holy writt aftir þe lettir, or aftir her owne feelyng, þan aftir þe verry vndirstondyng. And so by taastynge oonli of þe lettir þei maken manye bookis, but þei taasten not þe pith and þe mary of þe same lettre, for þei lacken þe liȝt þat I spak of . . . wherfore þei wondren, and fallen in grucchinge, for to se so manye rude folk and ydiotis of holy writt, as hem seemen. And ȝit naþelees þei ben so illumyned and liȝtned by þe liȝt aboue nature in knowleche of þe truþe, as if þei hadden stodied longe tyme þereynne. (188: 31–189: 5)

Catherine argues that Christ 'ravishes' (187: 16) where he will, sometimes to 'rude and boistous folk', but always distinguishing the meek (187: 21) who provide better counsel in spiritual matters than 'proud lettrid' clerks (189: 13). Catherine's great reverence for the priestly office is clear throughout her writings, but it is significant that her colloquies do not privilege those in orders for spiritual distinctions.

---

[35] Caroline Walker Bynum, *Holy Feast and Holy Fast: the Religious Significance of Food to Medieval Women* (Berkeley, CA.: UP, 1987), 169–77.

Perhaps the Middle English translator of Catherine's *Dialogue* felt uncomfortable with this bold recognition of mystical illumination, as well as Catherine's invitation to psychic and psychosomatic religious experience. His decision to allegorize her colloquies and thus restructure them according to the divine hours is problematic, as a shift in *ordinatio* or a reformulation of the rubric is essentially a movement away from if not the original mystical utterance, then at least Raymond of Capua's conceptualization of six treatises, and thus an editorial move.[36] Originally, Catherine's treatise on 'Tears' had its own place in the colloquies; by appending this treatise to the fourth chapter on 'Prayer', the translator potentially diminishes its importance as a type of holy behavior; furthermore, by making it the fifth chapter in the section on 'Prayer', the translator places it logically behind the sections on false visions, deceitful spiritual comfort, and wicked spirits. Tears become an essentially private form of prayer according to this reformulation. While the Middle English translation is largely faithful, such editorial decisions need to be scrutinized carefully in light of recent research on reception and transmission as literary criticism.

Roger Ellis has shown, for example, how variously, and subtly, St Bridget's *Revelations* were culled by compilers; one translator adapted, indeed extended, Chapter I: vii, 'which considers the virtues of the soul using imagery of clothing' in a sermon on the Assumption for a group of nuns.[37] Modern readers will hardly be surprised by the clever interpolations from *Troilus and Criseyde* in a manuscript of the *Disce mori* (Patterson, 188–99). Lee Patterson's exposition argues for the complexity of the reception of secular poetry, even in religious circles, and reconfirms the circulation of 'elite' materials, spiritual or secular, between religious houses and prominent families. That 'visions', dialogues transmitted from the Divine to a passive receptor like Catherine or Bridget, received the same treatment is intriguing and requires further study. What is clear is that extracts and adaptations, alterations and 'tamperings', to use Ellis's apt description, indicate an entirely different sense of textual coherence and authority than we are familiar with. Roger Ellis speculates that 'the irony of choosing a text because of its authority and then rewriting it to make it more relevant or dramatic seems not to have struck' the author of the Bodley *Meditaciones* (Ellis, 181). My guess is that such emendation was not perceived as tampering at all, just as *The Orcherd* translator does not seem to see a discrepancy between Catherine's injunctions to an active life of charity and his own injunction in the Prologue to serve Our Lady 'oonli to rede and to sunge as hir special seruauntis' (Prologue: 5). In other

---

[36] Stephen Nichols describes competing interpretations as reflected in manuscript production as 'systemic rivalry' in 'Philology in a Manuscript Culture', *Speculum* 65:1 (1990), 7.
[37] Roger Ellis, ' "Flores ad Fabricandam . . . Coronam": an Investigation into the Uses of the Revelations of St Bridget of Sweden in Fifteenth-Century England', *Medium Aevum* 52 (1983), 175.

words, even when a text convincingly achieves the univocality of mystical utterance, in which the speaker is voicing God's will – certainly the case with Catherine's *Dialogue* – translators do not necessarily preserve this 'sacred' coherence. Adapting these lengthy and often repetitious texts as doctrinal works rather than mystical utterance, compilers felt free to edit, omit, and select: a 'work's lack of concern for formal structure meant that a revelation could be removed from its context, usually, without difficulty' (Ellis, 166). The aim of the Middle English translator of *The Orchard* is not to encourage mystical experience through dramatic reading, but to provide nuns with small portions of doctrinal food for contemplation and meditation. In a sense, Catherine's effusive, repetitious, and sometimes circular colloquies on the relationship between visionary activity and charitable action become merely cautionary in *The Orchard*, as opposed to issues of central importance and anxiety.

A translator in a manuscript culture considered, then, the needs of his audience, or dictated those needs if his clerical and monastic duties made him aware of the dangers of unsupervised mystical reading. This devotional paternalism, acute in an England experiencing heretical dissension, manifested itself in interesting ways in the new marketplace of early printed books. Caxton, for example, 'ignored the vernacular writings of the English mystics' as risky propositions.[38] Nonetheless, both he and Wynkyn de Worde responded to the demands of powerful patrons, who, like the spiritual elite sponsored by the Carthusians, developed a taste for pious and even mystical works. The excerptor of Margery's *Book*, printed by de Worde in 1501, exhibits the same kind of editorial freedom we see to a small degree in *The Orchard* and widely in compilations of Bridget's *Revelations*. In keeping with the conservative nature of English spirituality, the excerptor presents a reinterpretation of Kempe that 'strips away the mystical, radical, physical and public aspects of Kempe's visions'.[39] Kempe's voice is diminished, while the instructional nature of Christ's colloquies are heightened (Holbrook, 32). Weinstein and Bell's emphasis on martyrdom as a defining characteristic of English sanctity seems valid in Margery's case, for the excerptor extracts material from Chapter 14 in such a way as to diminish 'the threat Kempe poses to conservative clerics . . . the excerpts imply that Kempe wants martyrdom' (Holbrook, 33). Significantly, the excerptor ignores the mystical or paramystical and particularly sensory and erotic manifestations of grace Kempe so cherished. The compilation thus produces a nontheatrical form of spirituality, private, meditative, self-contained, and reclusive, that would be particularly

---

[38] See George R. Keiser, 'The Mystics and the Early English Printers: the Economics of Devotionalism', *The Medieval Mystical Tradition in England* IV, ed. Marion Glasscoe (Cambridge: D.S. Brewer, 1987), 9.
[39] Sue Ellen Holbrook, 'Margery Kempe and Wynkyn de Worde', *The Medieval Mystical Tradition in England*, 34; and Lochrie, 203–35.

acceptable to English religious authorities. Good works are not the theatrical *imitatio* of Italian mendicant spirituality, but rather the generous patronage of religious orders, the financing of chapels (as was historically the case with powerful fifteenth-century women like Margaret, Lady Hungerford, and Anne Harling) and service to the parish and community through institutionalized channels.[40]

Kempe's literalmindedness has long incurred criticism, even contempt, from scholars who have rigidly accepted this conservative, insular spirituality as the norm – a 'norm' that we are increasingly beginning to recognize as a construction of late medieval religious authorities anxious to stem reform. I have argued elsewhere that Kempe was influenced by an earlier Franciscan meditative tradition that predisposed her to autobiography; but even apart from cultural influence, she recognized the spiritual dynamism of apostolic living also at the heart of a mendicant Christocentric anthropology. This is not mere literalism.[41] Kempe understood the relationship between visions and charity, the necessity of integrating the active life and contemplative, that is forcefully conveyed in *The Orcherd*. The writings of and about Continental women and the practice of visual meditation no doubt predisposed her toward this synthesis, despite the practical discouragement she sensitively recognized through the lack of spiritual models in her daily experience. Her predisposition, however, does not account entirely for evangelical courage, or eccentricity (depending upon one's point of reference). Margery's *Book* is noteworthy in that it attempts to reconcile mendicant piety, still very much influential on the Continent, with the new monastic or Carthusian-dominated lay piety of fifteenth-century England. Her failure of reconciliation is not surprising, and her contemporaries' fear of religious experimentation is well documented throughout the *Book*. David Wallace points out:

> Her personal style of devotion would not, I believe, have seemed particularly outlandish in medieval Siena . . . her mixing of sacred, secular and domestic imagery parallel that of Bianco de Siena and Catherine herself. Within Catherine's circle there was genuine understanding of the differing forms of religious expression that were natural to differing social classes; and much of this understanding stemmed from the experience and

---

[40] See Eamon Duffy, *The Stripping of the Altars: Traditional Religion in England c.1400–1580*, Chapter Four, 'Corporate Christians', and Chapter Seven, 'The Devotions of the Primers', for discussions of these acceptable forms of English piety. Also see Chapter Four, 'In Search of East Anglian Devotional Theatre: Four Lives', in Gail McMurray Gibson, *The Theatre of Devotion: East Anglian Drama and Society in the Late Middle Ages* (Chicago: UP, 1989).

[41] For a discussion of Kempe's sources and possible literalistic interpretation see Roger Ellis, 'Margery Kempe's Scribe and the Miraculous Books', *Langland, the Mystics and the Medieval English Religious Tradition*, ed. Helen Phillips (Cambridge: D.S. Brewer, 1990), 161–175.

developments of Catherine herself . . . There were, however, limited attempts at such cultural mediation in England.[42]

Margery's experience in Italy confirmed a vocation of *imitatio* highly unusual in England, thus we cannot blame her confusion entirely upon 'literalism' or a lack of cosmopolitan sophistication. She hoped to witness to a divinely authorized apostolic injunction, and her notion of truth could not negotiate cultural relativism. The Friar Minor with whom she traveled to Assisi, who gave her full and admiring approval after she confessed her 'holy inspiracyons & hy contemplacyons', was, after all 'an Englyschman, & a solempne clerke he was holdyn' (79: 10–13). The Friars at home who persecuted her were, in her estimation, obviously false friars – a conclusion Langland also makes about English friars. The wealthy gentlewoman, Margaret the Florentine, who seeks Margery's prayers, viewed her poverty as a sign of sanctity; she insisted upon feeding Margery on Sundays and serving her English guest with her own hands (93: 25–30). Consider, in contrast, the extensive speculation about the motives Rolle had in accepting the patronage of the Dalton family; Rosamund Allen argues that Rolle's 'Office dwells on these events because they show just how very untypical of his time (and by inference, how saintly) Rolle was'.[43] It may have been customary for gentlemen and women to feast with churchmen in England, but this generosity was hardly extended to the religious fringe. If Margery gained a sense of authority and confirmation from such privileges abroad, where the Italian model of sanctity prevailed, it is no wonder that she and her contemporaries were confused at home. In fact, all of the 'theatrical' aspects of religion, such as public witnessing, wearing distinctive clothing, preaching and begging, and penitential weeping figure prominently in the forging of a spiritual persona in fourteenth- and fifteenth-century England; they are agonizing issues for the mystics and visionaries who self-consciously traversed the borders of English religious respectability.

While the case of Elizabeth Barton is too complex to address fully here, the meagre documents concerning her religious career are important in that they underscore an anxiety about ecstatic reading, or misreading of *The Orcherd of Syon*. Around Easter time in 1525, Elizabeth Barton, a servant girl, suffered from an acute illness that produced visions. Her visions were prophetic, but unlike Margery Kempe or Julian of Norwich, Elizabeth imprudently confided them too quickly and complied in their recording.[44] Elizabeth's mariological visions directed greater support for

---

[42] 'Mystics and Followers in Siena and East Anglia: a Study in Taxonomy, Class and Cultural Mediation', *The Medieval Mystical Tradition in England* III, ed. Marion Glasscoe (Cambridge: D.S. Brewer, 1984), 165.

[43] Richard Rolle, *The English Writings*, ed. and trans. Rosamund S. Allen (Mahwah, NJ: Paulist Press, 1988), 16.

[44] See Denton A. Cheney, 'The Holy Maid of Kent', *Transactions of the Royal Historical*

the Marian shrine at Court Street, where she fell into a public trance before three thousand witnesses and learned of her own vocation as a nun. The shrine, in turn, became a noted place of pilgrimage.

These phenomena in themselves are interesting in view of patterns in mariological visions that proliferate in the nineteenth century and exist even today. Victor Turner has noted the chiliastic or apocalyptic character of 'apparitional' shrines which developed during the early industrial revolution.[45] Nineteenth-century Marian apparitions tended to occur at moments of political crises revealing, I would argue, major shifts in epistemology. They also tended to produce what Turner describes as 'a considerable populist literature, often chiliastic in tone' (209). Like those experienced at Lasallette and Lourdes, the Maid of Kent's visions point to rifts in the social fabric and political structure that invite the unauthorized or disempowered to speak (Lochrie, 97–134). Just as Catherine of Siena provided her sponsors with divine ammunition against heresy and dissent, Elizabeth Barton rather naïvely (in contrast to Kempe and Julian) embraced the prophetic role. The sermon preached publicly against the Maid of Kent, delivered at St Paul's Cross on November 23, 1533, suggests that her detractors were acutely aware of the potential dangers of mystical texts. False or imaginative reading is imitative; at best, the proclaimed visionary is socially disruptive, and, at worst, she (or he) produces heretical texts.

We need to remember that this very principle of literal 'imitative' reading engendered mendicant devotional writing (such as Bonaventure's *Lignum Vitae*) and hagiography. Bonaventure, for example, ascended Mt Alverna, where Francis received the stigmata (in imitation of Christ), deliberately hoping to receive mystical illumination; the result was the *Itinerarium*. Imitation of Catherine or Bridget, however, can only be theatrical or dissembling in a fifteenth-century religious climate sufficiently anxious, due to the Lollard heresy, about orthodoxy and appearances. In the 'Sermon against the Holy Maid of Kent', Elizabeth is accused of acting, of imitating a mystic; feigning trances, she makes a public spectacle of her body, 'wresting her body and her arms as she had been in a pang of sickness' (Whatmore, 466). In addition, she advocates extreme penance, sometimes encouraging excess fasting, hairshirts, and discipline through chains. Finally, her example incited others 'to prepare themselves to be worthy to preach and declare her false and mischevious revelations'

Society, new series 18 (1904), 107–29. Also see the essay by Watt in this volume. The text of the sermon preached against Elizabeth Barton may be found in L.E. Whatmore, 'The Sermon Against the Holy Maid of Kent, Delivered at St Paul's Cross, 23 November, 1533 and at Canterbury December 7', *English Historical Review* 58 (1943), 463–75.

45 See Victor Turner and Edith Turner, *Image and Pilgrimage in Christian Culture* (New York: Columbia UP, 1978), 163. Also see Thomas A. Kselman's intriguing discussion of Marian devotion, bourgeois family life, and incipient nationalism in *Miracles and Prophecies in Nineteenth-Century France* (New Jersey: Rutgers UP, 1993).

(469). The 'Sermon against the Holy Maid of Kent' directs its criticisms not only at Barton's presumptuousness as a prophet, but at this error in the larger framework of a devotion deemed foreign by authorities. Dr Bocking, her confessor, is blamed for exposing her in daily doses to the *Revelations* of St Bridget and to Catherine of Siena's writings (469). Such books are dangerous to the ignorant who, after exposure, may mistakenly imitate or imagine these phenomena. Recalling for a moment Catherine's discussion of proud priests and illumination, we need not wonder at this anxiety. Whereas the Carthusians mediated a revised form of contemplation as a prayerful, exemplary discipline, Catherine advocated dramatic penitential suffering for all Christians in imitation of Christ. And she clearly accepted and encouraged the followers, her family, who wished to share this life with her. Whereas Raymond of Capua marvels at Catherine's inedia, the author of the 'Sermon against the Holy Maid of Kent' protests that Barton urges fasting 'that the sharpness of their bones had almost worked through their skin', – clearly a sign of fanatical excess rather than devotion. Indeed, Margery Kempe's own difficulty with fasting, hairshirts, and other kinds of physical penance, when she was so influenced by Continental models in general, suggests how impervious English devotionalism was to dramatic elements of Continental women's piety.

Like Margery's 'hysterical' reading, the Maid of Kent's 'misreading' most likely encouraged a visionary response – a natural result of monastic *lectio* outside of the textual community of the cloister; although without Barton's book, we cannot ever know exactly how influential Catherine of Siena was in providing doctrinal or prophetic constructs, literary metaphors, or even a sense of literary structure for Barton. It is clear, however, that Catherine's bold maneuvering in conciliar politics, through prophecy, preaching, and mendicant *imitatio*, would have provided Barton with a model of success, or at least the validation of such evangelical activities as a testimony to visions. Similarly, Margery's 'reading' and meditation enabled her to construct a textual community peopled by saints and past visionaries like Marie d'Oignies, whose credibility depended upon charitable works as a response to visions. Perhaps Margery was fortunate in the grudging nature of her spiritual advisors; her spiritual community, in anticipation of the Communion of Saints, appears to have provided her with comfort and acceptable female models of devotion. In contrast, Barton's Dr Bocking is accused in the sermon of behaving very much like Raymond of Capua – of providing ambitious spiritual models for his charge and moving her 'very often and busily to make petition to God and to have revelations in manifold manner' (469). The author of the 'Sermon against the Holy Maid of Kent' claims that when visions were withdrawn from her, Bocking reproached her, causing the Maid to feign visions. In anticipation of such ecstatic reading, the humble translator of *The Orchard* wished to moderate the use of the visionary work he was translating, and his Prologue recasts the work for moral and doctrinal instruction. Like the translator of *The Chastising of God's Children*, the translator of *The Orcherd* advocates ghostly comfort and, in doing so, subtly discourages pious fantasizing or recreation of ecstatic experience.[46]

Much scholarship remains to be done before we can fully assess how English readers received the writings of Catherine of Siena. Thus far, we can speculate that the *Dialogue*, although diminished and modified through translation and editing in its fifteenth-century English reception, may have moved one women to embrace an apostlic life and record visionary experience, and provided others, perhaps wiser, with a model of contemplative, albeit silent, virtue.

---

[46] See Elizabeth Psakis Armstrong, 'Informing the Mind and Stirring up the Heart: Katherine of Siena at Syon', *Studies in St Birgitta and the Brigittine Order*, vol. 2, 172–4.

The Prophet at Home:
Elizabeth Barton and the Influence of
Bridget of Sweden and Catherine of Siena

DIANE WATT

Elizabeth Barton, the 'Holy Maid of Kent', had been prophesying for over eight years before she began to utter predictions concerning Henry VIII's divorce from Katherine of Aragon, but it was only then, when she became openly involved in the opposition to the royal divorce, that the authorities decided to put a stop to her activities. Her prognostications against the King, and in particular her assertion that if he went ahead with his plans and remarried then he 'shulde not be kynge of this Realme by the space of one moneth after, And in the reputacion of God shuld not be kynge one day nor one houre' brought her international fame, or notoriety.[1] In the autumn of 1533, Barton was arrested and for three months subjected to a series of examinations. Then, on 23 November 1533, along with her confessor Dr Edward Bocking and a number of their adherents, she was made to do penance at St Paul's Cross in London. Two weeks later the ritual was repeated in the precincts of Canterbury Cathedral. The Spanish Ambassador, Eustice Chapuys, described the purpose of these public performances as being 'to blot out from the people's minds the impression they have that the Nun is a saint and a prophet'.[2] Clearly, the government feared that Barton had attracted some sort of popular following, and it became necessary to expose her as a heretic and a criminal. In March 1534 Barton was attainted of treason for inciting insurrection within the realm, and the following April she was hanged at Tyburn alongside Bocking and four others. Although historians have tended to minimise the significance of Barton's contribution to the conservative resistance to the Reformation

---

[1] 25 Henry VIII, c12, printed in *Statutes of the Realm*, ed. A. Luders *et al.* (London: Dawson, 1963), vol. 3, 446–51; 446.
[2] *Calendar of Letters, Despatches, and State Papers, Relating to the Negotiations between England and Spain*, ed. G. A. Begenroth *et al.* (London: HMSO, 1862–1947), vol. 4, part 2, no. 1154.

and very few give detailed accounts of her life and prophecies,[3] at the time, Barton's execution was something of a *cause célèbre*. Amongst those implicated in the affair were Sir Thomas More and Bishop John Fisher. The former succeeded in defending his relations with Barton to Cromwell (who was leading the investigation); the latter did not, and his name was included in the indictment against her. In a letter written a year after the event, John Mason linked Barton's death to Fisher's martyrdom and commented, 'What end this Tragedy wyll com to God wot. Iff that may be callid a Tragedye *quae inceperit a nuptiis*'.[4] Elizabeth Barton was, in fact, an exceptional figure in English history, both as one of only very few Catholic women to die for opposing Henry VIII, and, as I hope to show, as a pre-Civil War female political prophet.

Recent scholarship has revealed that prophecies proliferated at times of discontent and rebellion.[5] Prophecy functioned as a form of political commentary and protest, but sometimes it not only articulated, but also *inspired* social and political unease. In 1521 Edward Suffolk, the third Duke of Buckingham, was executed after the revelations of a Carthusian monk encouraged him in his aspirations to the throne. Indeed, sometime before Elizabeth Barton's arrest, Thomas More wrote a letter to her in which he tried to dissuade her from talking with anyone about affairs of the King or the state and to illustrate this warning he specifically alluded to Buckingham's downfall: 'I thinke you have harde how the late Duke of Buckingham moved with the fame of one that was reported for an holye monke and had suche talkinge with hyme as after was a grete parte of his distruction . . .'.[6] Thomas Cromwell was fully aware of the subversive power of prophetic discourse, arguing that 'if credence shuld be gyven to euery suche lewd person as wold affirme himself to haue reuelations from god what redyer wey were there to subuert al common welthes and good orders in the worlde',[7] while Eustace Chapuys observed that the English people were especially 'given to prophecies and divinations . . . and

---

[3] The best short narrative accounts of Elizabeth Barton's life and prophecies are those by David Knowles, *The Religious Orders in England* (Cambridge: Cambridge University Press, 1948–1959), vol. 3, 182–191; and A.D. Cheney, 'The Holy Maid of Kent', *Transactions of the Royal Historical Society*, ns vol. 18 (1904), 107–129. The only book-length study is Alan Neame, *The Holy Maid of Kent: The Life of Elizabeth Barton, 1506–1534* (London: Hodder and Stoughton, 1971).

[4] Henry Ellis, ed., *Original Letters Illustrative of English History* (London: Harding, Tripbook and Lepard, 1827), 2nd series, vol. 1, 58.

[5] Keith Thomas, *Religion and the Decline of Magic: Studies in Popular Beliefs in Sixteenth and Seventeenth Century England* (London: Weidenfield and Nicholson, 1971), 389–432. See also Sharon L. Jansen, *Political Protest and Prophecy under Henry VIII* (Woodbridge: Boydell Press, 1991).

[6] Elizabeth F. Rogers, *The Correspondence of Sir Thomas More* (Princeton: Princeton University Press, 1947), 465–6.

[7] Roger B. Merriman, *Life and Letters of Thomas Cromwell* (Oxford: Clarendon Press, 1968), vol. 1, 375.

thereby exceedingly prone to riots and revolutions'.[8] However, this problem was by no means peculiar to England. By the early sixteenth century figures like Joachim of Fiore, Amadeus of Portugal and Girolamo Savonarola were extremely influential, especially in Italy, and the spread of prophecy throughout Europe was perceived to have become such a serious concern that the Fifth Lateran Council (1512–1517) issued decrees which were intended to circumscribe its abuses: members of the clergy were forbidden to date forthcoming catastrophes; and they were banned from deriving such predictions from scriptural interpretation or claiming that they were received as divine inspiration.[9]

Elizabeth Barton's example illustrates that prophecy could offer women as well as men an opportunity for direct involvement in the public sphere on a national level. This raises the question of what precedents existed for such female intervention. In the second half of the fourteenth century, two women in particular emerged as important figures in European politics: Bridget of Sweden (1303–1373) and Catherine of Siena (1347–1380). Although St Bridget is now most famous for having founded the Brigittine Order, she first came to the attention of her contemporaries when she accurately predicted the arrival of the plague in Sweden, and she became renowned throughout Europe for her apocalyptic prophecies and visions, many of which were concerned with the iniquity of secular governments and the corruption of the Roman Church. Bridget wrote letters to and prophesied about, amongst others, King Magnus of Sweden, the Holy Roman Emperor Charles IV, and Queen Joanna of Naples. During the Babylonian Captivity, she warned both Clement VI and Urban V to leave Avignon, and she requested the papacy to bring about an end to the war between France and England. Likewise, St Catherine acted as an intermediary between the papacy and the rebellious city of Florence, and she is credited with having persuaded Gregory XI to return to Rome. When the Great Schism broke out after his death, she took the part of Urban VI, actively seeking support for his cause.

Are there any indications that English holy women took part in similar activities in the centuries leading up to the Reformation? Certainly there were quite a number of women who became known for their miracles and visions. To give some examples, the theologian Thomas Netter, in his *Doctrinale*, described a pious fifteenth-century Norfolk woman called Joan the Meatless who survived by eating the bread of the sacrament and was able to discern a consecrated host from an unconsecrated one;[10] while a century later, Thomas More, in his *Dialogue Concerning Heresies*,

---

8 *CSP Spain*, vol. 4, part 2, no. 1154.
9 Nelson H. Minnich, 'Prophecy and the Fifth Lateran Council (1512 1517)', in Marjorie Reeves, ed. *Prophetic Rome in the High Renaissance Period* (Oxford: Clarendon Press, 1992), 63–87; 85–6.
10 Thomas Netter, *Doctrinale antiquitatum fidei catholicae*, ed. F.B. Blanciotte (Venice, 1757–59), vol. 2, 376–7.

discussed Elizabeth the so-called 'Holy Maid of Leominster' who, although she subsequently was exposed as a fraud, became famous after fasting for a long time and performing Eucharist miracles.[11] Yet even though Elizabeth of Leominster became the focus of public attention, neither she nor Joan of Norfolk seems to have been associated with divinely inspired utterances of any sort. Another example, taken this time from the early-sixteenth century, and more closely linked to Barton's case, is that of Anne Wentworth. Wentworth is also cited by Thomas More in his *Dialogue*, this time as a genuine holy maid.[12] As an adolescent Wentworth was afflicted by a form of prophetic madness which was cured during a pilgrimage to the shrine to the Virgin in Ipswich:

> She prophesyed and tolde many thynges done and sayd at the same tyme in other places whiche were proued trewe and many thynges sayd lyenge in her traunce of suche wysdome & lernyng that ryght connyng men hyghly meruayled to here of so yonge an vnlerned mayden whan her selfe wyst not what she sayd suche thynges vttered and spoken as well lerned menne myght haue myssed with a longe study.[13]

Wentworth's story bears a remarkable similarity to Barton's earliest paramystical experiences which began in 1525 when Barton was nineteen years old. The fullest surviving account of these experiences occurs in William Lambarde's *A perambulation of Kent* (1576).[14] According to Lambarde, Barton was stricken by illness, then began to prophesy during fits and trances, characterised by bodily and facial contortions, and was later healed at a local Marian shrine in the village of Court-at-Street near Aldington in Kent. Lambarde gives a fairly detailed report of Barton's first revelations:

> She told plainly of diuers things done at the Church, and other places where she was not present, which neuerthelesse she seemed (by signes proceeding from her) most liuely (as it were) to beholde with her eye: She tolde also, of heauen, hell, and purgatorie, and of the ioyes, and sorrowes that sundry departed soules had, and suffered there: She spake frankly againste the corruption of manners and euill life: She exhorted repaire to the Churche, hearing of Masse, confession to Priestes, prayer to our Lady and Sainctes, and to be short, made in all pointes, confession and confirmation of the Popish Creede and Catechisme, and that so deuoutly and discretely (in the

---

[11] Thomas More, *A Dialogue Concerning Heresies*, ed. T.C. Lawler, G. Marc'hadour and R.C. Marius, The Yale Edition of the Complete Works of Thomas More 3 (New Haven: Yale University Press, 1981), part 1, 87–8.

[12] More, part 1, 93–4.

[13] More, part 1, 93.

[14] William Lambarde, *A perambulation of Kent: conteining the description of that shyre* (1576) sigs. T2v–T5r.

opinion of mine authour) that he thought it not possible for her to speake in that manner.[15]

Yet, while both these young women impressed spectators with their psychic abilities and seemingly profound insights, it appears that neither Wentworth's utterances nor Barton's early revelations had an *overtly* political agenda. In fact, before Elizabeth Barton began to prophesy about Henry VIII's actions and policies, there is little reason to think that other English holy women showed any interest in matters of government. The anonymous author of the fifteenth-century *Revelation of Purgatory*, which describes a woman's vision of the pains experienced by a sinful nun, may well reflect the influence of St Bridget's revelations, but it does not address issues relating to national politics,[16] and even the devout lay-woman Margery Kempe, who is generally recognised to have had St Bridget as a spiritual model, was very much a *local* prophet, concerned only with questions involving her immediate communities.[17]

If there was no tradition of women political prophets in late medieval England, then it follows that Barton may well have been influenced instead by Continental models of sanctity. The suggestion that St Bridget and St Catherine may actually have inspired Barton's political involvement is not a new one, but in this paper I would like to consider this possibility in more detail than it has been formerly.[18] However, in examining this issue I am faced with one fundamental problem: the unreliability of the evidence about Barton's visions and predictions. It appears that in the years leading up to Barton's execution, her supporters produced a number of books about her revelations. We know something about two of these works.[19] Firstly, there was a printed tract describing Barton's early prophetic career which began when she was working as a servant in the household of a steward of the archiepiscopal estates in Kent. Secondly, there was a large manuscript, written it seems in Latin, in which Barton's confessor, Edward Bocking, had assembled the miracles and revelations which occurred after she had been professed as a nun at the convent of St Sepulchre in Canterbury, and which no doubt included some of her more politically-contentious revelations. Neither the printed tract nor the manuscript survived the censorship which followed Barton's arrest. All that

---

[15] Lambarde, sig. T3v.

[16] *A Revelation of Purgatory*, in C. Horstmann ed. *Yorkshire Writers: Richard Rolle of Hampole and his Followers* (London: Swan Sonnenschein, 1895–6), vol. 1, 383–92.

[17] See, for example, Kempe's prophecies concerning the controversy over the granting of certain privileges to the Chapel of St Nicholas in her home town of Lynn: Sanford B Meech and Hope Emily Allen, eds., *The Book of Margery Kempe* (Oxford: EETS 212, 1940), 58–60.

[18] See, for example F.R. Johnson, 'The English Cult of Saint Bridget of Sweden', *Analecta Bollandiana*, vol. 103 (1985), 75–93; 88 and Neame, 151.

[19] See E.J. Devereux, 'Elizabeth Barton and Tudor Censorship', *Bulletin of the John Rylands Library*, vol. 49 (1966), 91–108.

now exists is an unsigned Latin fragment which may be a draft of the prologue to Bocking's book.[20] As a result, in reconstructing Barton's life and prophecies, we are almost entirely reliant on documents relating to her trial. These include the Act of Attainder against Barton and her associates;[21] a draft of the sermon which was delivered at their public penance;[22] and the correspondence of suspects and witnesses like Sir Thomas More or Thomas Goldwell, the Prior of Christ Church, Canterbury, the monastery where Bocking held office of cellarer.[23] In addition to this contemporary material, there is the Protestant propaganda which was circulated against Barton after her execution.[24] Some of these documents are clearly of more use than others. Goldwell's testimony is of especial interest because he acknowledges having read some of Bocking's writings about Barton, but it should not be forgotten that it was in Goldwell's interest to cooperate with the investigators and produce the sort of statement which would satisfy them, even if it had to be done at the expense of what he believed to be the truth. Nonetheless, it is important not to overstate the problems surrounding the nature of the evidence. Although it is obviously impossible to disentangle Barton's experiences from the way they were constructed by her contemporaries and by subsequent writers, many of whom were determined to prove that she was a fraud, heretic and traitor, much of our information about feminine sanctity in the Middle Ages comes from comparable sources, such as saints' lives, and the records of canonisation processes, which were, of course, simply another form of trial. As Dyan Elliott points out, even in the case of officially recognised saints 'it is ultimately unproductive to attempt a definitive separation of a saint's experience, its hagiographical representation, and its ultimate assimilation by the church as an exemplar of sanctity'.[25] What is more, a rather different, and much more positive picture of Barton emerges from the letters written by her supporters such as Henry Man, Procurator of the Charterhouse of Sheen, and Henry Gold, parish priest of St Mary,

---

[20] Public Records Office, State Papers 1/80, f. 140r (*Letters and Papers, Foreign and Domestic, of the Reign of Henry VIII*, ed. J.S. Brewer, J. Gairdner and R.H. Brodie (Vaduz: Kraus, 1965), vol. 4, no. 1468 (6)), edited in J.R. McKee, *Dame Elizabeth Barton, OSB, the Holy Maid of Kent* (London: Burns, Oates and Washbourne, 1925), 60–3.

[21] *Statutes*, vol. 3, 446–51.

[22] L.E. Whatmore, 'The Sermon against the Holy Maid of Kent and her Adherents, delivered at Paul's Cross, November the 23rd, 1533, and at Canterbury, December the 7th', *English Historical Review*, vol. 58 (1943), 463–75.

[23] See Rogers, especially 464–6 and 480–88; and Thomas Wright, ed. *Three Chapters of Letters Relating to the Suppression of Monasteries* (London: Camden Society, os 26, 1843), 19–22.

[24] See, for example, Richard Morison, *Apomaxis calvmniarum* (1537) sigs. T1r–V2v.

[25] Dyan Elliott, *Spiritual Marriage: Sexual Abstinence in Medieval Wedlock* (Princeton: Princeton University Press, 1993), 208.

Aldermary;[26] or from recusant histories like that by Nicholas Sanders, published in 1585.[27]

Throughout the following discussion of the question of the extent to which Barton is likely to have emulated the Continental saints, these problems of evidence should then be kept in mind. Amongst the documents relating to Barton's trial, there is only one occasion when a direct connection is actually made. This occurs in the draft of the sermon written for Barton's public penance and first delivered by John Capon in Canterbury, and later by Nicholas Heath in London. According to this sermon, Barton had already made a confession before the King's Council that her prophecies and revelations were feigned, 'wherein she used much craft to make and devise them consonant and agreable to the minds of them who were resorting unto her, with the help of Dr Bocking, her ghostly father'.[28] The sermon goes on to assert that

> [Bocking] daily rehearsed matter enough unto her, out of St Bridget's and St Catherine of Senys revelations, to make up her fantasies and counterfeit visions, and moved her very often and busily to make petition to God to have revelations in manifold matter. And when she ceased any while of shewing new revelations unto him, he was wont to say unto her: 'How do you live now? Virtuously? Meseemeth God hath withdrawn His grace from you, that ye have no revelations this season.' Whose words caused her to feign many more revelations than she else would.[29]

The sermon sets out to discredit Barton and her associates by asserting that Bocking deliberately tried to induce her to prophecy. The accusation that Bocking taunted her if she failed to receive revelations obviously gives fuel to the prevailing idea amongst modern historians that Barton was merely the pawn of conservative churchmen. The Latin prologue implies that Barton dictated her revelations to Bocking because their relationship was one of particular intimacy:

> quomodo igitur omnia que presenti libello magna parte conscripta sunt iuxta narracionem ipsuis qua vni spirituali viro de de [sic] ordine sancti benedicti sacre theologie professori quem pre ceteris familiarem habebat singula exposuit cum eadem ab inquirentibus multa occultaret eo quod esset timorata valde et humilima spiritu huic diligenter omnia inuestiganti et memorie ea tradere cupienti humane salutis et dilectionis gratia ut diuina et celesti dispensacione cuncta familialiter enarrare coa conata est.[30]

---

[26] PRO, SP 1/77, f. 237r (*L&P*, vol. 6 no. 835); PRO, SP 1/79 f. 76r (*L&P*, vol. 6 no. 1149 (2)); and PRO, SP 1/73, ff. 77v–78r (*L&P*, vol. 5 no. 1698 (1) and (2)).

[27] Nicholas Sanders, *De origine ac progressu schismatis Anglicani* (Cologne, 1585), ff. 74r–74v.

[28] Whatmore, 469.

[29] Whatmore, 469.

[30] McKee, 62.

As Barton's confessor and spiritual biographer, Bocking was clearly in a position to manipulate the young nun, yet there exist obvious precedents for similar activities going on under rather less sinister circumstances. A very well-known example is Margery Kempe, who reports that she too listened to her priest reading from St Bridget's book along with other spiritual texts.[31] As is clear from *The Book of Margery Kempe*, it was not uncommon for medieval women to internalise the models of sanctity they encountered in saints' lives,[32] and it was in the interest of both Kempe's priest (who was also her amanuensis) and Barton's confessor Bocking that they should present their spiritual protégées as being in the same class as figures of religious authority. It is not then necessary for us to dismiss out of hand the evidence of the penitential sermon as simply defamatory. It is perfectly plausible that Barton was familiar with the prophecies of both St Bridget and St Catherine in some form. Well before the 1520s, the works of both saints were certainly reasonably accessible: in the first decades of the fifteenth century, the Brigittine convent of Syon had in its possession vernacular translations of the huge collection of St Bridget's revelations known as the *Liber Celestis* and St Catherine's long religious treatise, *Il Dialogo*; and by the end of the century, records of lay women's ownership of books of the life and revelations of the former saint provide just one indication of a flourishing Brigittine cult in England.[33]

In establishing a connection between Barton and these Continental women prophets, it is also relevant to note that Barton had direct links with Syon Abbey. Syon was a centre of late medieval feminine devotion and shared with the neighbouring Charterhouse at Sheen an interest in the study and dissemination of mystical texts; it has even been argued that the Brigittine nuns might have had an interest in Wynkyn de Worde's publication of extracts of *The Book of Margery Kempe*.[34] In the early Reformation, Syon was also a centre of opposition to the Act of Supremacy, and according to notes taken during Barton's investigation, her prophecies were told to Abbess Agnes Jordan; the confessor of Syon John Fewterer, the scholar and future martyr Richard Reynolds, and a number of women there including the wife of the Lieutenant of the Tower, Lady Kingston.[35] Indeed, Agnes Jordan was said to be one of a number of figures who requested Barton to present on her behalf petitions to the Virgin Mary.[36] What is more, Barton herself confessed that the Abbess of Syon had

[31] *Kempe*, 39, 143.
[32] See Clarissa W. Atkinson, *Mystic and Pilgrim: The Book and the World of Margery Kempe* (Ithaca: Cornell University Press, 1983), 168–79.
[33] See Johnson, 79–82, 85–7.
[34] S.E. Holbrook, 'Margery Kempe and Wynkyn de Worde', in Marion Glasscoe, ed., *The Medieval Mystical Tradition in England*, Exeter Symposium 4 (Cambridge: D.S. Brewer, 1987), 27–46; 42.
[35] *L&P*, vol. 6 no. 1468 (1).
[36] PRO, SP 1/73, ff. 27v–28r (*L&P*, vol. 5 no. 1698 (2)).

encouraged her to meet the Marchioness of Exeter, whose antipathy to the King was well-known,[37] and subsequent government investigations uncovered evidence which suggests that such meetings were indeed treasonous in intent.[38] Thomas More reported that certain of the monks at Syon were somewhat suspicious of Barton and of the things that she said,[39] but this did not prevent her from receiving an enthusiastic reception at Sheen.[40] In a letter written less than a year before Barton's execution, the Procurator, Henry Man, declared that the knowledge of her pious works was more edifying to his soul than anything that he had read in Holy Scripture.[41] Barton's adherents exchanged letters and gifts and prayed for one another, forming a closely-knit group reminiscent of the *famiglia* which surrounded both St Bridget and St Catherine. Henry Man praised Barton as one who nurtured her spiritual children, feeding and fostering them in virtue,[42] and according to another Sheen Carthusian, she was to her supporters a good and devout mother.[43] It is then quite probable that Barton's connections at Syon and Sheen would have played a significant part in her spiritual development.

If the likelihood that Elizabeth Barton was familiar with the writings and lives of Bridget and Catherine is then a very real one, it follows that the influence of these saints should be apparent, at least to some extent in the miracles and revelations attributed to her. Despite the disparate and often hostile nature of the evidence, a fairly coherent picture of Barton's life does emerge. In certain respects it seems that her experiences differed quite radically from either of her Continental predecessors. There is no suggestion in any of the sources that she showed any signs of remarkable piety during her childhood; nor does she appear to have indulged in the sort of extreme asceticism which we find associated with both saints. Whereas Bridget would sleep on the floor, deprive herself of food and drink, tie a knotted girdle around her waist, chew the bitter-tasting herb gentian, and drip burning wax on her arms,[44] the penitential sermon states that Barton herself remained 'fat and ruddy' while her supporters were encouraged to fast, to wear hair shirts and iron chains, and to perform other penances in order to make themselves worthy to preach her revelations.[45] On the other hand, in the tradition of visionaries like Catherine of

---

[37] PRO, SP 1/80, ff. 142r–143v (*L&P*, vol. 6 no. 1468 (7)).
[38] See PRO, SP 1/138, f. 210r (*L&P*, vol. 13, part 2, no. 802); SP 1/139, f. 16r (*L&P*, vol. 13, part 2, no. 827 (2)); SP 1/139, ff. 77r–77v (*L&P*, vol. 13, part 2, no. 831 (1.4 and 1.5)); SP 1/140, ff. 5r–8v (*L&P*, vol. 13, part 2, no. 961 (2)).
[39] Rogers, 484.
[40] Rogers, 485–6.
[41] PRO, SP 1/79, f. 76r (*L&P*, vol. 6, no. 1149 (2)).
[42] PRO, SP 1/77, f. 237r (*L&P*, vol. 6, no. 835).
[43] PRO, SP 1/80, f. 146r (*L&P*, vol. 6, no. 1468 (8)).
[44] See, for example, Johannes Jørgensen, *St Bridget of Sweden*, trans. Ingeborg Lund (London: Longman, Green and Co.: 1954), vol. 1, 61–3.
[45] Whatmore, 469.

Siena who, for much of her life, endured almost constant physical pain even after her public healing, Barton was afflicted by an illness which Thomas Goldwell observed recurred 'abowte the conception of our lady' and caused her 'to lye thre of iiij. dayes without mete or drynke'.[46] The jaw-locking and writhing which accompanied Barton's ecstatic trances were also somewhat akin to the paralysis which afflicted Catherine, causing her eyes to shut tight, her neck to stiffen, and her fingers to clench 'so tightly that it was as though they were nailed there, and it would have been easier to break them than force them open',[47] while the heavenly lights, beautiful voices and melodies, and feeling of inner joy which Barton regularly experienced resembled the physical and emotional sensations of warmth and rejoicing which St Bridget felt at the time when Christ dictated her Rule to her.[48]

St Bridget and St Catherine were miracle workers who possessed marvellous abilities to heal the sick, discern hidden sins and convert the recalcitrant, and St Catherine's renown was such that members of her *famiglia* were given special permission to absolve those who came to visit her.[48] Barton was requested by her devotees to intercede for their physical and spiritual well-being, and sinners stricken by guilt who felt the need to come and speak with her were amazed by her ability to read the secrets of their hearts.[50] She was reputed to have received regular heavenly visitations[51] and at one time several letters were in circulation said to have been produced in Heaven and given to her by an angel.[52] One such letter, supposedly written by Mary Magdalen, and preserved as a relic in Canterbury, warned a London widow that she and her husband would be damned unless certain gold which had been hidden away by the dead man was donated to the Church.[53] Again we might find in this evidence of a link with St Bridget: during her canonisation process a witness reported that the secrets of a man's life were revealed to St Bridget in a miraculous letter, which, on the instructions of the Virgin Mary, she had given to the recipient.[54]

Following precedents set in medieval saint's lives, Barton not only experienced visions and performed miracles, but, according to Thomas

---

[46] Wright, 21.

[47] Raymond of Capua, *The Life of St Catherine of Siena*, trans. George Lamb (London: Harvill Press, 1960), 113.

[48] *Statutes*, vol. 3, 448; Jørgensen, vol. 1, 182.

[49] Raymond of Capua, 217.

[50] Rogers, 486.

[51] Morison, sig. T4r; Wright, 14–18; and *Statutes*, vol. 3, 448.

[52] J.E. Cox, *The Works of Thomas Cranmer* (Cambridge: Parker Society, 1846), vol. 2, 273–4.

[53] Whatmore, 471. Cf. *Statutes*, vol. 3, 448; Wright, 18.

[54] Roger Ellis, 'The Divine Message and Its Human Agents; St Birgitta and Her Editors', in James Hogg, ed., *Studies in St Birgitta and the Brigittine Order*, *Analecta Cartusiana* 35:19 (Salzburg, 1993), vol. 1, 209–33; 232.

Goldwell, was also 'meny tymes trobeled with her gostely enmy'.[55] Barton herself confirmed to Thomas More that the devil had appeared to her as a bird flying around her room.[56] The penitential sermon and the Act of Attainder made much of Bocking's stories of such matters: stinking smoke rising from the nun's cell was an indication of a diabolical presence, and in one of his attacks the devil burnt the veil which Barton was wearing.[57] This last episode might be compared to a series of incidents recorded by Raymond of Capua in which Satan tried to set fire to Catherine of Siena's veil and hair but did not succeed in distracting her from her ecstasies.[58] The fleshly temptations of women saints were often dwelt on by their hagiographers. Prior Goldwell stated that he had read that Barton was often 'moved . . . to incontynency, and to unclene levying',[59] and another source notes that she had been troubled by a vision of Satan copulating with a woman on the bed in her cell.[60] Yet although the sermon and the Act exploited every opportunity to insinuate that Barton was engaged in immoral activities by referring to her claims that the devil appeared to her as a man 'wantonly aparelled'[61] and attempted to seduce her 'like a jolly gallant',[62] Raymond of Capua also said of St Catherine of Siena that

> She confessed to me that there were so many hordes of devils in her cell – she could almost see them with her own eyes – rousing so many vile thoughts in her mind, that for a time at least she was glad to get out of it and take refuge in church. . . . But when she returned to her little room they were still there, talking and acting in the most licentious manner and attacking her like a swarm of maddening flies.[63]

The devil's attack on Barton was typical of the sort of tests to which even the most virtuous of holy women were subjected.

In some respects at least it appears that Elizabeth Barton's miracles and temptations conform to Continental patterns of feminine piety, but it is the determination with which she championed the Church against bishops, the King and even the Pope, obtaining interviews with some of the most powerful people in the realm in the process, which is most reminiscent of the activities of St Bridget and St Catherine. Just as these saints had turned bishops and monks away from their corrupt practices, so Barton attempted to manipulate the English churchmen who were facilitating the divorce. It appears that Archbishop Warham, who first came into contact with Barton

---

55 Wright, 21.
56 Rogers, 405; cf, *Statutes*, vol. 3, 448.
57 Whatmore, 469.
58 Raymond of Capua, 114–15.
59 Wright, 21.
60 Wright, 17.
61 *Statutes*, vol. 3, 448.
62 Whatmore, 471.
63 Raymond of Capua, 93.

when he sent a commission to examine her at the time of her marvellous illness in 1525, subsequently interviewed her on a number of occasions, and through Warham, she obtained a meeting with Cardinal Wolsey.[64] Possibly through Wolsey, Barton gained admission to the King himself who at first seems to have granted her his favour: one anonymous document produced during the investigation claims that the King offered to make Barton an abbess, and Anne Boleyn asked her to remain at Court in attendance upon her.[65] Yet as the King's 'Great Matter' came to a crisis and Barton's prophecies became increasingly politically contentious, she lost any royal support she might initially have enjoyed. Perhaps inspired by both Bridget and Catherine who wrote letters to the papacy as well as to various sovereigns and leaders, Barton sent messages to Clement VII encouraging him to stand against the English King.[66] She communicated directly with his ambassadors;[67] and, at least according to the Protestant writer Richard Morison, one of them pledged the Pope's support, prostrating himself in front of her, and kissing her feet.[68] The precedents of St Bridget and St Catherine may well have not only empowered Barton to venture into the public sphere, but also prepared her audiences to listen to her.

The revelations attributed to Barton, and attested to in a range of different sources, go some way to confirming that St Bridget and St Catherine became her role models. Again like Saint Bridget and Saint Catherine, Elizabeth Barton put pressure on secular as well as ecclesiastical leaders to reform their conduct and policies. While Bridget and Catherine were concerned by the corruption within the Roman Church, Barton is recorded to have spoken against the removal of its liberties,[69] and an angel commanded her to warn Henry against depriving the Pope of his rights, estates and revenues.[70] Furthermore, she insisted that it was Henry's duty to destroy both the Protestant heretics and their publications.[71] Barton was outspoken in her approach: a fifteenth-century *vita* of Bishop John Fisher, relates that during the early divorce negotiations, she was granted an interview with the King at Hanworth, at which time she attempted to discourage him from pursuing the course he had taken, 'for the safety of his soul and the preservation of the realm'.[72] Just as St Bridget had spoken in apocalyptic terms of the judgement to come and warned of the terrible

---

[64] PRO, SP 1/50, f. 163r (*L&P*, vol. 4, part 2, no. 4806).

[65] PRO, SP 1/80, f. 138r (*L&P*, vol. 6, no. 1468 (5)).

[66] Barton's communications with the Pope are mentioned in a considerable number of sources, for example, Cox, vol. 2, 273.

[67] *Statutes*, vol. 3, 449–50.

[68] Morison, sig. T4v; see also PRO, SP 1/143, f. 205r (*L&P*, vol. 14, part 1, no. 402).

[69] Cox, vol. 2, 273.

[70] Wright, 14.

[71] Wright, 14. Cf. Cox, vol. 2, 273; and Morison, sig. T3v.

[72] Richard Hall, *Vie du bienheureux martyr Jean Fisher*, ed. Fr van Ortroy (Brussels: Polleunis and Ceuterick, 1893), 251.

punishments which would befall those who did not listen to her,[73] so Barton reproached Warham and Wolsey for their sins,[74] and she issued the Archbishop and Cardinal with threats of the divine retribution which would follow if they continued to support the King in his plan to re-marry.[75] According to Thomas More, Barton had told Wolsey that she had seen a vision of the three swords which God had placed in his hands:

> The firste . . . was the orderinge of the spiritualtie vnder the Pope, as Legate, the seconde the rule that he bare in order of the temporaltie vnder the Kinge, as his Chauncellor. And the third, she saide, was the medlinge he was put in truste with by the Kinge, concerninge the greate matter of his marriage.[76]

Her interpretation made it clear that Wolsey's first responsibility was to the Church and she warned of the dire consequences which would follow if this power was misused. Barton also threatened Clement VII that God would plague him if he failed to rule in favour of Katherine of Aragon,[77] and told him that there was a great stroke of God suspended above his head.[78] If the threat of stirring up rebellion in her own country did not restrain St Bridget, who predicted that 'the king who is now reigning [Magnus] shall lose the kingdom and all his house with him',[79] neither did it impose any limits on Barton. The Act of Attainder claims that she had not only announced that Henry VIII's reign would end if he went ahead with the divorce, but that she had also prophesied that, no matter the outcome, the Princess Mary would not be deprived of her birthright, but 'shuld prospere and reigne in this Realme, and have many fryndes to susteyne and maynteyne her'.[80] For Barton, as for St Bridget and St Catherine, the law of God was above the law of man, and had to be enforced whatever the cost.

The strongest indications of the Continental influence on Barton are her visions of heaven, hell and purgatory. St Catherine and St Bridget both had visions of beyond the grave, interceded for souls which they saw in tor-ment, and were assured of the salvation of others, and St Catherine knew that her beloved confessor had been granted eternal life.[81] Similarly, the extract of Bocking's book seen by Prior Goldwell had told of the fate of 'dyvers that were ded' including Bocking's uncle and a former servant of Christ Church; described the prayers and devotions which would rescue

---

[73] See, for example, Jørgensen, vol. 1, 202–4.
[74] Thomas Cranmer, *A Confutation of Unwritten Verities* in H. Jenkyns ed., *The Remains of Thomas Cranmer* (Oxford: Oxford University Press, 1833), vol. 4, 241.
[75] See Whatmore, 467; and Cox, vol. 2, 273.
[76] Rogers, 482; and cf. Wright, 15.
[77] Wright, 20.
[78] Cox, vol. 2, 273; cf. Wright, 16.
[79] Jørgensen, vol. 2, 118; see also 149–51.
[80] *Statutes*, vol. 3, 450.
[81] Raymond of Capua, 174.

them from their purgatorial sufferings;[82] and Barton received revelations concerning Bocking's death and glorification, and also her own martyrdom.[83] A number of her later visions may have been directly inspired by descriptions in St Bridget's *Revelations* of the sufferings of intransigent bishops, and popes. St Bridget, for example, received a revelation that Urban V (who had failed to grant full approval to her Rule) was in purgatory, but had escaped its worst torments: 'This soul is not among those who have to suffer the severest punishments in purgatory, but it is among those who daily come nearer to the face of God.'[84] Barton claimed to have foreknowledge of Wolsey's fall, which she declared to be the consequence of his disobedience of the commands which she had given him.[85] After his death in 1530 she was able to describe the fate of his soul. The penitential sermon gives one version of her revelations on this matter: '[the] Lord Cardinal came to his death before God would have had him by the space of fifteen years; and therefore Allmighty God hath given no sentence upon him, but will defer it till those years be expired which it was the will of God he should have lived in the world'.[86] However, Thomas More had heard that Wolsey was brought to heaven by Barton's prayers,[87] and another source agrees that he was saved by Barton's intercession and gives this summary of her vision of his fate:

> syns he dyed she saw the disputacion of the devylles for his sowylle, and how she was iij. tymes lyfte up and culd not se hym nether in hevyn, hell, nor purgatory, and at the last where shew saw hym, and how by hur pennaunce he was browght unto hevyn . . .[88]

Even kings were not exempt from such harsh judgements: again like St Bridget, who had a vision of King Magnus of Sweden's judgement before God and heard him be sentenced to eternal damnation ('Therefore shall all that is good in thee be taken from thee and be given to one who shall come after thee'),[89] Barton received a revelation that Henry VIII would not achieve salvation and claimed that she had seen 'the particular place and spot destined to him in hell'.[90] Not content with simply imitating the prophecies of her predecessors, Barton apparently went beyond the bounds of church doctrine, as the penitential sermon accuses Bocking of saying that she had received a revelation that there was another place of

---

[82] Wright, 21.
[83] Wright, 17.
[84] Jørgenson, vol. 2, 222.
[85] Wright, 15.
[86] Whatmore, 470.
[87] Rogers, 482.
[88] Wright, 16.
[89] Jørgenson, vol. 2, 179–82; 182.
[90] *CSP Spain*, vol. 4, part 2, no. 1149.

eternal punishment which was neither hell nor purgatory.[91] Nonetheless, while most of Barton's prophecies and visions of purgatory and hell echo those in St Bridget's in particular, it is when one comes to look for more specific illustrations of the influence of Bridget or Catherine on Barton's predictions and visions that the full limitations of this evidence really manifest themselves, and it has to be acknowledged that Barton's prophecies are not recorded in enough detail for this influence to be categorically proven.

God's anger at Henry VIII during his attempted reconciliation with the French king in October 1532 was demonstrated to Barton in an openly seditious eucharistic vision which once more echoes the revelations of earlier European women saints.[92] A number of sources record that Barton claimed to have been miraculously transported from her convent to the Church of Our Lady in Calais where she remained invisibly present during the mass. As the King prepared to receive the bread of the sacrament an angel took it out of the hands of the priest and offered it to Barton instead. Miracles in which the Eucharist is brought to the recipient by divine means are not unusual, especially amongst women mystics and saints,[93] and again a parallel can be found in the life of one of her predecessors. Raymond of Capua describes an occasion when a particle of consecrated bread which had fallen from the chalice apparently flew straight to Catherine of Siena at the other end of the church.[94] It was also reputed of Barton's contemporary, the Holy Maid of Leominster, that during mass the host often appeared to rise miraculously from the paten held by the priest and place itself in her mouth.[95] Nonetheless, the political dimension to this example of Barton's miraculous abilities does give the impression that Barton had Catherine of Siena in mind as a role model. Catherine of Siena's miracle occurred after she had been discouraged from receiving the sacrament by her companions who knew that her trances displeased some of Raymond's fellow friars. Thus clerical authority could be seen to be circumvented by divine intervention on behalf of the woman dedicated to serving God. Likewise, Elizabeth Barton's Eucharist vision confirmed her prophecies against the King: for Henry VIII to be deprived of the host in this way was a sign that he was no longer a member of the community of Church and may have been intended as a prediction of his excommunication. Barton's own reception of the host from the angel attested to her role as God's chosen messenger.

I have argued in this paper that Elizabeth Barton's prophecies and visions reveal that in taking upon herself the role of political prophet she

---

91 Whatmore, 470.
92 *Statutes*, vol. 3, 448; cf. Wright, 15, 20; and Rogers, 483.
93 Caroline Walker Bynum, *Holy Feast and Holy Fast: the Religious Significance of Food to Holy Women* (Berkeley: University of California Press, 1987), 77 and *passim*.
94 Raymond of Capua, 286–91.
95 More, part 1, 87.

followed the examples set by Bridget of Sweden and Catherine of Siena. However, by the time of her execution, her prophecies had been discredited, her reputation destroyed, and her followers dispersed, and under such circumstances it is not surprising that her influence was short-lived. While some women in Barton's immediate circle imitated her (her own sister is said to have collected the blood from Christ's side in a chalice and warned of the plagues which would come to the city of London;[96] and in response to Barton's prayers another female devotee was visited by an angel),[97] in the decades after her execution, the closest parallels are once again found not in England but in central Europe, especially Spain and Italy. In these countries, in spite of the fact that they were sometimes persecuted by the Inquisition, *beatas* often held a great deal of control over religious and political leaders. These holy women resemble Barton in that they too claimed the authority to give advice on matters relating to the public as well as the private arena; a number of them are known to have consciously emulated earlier female saints.[98] In Reformation England the patterns of female piety were rather different. Although many Protestants, like the martyr Anne Askew (executed 1546), confident that they possessed the spirit of God, defended their right to instruct others in the true faith and refused to be silenced by the laws of the land, following the dissolution, recusant women such as Margaret Clitherow (executed 1586) largely confined their acts of rebellion to the household, converting family and friends, organising devotions and harbouring priests. To reiterate the point I made at the start, as a woman political prophet Barton is a unique figure, set apart not only from earlier English visionaries and from her contemporaries, but also from her successors by the active part which she played in the resistance to Henry VIII's reforms.

---

[96] Wright, 18.

[97] Wright, 17.

[98] See, for example, Mariá Vela y Cueto, discussed by Milagros Ortega Costa in 'Spanish Women in the Reformation', in Sherrin Marshall, ed., *Women in Reformation and Counter-Reformation Europe: Public and Private Worlds* (Bloomington: Indiana University Press, 1989), 89–119; 103–105. See also Jodi Bilinkoff, 'A Spanish Prophetess and Her Patrons: The Case of María de Santo Domingo', *Sixteenth Century Journal*, vol. 23 (1992), 21–34.

Auctricitas? Holy Women
and their Middle English Texts

IAN JOHNSON

This essay considers the nature of some apparent conferrals and negotiations, in some fifteenth-century texts, of forms of *auctoritas* on or by women as generating or underpinning literary texts, an authority albeit refracted, as a rule, through male vernacularisers or amanuenses. Such discourses present extreme constructions of women, as special cases ostensibly raised up in power and respect.

For the Middle Ages the terms *auctor* and *auctoritas* are the masculine/general terms for originating and governing cultural and textual power. From such authority derives a continuum of roles, as conceived by contemporary learned literary theory: *commentator, compilator, predicator, scriptor, rhetor* and so on.[1] Vernacular male writers were not, as a rule, *auctores*. No surprise then that Hoccleve, in his *Dialogus cum Amico*, a

---

[1] For discussion of such academic literary theory and its implications for vernacular literary culture, see generally A.J. Minnis, *Medieval Theory of Authorship: Scholastic Literary Attitudes in the Later Middle Ages* (London: Scolar Press, 1984), esp. 94–5; M.B. Parkes, 'The Influence of the Concept of *Ordinatio* and *Compilatio* on the Development of the Book', in *Medieval Learning and Literature: Essays presented to R.W. Hunt*, ed. J.J. Alexander and M.T. Gibson (Oxford: Clarendon Press, 1978), 115–41, esp. 127; Ian Johnson, 'The Late-Medieval Theory and Practice of Translation with Special Reference to Some Middle English Lives of Christ' (Ph.D., diss. Bristol, 1990), esp. 1–27, 49–159; 'Prologue and Practice: Middle English Lives of Christ', in *The Medieval Translator: The Theory and Practice of Translation in the Middle Ages: Papers read at a conference held 20–23 August 1987 at the University of Wales Conference Centre, Gregynog Hall*, ed. Roger Ellis *et al.* (Cambridge: D.S. Brewer, 1989), 69–85, esp. 69–75; the section on academic literary theory and Middle English literary translation in *The Cambridge History of Literary Criticism*, ed. A.J. Minnis (Cambridge, CUP, forthcoming); *The Medieval Boethius: Studies in the Vernacular Translations of* De Consolatione Philosophiae, ed. A.J. Minnis (Woodbridge: D.S. Brewer, 1987) for studies in the use of commentary-tradition and the importance of academic literary attitudes in the vernacularisation of the most important *auctor* outside the Bible; and see generally Rita Copeland, *Rhetoric, Translation and Hermeneutics in the Middle Ages: Academic Traditions and Vernacular Texts* (Cambridge: CUP, 1991). See also, for discussion of women negotiating masculine literary authority, *Women's Writing in Middle English*, ed. Alexandra Barratt (London: Longman, 1992), 1–16.

work with a homosocial *titulus* if ever there was one, enforces with lad-
dish irony the hopelessly whimsical paradoxicality of the notion of feminine *auctoritas*:

> The wyf of Bathe, take I for auctrice
> Þat wommen han no ioie ne deyntee
> Þat men sholde vp-on hem putte any vice . . .[2]

But were there, perhaps, some unwhimsical, irony-free cultural spaces for
the *auctrix*, a possibility that in some patriarchally delimited ways there
were gaps for a gendered authority, which might be termed **auctricitas*,
and licensed with some relative autonomy or agency? To this end it seems
appropriate to look at some Middle English manifestations of holy
women, dead or alive, in their roles as producers and conduits of authoritative meaning in accordance with contemporary orthodoxies. It is right and
proper, before moving on to consider other saints, lesser females and their
male amanuenses and translators, to start with the most powerful woman
of all, the Virgin Mary, together with a saint on whom she has a particular
textual bearing, St Bridget of Sweden.

I. Holy Women and their Words

1. *The Virgin Mary and St Bridget of Sweden as* Auctrices

The *Speculum Devotorum*, a Carthusian prose compilation by an unknown
monk of Sheen (probably composed before the middle of the fifteenth
century and no earlier than 1410), was intended for a religious woman,
probably a 'goostly syster' of Syon Abbey.[3] It is a meditative Life of Christ
– narrative, imaginative, exegetical, moralising and prayerful. It exists in
two manuscripts and shows considerable awareness of contemporary academic literary theory, as its prologue and intermittent self-exegesis witness.[4]

---

[2] Thomas Hoccleve, *Dialogus cum Amico*, 694–6, in *Hoccleve's Works: I. The Minor
Poems*, ed. F.J. Furnivall (London: EETS, ES 61 1892).
[3] *The Speculum Devotorum of an Anonymous Carthusian of Sheen*, ed. James Hogg,
Analecta Cartusiana, 12–13 (Salzburg: Universität Salzburg, 1973–74). For an earlier,
more complete edition of the text, which unlike Hogg's, includes the last four chapters, see
Bridget Anne Wilsher, 'An Edition of "Speculum Devotorum", a Fifteenth Century English Meditation on the Life and Passion of Christ, with an Introduction and Notes' (M.A.
diss. London, 1956). Hogg's edition is cited unless otherwise specified.
[4] For basic information about this work I am grateful to have had access to Professor
Hogg's unpublished typescript introduction to his edition. For discussion of the literary
attitudes and translation methods of this work, see Johnson, 'Late-Medieval Theory',
300–86, and 'Prologue and Practice', 75–80. See also generally Wilsher's introduction and
notes.

In this 'Myrowre to deuout peple' (as it is entitled in the *proheme* (5), indicating a general as well as a gendered one-woman intended reader-ship), the figure of Mary is not only an exemplary role-model for medita-tion and devotion, she is also acknowledged as an *auctrix* behind the evangelical *auctores*, for it was she who told them the details of the Nativity and Infancy of Christ. Subsequently, instead of going straight to Heaven with her risen son, she stayed on earth and fulfilled her authorial role:

> And how gret desyre also trowe ȝe hadde sche to haue goo wyth hym. God wote a lone. Not wythstandynge hyt was necessarye þat sche schulde a byde ȝette in erthe for the conforte of the dyscyplys. & also to the informynge of the euangelystys of the incarnacyon. & the ȝougthe of oure lorde. for sche knewe þat best of alle othyre. (Wilsher, 378)

Mary has a real efficient causality in this work, not only in the gospel material but also in her revelations to 'approuyd wymmen' like St Bridget, revelations which also form an important part of the *Speculum Devo-torum*. Such visions, being granted by grace, are not to be regarded as mere additions to gospel materials; they are utterly central to the exposi-tion of the affective *sentence* of the *Vita*. The meditation on the Nativity is a case in point. For example, the birth is recounted summarily in the *narratio* (72–73), but expounded more elaborately and in immense detail at the next stage of *meditatio* by recourse to 'Brygytt'. She is credited with opening the gospel by revelation just as Nicholas of Lyre (another major source of this work) opens it by literal-sense commentary.[5] It is Bridget's special grace that she has access to the minute realities of the Biblical *mise-en-scène*, the actual events, which can then be recreated in the medi-tating soul of the reader by 'ymagynacyon':

> ȝytt more opynly how oure lorde was borne & alle the manyr therof oure lady schewde to seyint Brygytt ful fayre be reuelacyon, the whyche sche tellyth thus. (73)

The extraordinary loving detail and the anatomical and practical minutiae of birth and babycare which preoccupy the subsequent meditation are designed to have a considerable affective impact on the female reader and on the general audience to whom this work is also addressed. Care is taken to show how Mary has 'too smale lynnyn clowtys & too clene wollen clothys þat sche hadde browgth wyth here to wrappe inne the chylde' (74) at the ready before the birth. She does not, like most medieval women, squat to give birth but stands upright in dignified prayer and spiritual

---

[5] For a basic account of St Bridget and her importance, see Barratt, 84–5. For the *Speculum Devotorum*'s recourse to Mary and Bridget, and use of Nicholas of Lyre, see Johnson, 'Prologue and Practice', 75–80, and 'Late-Medieval Theory', 330–1, 364–7, 373–82.

ecstasy, without pain, swathed in light (75–76). The child appears on the ground before her, 'rygth clene fro alle manyr felthe & vnclennesse', as is also the 'skynne þat hyt cam out in lyinge besyde hym wrappyd togederys & rygth schynynge' (76). She addresses Him tenderly (76–77), and further affective description follows:

> ... wyth gret honeste & reuerence sche worschypyde the chylde & seyde to hym: Ʒe be welcome my god, my lorde, & my sone, & thanne the chylde wepynge & as hyt were quakynge for colde & hardenesse of the pauyment there hyt laye turnede hytself a lytyl & straugth out hys lemys sekynge to fynde refute & fauoure of the mothyr; the whyche the mothyr thanne toke vp in here handys & streynyde hym to here breste & wyth here cheke & here breste sche made hym hoote wyth gret gladnesse & ful tendyr modyrly compassyon; the whyche thanne satte downe vpon the grounde & putt here sone in here lappe & toke wyth here fyngrys craftyly hys nauyl, the whyche anone was kytte aweye, ne ther came ny likur or blode out therof, & anone sche beganne to suade hym vp dylygently, fyrste in the lytyl lynnyn clowtys & aftyr in the wollen, streynynge the lytyl body the leggys & the armys wyth a suadynge bonde the whyche was souwed in foure partyis of the ouyr wollen cloth; aftyrwarde forsothe sche wrappede & bonde abowte þe chylde ys heed the othyr tueyne smale lynnyn clowtys the whyche sche hadde arethy therfore. (77–78)

Bridget's revelation caters to theological proprieties and to the intense decorum of worship, tenderness and divine courtesy enacted in the developing relationship between Holy Mother and Child-God. Immediately He appears she renders Him His due, worshipping Him with the formal 'Ʒe' as 'God' and 'lorde', and then shifting the focus to His incarnation and the human intimacy of motherhood: 'my sone'. These words are the cue for the child to weep, to reciprocate her words by reaching out in all too human fashion for maternal comfort. Mary, advertised for the first time not as the 'virgyne' or 'Marye' but (twice) as 'the mothyr', expresses 'modyrly compassyon', exemplifying the *compassio* at the core of meditating (like the reader) on the Life of Christ. The scene then moves on from welcome and mutual recognition to the decorum of practical care. The word 'lytyl' is repeated in emphasis of the divine baby's paradoxical diminutiveness (but without the cloying sentimentalism of Chaucer's Prioress). The 'streynynge' of 'the lytyl body' with the cloths echoes the earlier 'streynyde hym to here breste', the tender intimacy of the maternal embrace being extended to the wrapping of the clothes. In her behaviour, Mary could be any exemplary late-medieval woman, displaying the best of mothering skills. Elsewhere in the early chapters of the *Speculum Devotorum*, attention is drawn to physical details and maternal attentiveness: for example she holds the baby (who 'was sumwhat fatt as chyldryn been') and supports his head properly: 'wyth here rygth hande sche helde vp the chyld ys heed' (104). Yet there is more to such meticulous emotive realization than perinatal affectivity alone. The details are, according to St Bridget, *what actually happened.*

Bridget's self-interpolation into the key textual locus of the Nativity is matched by her version of the Crucifixion, where the translator points out that:

> . . . sche tellyth hyt in here owen persone as sche seygth hyt doo þe whyche I turne here into the forme of medytacyon not goynge be the grace of god fro the menynge of here wordys. (267)

One central feature of the tradition of meditation on the gospels with pressing theoretical implications is the issue of whether and how to imagine events not explicit in the evangelists, and also any apparent contradictions between them. In the *Speculum Devotorum* is a version of the Crucifixion attributed to the evangelists and another based on the revelations of Bridget. The difference between them is not seen as embarrassing. Far from it-Syon was a Brigittine house, and the revelations of the saint carried a special authority there. The first, biblical, account tells how Christ was nailed to the cross lying on the ground; the second, Brigittine, version has Him ascending the cross and stretching out His arm willingly to be nailed. Each is rehearsed separately, in the ostensibly non-interventionist manner of medieval *compilatio*, with the following directions:

> How & in what wyse oure lorde was crucyfyed the euangelystys make no mencyon in specyal but in general. Wherefore I wole telle ʒow too manyrys, whyche of hem maye beste styre ʒow to deuocyon that takyth.
>
> (266)

Both 'manyrys' are fruitful, but the choice between them is left to *lectoris arbitrium*, reader-choice.[6] The Carthusian of Sheen underplays somewhat the first meditation on the manner of crucifixion, which is merely 'oo wyse as I trowe some deuout men haue ymagynyd' (267). He then loyally recommends the Brigittine version in preference to the other:

> Anothyr wyse ʒe maye thynke hyt aftyr seyint Brygyttys reuelacyon & þat I holde sykyrer to lene to, & þat ʒe maye thynke thus (267).

His crafty use of the word 'sykyrer' ('more secure') implicitly undermines the trustworthiness of the first version. Moreover, the 'Brigittine' narrative runs back into the mainstream narrative, thereby lending itself an equally mainstream veracity.

Authorities by their very nature attract apocrypha, and it is a measure of Bridget's authority that she was no exception. In MS Tanner 407, *The Commonplace Book of Robert Reynes of Acle* (1470–1500) is a tale, 'The

---

6 For discussion of this phenomenon, see Minnis, *Medieval Theory*, 201, and Johnson, 'Late-Medieval Theory', 170–3, 308–12.

Woman Recluse and the Wounds of Jesus', in which Jesus speaks to a woman recluse 'coueytinge to knowe the noumbre of the woundes of Oure Lord Ihesu Crist'. He instructs her:

> Sey euery day be an hooll yeer xv Paternoster and xv Aue Maria, and at the yeeris ende thow schalt han wurcheped euery wounde and fulfylled the noumbre of the same.[7]

Such prayers, she is told, will be greatly efficacious towards salvation, mitigate the pains of purgatory, aid the virtuous life, and benefit 'kynrede' mightily. 'An holy man' who dwells with her describes her revelation to an abbess. She transmits all this to her nuns, 'and bade hem seyn these orisones'. Significantly, it is a man, not the abbess or the holy woman, who authorises the use of these prayers. Some of the sisters, however, say their prayers less diligently than others. This is revealed to the holy man in a vision, in which he sees the sisters washing their 'precious stones' (i.e. saying their prayers) well or not so well according to their devotion. When told of this, the sisters mend their ways. Then:

> Afterward on a nyghte this holy man herde a gret noyse and an hidows crye, as all that was in the wode hadde ouerthrowen and be rent vp be the rotes. And he went oute of his celle, and coniured on of the ffendys þat he had herde, and badde that he schuld telle hym what that noyse ment. To whom the fende seyde, 'In this wode woneth an olde woman ful of many holy wordes and seyth an orison so plesyng to God of heuene wherthrowgh we taken ful oftyn gret harme. For with that orison sche getyth to God ful many soules þat were in oure power fast beforn . . . It is tolde that this wommanys name is Sent Bryde, the Quene of Swethe, þat ful many reuelaciouns and gret grace had of God'. (267–8)

The supernatural action and revelations are authenticated by a famous and sanctified name. This story is very common in the fifteenth century but, according to the editor of this commonplace book, Cameron Louis, the naming of the woman recluse as St Bridget of Sweden is found in only one other of the manuscript copies, Harley 2869. This identification having no apparent basis in fact, it is presumably intended to enhance the popularity and credibility of the tale, fitting in as it does with the (again-spurious) Brigittine tradition of the 'Fifteen Oes'.[8] Moreover, just as it was important that Orfeo was a king, and Elizabeth of Hungary royal, so also is Bridget crowned as Queen of Sweden. All in all, pious (mis)attribution is a symptom of authority and influence.

---

[7] *The Commonplace Book of Robert Reynes of Acle: an Edition of Tanner MS 407*, ed. Cameron Louis (London: Garland, 1980), 264.
[8] Ibid., editor's notes, 465.

2. *Valorising the* Auctrix *in Reception*

Just as it was appropriate to treat a holy woman's vision as authoritative by attaching it to a named saint, so was it appropriate to translate a literary work by a named saint as if it were one of authority. Medieval works of *auctoritas* were made, sustained and valorised by being refracted through the authorised hierarchy of contemporary literary roles and forms, such as commentary, compilation, or meditative reworking. Great works of authoritative *sentence*, in their superabundance of meaning and *utilitas*, demanded and were accorded a complementary variety of vernacular versions/performances so that justice could be done to the *sentence* for a particular audience. Thus the most authoritative *materiae* saw the greatest ranges of English versions, as, for instance, with Lives of Christ, a multiplex genre incorporating, amongst other manifestations, sparse gospel harmony, typological allegory, lyrical segmentation, affective meditation, sermonising and even *chanson de geste*.[9] An historically valid ideological measure of the functional importance and range of reception of a work of authority is its re-adaptation in various guises for different audiences, for whom it would take an intended appropriate form, be it changed greatly in style and structure or not. One gauge of a text's status and value is its propensity for compilation, as, for example with Catherine of Siena's *Dialogo*, which became in early-fifteenth-century England *The Orcherd of Syon*, made for Syon Abbey.[10]

The *auctrix* in question, Catherine, was already quite famous, and established as a considerable holy thinker and visionary. The translator makes it perfectly clear that these are pristine revelations, not worked up after the event but dictated while they were still happening. This gives the text the authentic character of a live unedited recording:

> Here begynneþ þe boke of diuine doctrine, þat is to seie, of Goddis techinge, ȝouen bi þe persone of God þe fader to þe intellecte of þe glorious virgyn, Seint Katerine of Seene, of þe Ordre of Seint Dominike, whiche was write as sche endited in her moder tunge, when sche was in contemplacioun inrapt of spirit, and sche heringe actueli and in þe same tyme tellinge tofore meny what oure Lord God spake in her. (18)

The translator (reflecting the common Latin title, *Liber Diuine Doctrine*) glosses 'diuine doctrine' not just as any holy lore but as *Goddis techinge*, directly expounded by Himself to her. The *Dialogo* takes on an elaborate

---

[9] For an account of the variety of this genre, see Elizabeth Salter, *Nicholas Love's Myrrour of the Blessed Lyf of Jesu Christ*, *Analecta Cartusiana* 10 (Salzburg: Universität Salzburg, 1974), 73–118, and for further discussion of this within the context of medieval literary theory, see Johnson, 'Late-Medieval Theory', 1–13.

[10] *The Orcherd of Syon*, ed. Phyllis Hodgson and Gabriel L. Liegey (London: EETS, OS 258, 1966), vol. 1.

Middle English *forma tractatus*, with the original revelations reshaped as an orchard. By giving a plan of the whole orchard in a 'kalender' (2–15), the translator enables the reader to review the summarising *capitula*, thereby taking in the entire work in its parts before choosing her own readerly routes through its various alleys, a feature shared with the *Speculum Devotorum*, which also offers its reader different ways of tackling the *materia* of the book with the help of a table of *capitula*, pointing out also that the reader 'mygthte þe sonnyr fynde that he desyryth moste, & the bettyr kepe hyt in mynde, & also redylokyr fynde hyt yf hym lyste to see hyt aȝen' (2), a function which holds good for *The Orcherd* too.

Although the compiler's labour is, in one sense, complete once the book is in the hands of his readers, he nevertheless presents himself as continuing to labour in the production of the text during its realisation in the process of reading. Conflating form and performance in the knowledge that prayers and grace transcend the limits of mere temporality, he asks that the prayers of the sisters pull his text into fruitful being:

> Grete laborer was I neuer, bodili ne gostli. I had neuer grete strengþe myȝtli to laboure wiþ spade ne wiþ schouel. Þerfore now, deuoute sustern, helpeþ me wiþ preiers. . . . Wiþ þis laboure I charge ȝou not but as ȝoure charite stiriþ ȝou. Wiþ þat vertu helpeþ me forþe, for hastly I go to laboure, in purpos to performe þis gostli orchard as it plesiþ almyȝti God to liȝtne my soule wiþ trewe felynge and clere siȝt. (16–17)

Only authoritative works of deep spiritual fecundity merit and sustain such comment and reshaping. Likewise, the compiler of the *Speculum Devotorum* felt 'sumwhat bore vp be . . . the merytys of hem that be þe mercy of god mowe be profytyd by my sympyl traveyle' (3). Thus, the text helps readers towards grace, who in turn can help to redirect grace towards the writer. Texts which use the economy of grace are texts of power indeed.

The metaphor of transplanting pre-existing materials is significant, as it tells us something about the ideology of moving a text of authority from one culture to another. Our compiler did not create the fruit; he merely gathers, sets and plants it (16); and as authority is re-arrangeable, his work may come to be corrected by 'betir lettrid clerkis' and 'trewe feelynge fadris' (421). He recognises the efficient causality of Christ and Mary (420) in the production of the work, acknowledging as his own only the *forma tractatus*, the orchardly *ordinatio* of *compilatio*, which he calls 'my symple deuyes' (420). Modern critics are frequently interested in seeing vernacular versions of foreign texts as forms of cultural self-aggrandisement and even self-authorisation, in which translations displace originals. In this case, however, the power of the *auctrix* and her work are not so much displaced as witnessed to and valorised by their very compilability and by the belief in this work as necessary or beneficial to an English readership. As much as the vernacular culture appropriates, so do the source-culture and text demand a place in the vernacular (sub)culture which they seek to affect, and *do* affect. The authority of Catherine of Siena is thus extended (i.e., transplanted and re-arranged) into Middle English. The *sentence* is preserved though the form (*forma tractatus*) is changed. In fact the form is redesigned to render more effective the *sentence* of the source, so that it and the source-culture penetrate more powerfully into the target-culture.

Likewise, the works of another woman visionary, St Bridget, are re-arrangeable. However, it is not merely a case of transposing passages within Bridget's individual works. Sometimes, as we have seen with the Nativity and Crucifixion in the *Speculum Devotorum*, extracts are interpolated into non-Brigittine materials. Such anthologising and excerpting of *auctoritates* (**auctricitates*?) enable a flexible and strategic dispersal and application of authority into various *loci* of vernacular literary culture. It is also indicative that a text is authoritative when it can be safely and profitably made subject to meditative amplification by the vernacular reader. In the following example, again from the *Speculum Devotorum*, though Bridget's words are little changed in being Englished, they are declared to be subject to desirable amplification by the meditating reader. Such expansion is deemed necessary to realise the authoritative *sentence* of her text. On this occasion, expansive meditative interpolation serves to fill in gaps left by the gospels on the vague subject of what Christ did in His youth:

> These be the wordys þat oure lady hadde to seyint Brygytt of the ʒougthe of oure lorde Ihesu cryste . . . the whyche I haue drawe here into englyische tonge almoste worde for worde for the more conuenyent forme & ordyr of these sympyl medytacyonys & to ʒoure edyfycacyon or eny othyr deuout creature þat can not vndyrstande latyn; the whyche ʒe maye thynke vndyr forme of medytacyon as I haue tolde ʒow of othyre afore; for thowgth hyt be schortly seyde here vndyr a compendyus manyr, ʒytt hyt maye be drawe ful loonge in a soule þat can deuoutly thynke & dylygently beholde the werkys of oure lorde that be conteynyd therinne . . . (145–6)

The topics specified for meditation, the various virtues shown by Christ, the Virgin and Joseph, according to which the text is to be 'drawyn out', are then indicated (146). It is significant that the same term, 'drawe', is used of both translation and meditation. As *fidus interpres* the translator follows the words of the source in front of him, but changes its form, recognising that its *sentence* requires an effort of meditative exposition to do it justice.

Compilation, meditation, excerption and interpolation are all discourses suitable for sustaining works of authority in the vernacular. The application of such prestige forms to the texts of holy women likc St Bridget and Catherine of Siena are fair measures of cultural power. But what strategies of authority were open to women of lesser stature, women actually producing Middle English texts?

II.   Living English Females: Holy Texts as Women's Work

So far we have concentrated on foreign saints and the strategies to preserve authority taken by male writers to accommodate them in the vernacular. But what about those Englishwomen who bore responsibility for
works in their own tongue, most notably Margery Kempe and Julian of
Norwich? Both women had revelations, and in causing texts to be written,
had to negotiate the masculinist minefield of *auctoritas*.

Margery was concerned to clear her revelations with appropriate
authorities, by checking herself and her revelations out with clerks, ancho-
rites and anchoresses, including Julian of Norwich.[11] The impression of
authenticity in her revelations is helped by the fact that they take the form
of a *reportatio* made by a male amanuensis. The genuineness of Margery's
experiences is further 'proved' by the assaults of the devil on the eyesight
of this man, whose vision recovers with God's grace aiding the good deed
of scribal work:

> Sche seyd hys enmy had envye at hys good dede & wold lett hym yf he
> mygth & bad hym do as wel as god wold ȝeue hym grace & not levyn.
> Whan he cam a-geyn to hys booke, he myth se as wel, hym thowt, as euyr
> he dede be-for . . . (5)

God tells Margery that she and her amanuensis please Him by their book-
production, so much so that He accepts the prayers which Margery would
have said but was prevented from saying when occupied in making the
book (216). In similar vein both Margery and 'hir writer' have confirma-
tory holy experiences while engaged in the task: both weep, and Margery
perceives 'a flawme of fyer a-bowte hir brest ful hoot & delectabyl, . . . a
swet brydde syngyn in hir ere, . . . swet sowndys & melodijs', visitations
from Christ, His mother and the saints, and immediate remission from
illness during the writing process (216). Though Margery is celebrated as
an awkward or eccentric character, she is conventional in her revelations,
with her homely daily routine of 'holy medytacyon of hy contemplacyon
& of wonderful spechys & dalyawns whech owr Lord spak and dalyid to
hyr sowle' (2, also 215). The cliché-ridden, or perhaps cliché-driven,
conventionality of her visions and holy conversations might arouse accu-
sations that they are concocted by formula. This may be true but it does
not necessarily work against the authority of her visions. Medieval theory
of imagination and meditation commonly held that God, in order to communicate with humanity, uses corporeal discourse, and this necessarily
includes the conventions (however shopworn) that are part and parcel of

---

[11] *The Book of Margery Kempe*, ed. Sanford Brown Meech and Hope Emily Allen (London: EETS, OS 212, 1940), 3, 42–43.

all human discourse.[12] It is proper that God condescend to Margery in such familiar revelations in order to be understood, stirring her *affecciouns* and those of other *simple soules* according to their capacities.

It is concomitantly 'proper', furthermore, that a male amanuensis should guarantee, witness to, and enable the *authority* of the *Book* in its initiation and dissemination. As such, he is in a tradition of male amanuenses dictated to by female figures of authority, or rather, writing them up – the man interposing between the holy woman and the sanctified written 'record', between the saint's life and the saint's *Life*, between what she may have said, done or willed and what she 'officially' or institutionally said, did or willed. But just how honest, how accurate, how non-interventionist this or any male amanuensis is with his 'dictating' female is a tricky question requiring further study. How much of what Margery or any other female visionary experienced and expressed found its way into her book in the way in which she might have liked it is impossible to know, especially if she was looking in the first place to others, male or female, to give meaning, sanction and authority to her visions and stirrings.

Julian of Norwich is credited with being more of a writer of her own work than Margery is of hers. She has more theological sophistication in her negotiation of gendered authority, taking pains to show her obedience to Holy Church:

> But in althing I leve as holy church levith, preachith and teachith; for the feith of holy church the which I had aforn hand understonden and, as I hope, by the grace of God wilfully kept in use and custome, stode continualy in my sight, willing and meneing never to receive onything that might be contrary therunto.[13]

It is, however, made clear that hers are indeed divine revelations: 'I conseyvede treulye & myghttyllye that itt was hymselfe that schewyd it me withowtyn any meen' (Beer, 43, cf. 48). Revelation, being a supralinguistic experience, cannot easily be accommodated to the frailties of corporeal discourse, so the reader needs the compensating grace of God to raise the soul up towards divine understanding through love/charity. The function of the text is to stir the reader's charity and *affecciouns* so that the soul becomes subject to grace. Who loves more, understands more, 'for the shewing I am not goode but if I love God the better; and in as much as ye love God the better it is more to you than to me' (Glasscoe, 10). The same charity unites her with God, with her readers, and stirs her to publish

---

[12] For further information on this subject see *Medieval Literary Theory and Criticism c.1100–c.1375: the Commentary-Tradition*, ed. A.J. Minnis and A.B. Scott ass. David Wallace (Oxford: Clarendon, 1988), 165–96.

[13] Julian of Norwich, *A Revelation of Divine Love*, ed. Marion Glasscoe (Exeter: U of Exeter P, rev. edn 1986), 10. For the shorter version, see *Julian of Norwich's Revelations of Divine Love: The Shorter Version ed. from BL Add. MS 37790*, ed. Frances Beer, Middle English Texts 8 (Heidelberg: Carl Winter, 1978).

her showings. She feels unequal to the task of expounding her own visions and therefore hopes that God will Himself intervene to help her readers to 'take it mare gastelye and mare swetly than I can or maye telle it ȝowe' (Beer, 48). That 'in alle this I was mekylle styrrede in charyte to myne evyncrystene' exculpates her by dint of charitably pure *entent* (Beer, 48).

With orthodox meekness both mystical and 'womanly', it is not her meaning but that of God which generates the text and transcends its/her human limitations. Without undermining, and in order to confirm, the *auctoritas* of her showings, Julian rejects any idea that the text arises from her own personality or merits. She eschews the named and blessed selfhood of the *auctor* by speaking in the persona not of an agent of meaning but that of a humble consumer, witness and occasion of it. Like a compiler, she is a conduit for meaning, disavowing creation, assertion, ownership or control of it. In her Long Text, despite her protestation of expository inability, she has a role like that of a commentator/meditator, elucidating by grace-aided exposition the *sentence* immanent in her visions. This, naturally, creates an impression of authority in her revelations, inasmuch as they are predicated and treated as *sentence*-laden *materiae* requiring such treatment. Julian draws on standard 'non-assertive' interpretative and valorising procedures available in general/masculine culture, procedures which tie in felicitously and invisibly with gendered submissiveness. All remains God's meaning. Her showings are to be taken in the persona of all fellow Christians: 'For y mene in the person of myne evyncrystene' (Beer, 47). As she puts it in the longer version:

> Methowte this vision was shewid for hem that should leven. And that I sey of me I sey in the person of al myn evyn cristen, for I am lernyd in the gostly shewing of our lord God that he menyth so. (Glasscoe, 10)

Julian is just another amongst 'evyn cristen', occupying the same place in the semiotic process as all those who read her text. Her showings are intersubjective and are intended to be shared as 'schewyd in generalle & nathynge in specyalle' (Beer, 49, 64). Her self-obliteration in incorporation into the general mass of Christian souls is the starting-point of meaning, her true identity paradoxically depending on her subsumption through charity and hope into the unified body of all those who shall be saved:

> . . . for if I loke singularly to myselfe I am right nowte; but in general, I am in hope, in onehede of charitie with al myn evyn cristen; for in this onehede stond the life of all mankinde that shall be savid. (Glasscoe, 10)

It is the will of God, which takes precedence over her earthbound female feebleness, that she should communicate her showings to others (cf. Beer, 48). For her, claims to authority are duties to authority. Yet, in a sense, she is freed by her submission to subsequent correction, for she can do what she is stirred to do, comfortable in the knowledge that if it offends, her work can be changed without blame, especially as she is protected by her pure and charitable intentionality.

III. Female Hagiography: Actants and *Auctrices*

1. *A Living Canon of Dead European Females?*

Julian had no pretences to primary efficient causality in her *Showings*. There were, however, holy women who really did, so it seemed to late-medieval culture, direct the writing up of their lives, visions and teachings – the saints in heaven. The company of hallowed departed females, women better read when dead, looked down from heaven on the compilers and *makers* mediating to new generations their revelations, their preaching and their life-stories. These saints, though as historical personages they had as a rule been born, lived and been martyred in pre-medieval times under skies less grey than ours, were nevertheless imagined as contemporary idealised medieval Western European women of immense power, personality and credibility. To translate a saint's life was effectively to serve her, who had powers to guide the pen of the hagiographer.

Osbern Bokenham's compilation of Englished women saints' Lives, the *Legendys of Hooly Wummen* (1440s) is an appropriate place to initiate an examination of the literary *auctricitas* of women saints, because his work incorporates key features of gendered authority, such as the efficient causality of the saints in the making of hagiographic texts, the self-interested and affective relationship between saint and writer, the personal experience of the writer of the saint's gracious powers, and the spiritual puissance immanent in hagiographic textuality itself.[14] Bokenham shows frequent awareness (not least in an extravagant Aristotelian Four Causes prologue) of a bilocated authorship in which he is aided by saintly grace. Like other Middle English writers of holy works, he not only asks, at the beginning and/or end of legends, for the saints and the Holy Ghost to intercede for a heavenly pardon, but also beseeches their efficiently causal help in making the literary product.[15] Take, for example, his request to Katherine Denston to pray to the Virgin Mary at the beginning of his Life of St Anne:

[14] Osbern Bokenham, *Legendys of Hooly Wummen*, ed. Mary S. Serjeantson (London: EETS, OS 206, 1938).
[15] For discussion of the tradition of the Aristotelian prologue and the concept of efficient causality as relevant to writers like Bokenham, see Minnis, *Medieval Theory*, 28–9, 75–84, 160–5; Johnson, 'Late-Medieval Theory', 104–37, and 'Tales of a True Translator: Anecdote, Autobiography and Literary Theory in Osbern Bokenham's *Legendys of Hooly Wummen*', in *The Medieval Translator 4*, eds. Roger Ellis and Ruth Evans (Exeter: U of Exeter P, 1994), 104–24.

> Preyth ye enterly þat blyssed virgyne,
> Whiche of seynt anne þe dowter was,
> That she vouchesaf som beem lat shyne
> Vp-on me of hyr specyal grace,
> And þat I may haue leyser & spaas,
> Thorgh help of influence dyuyne,
> To oure bothe confort & solace
> This legende begunne for to termyn, . . .
> And saue vs bothe from endles pyne. (1469–79)

St Agnes is appealed to for literary inspiration and for the reward of seeing her in heaven (4097–8, 4729–35), as is St Christine:

> Now I thee besech, o blyssyd Cristyne,
> Wych regnyst wyth cryst in his heuenly tour,
> As it is wele worthi, mercyful inclyne
> Thy petous erys on-to the translatour
> Wych þi legend compylyd, not wyth-out labour,
> In englyssh tunge; and help, lady, þat he
> Of his mortale lyf in þe last our
> Of his goosly [*sic*] enmyse may victour be. (3123–30)

Such verses should not be passed off as piety-tinged literary decorum. They can reasonably be viewed as genuine prayer. The power of the saints was a deadly serious business, and their intercession could make the difference between salvation and damnation, life or death, sickness or health, to say nothing of writing well or writing badly. Indeed, as Osbern tells us with his customary autobiographical garrulity, he has had melodramatic personal experience of saintly power, for St Margaret saved him from a nasty demise in a fen near Venice where a 'cruel tyraunth' drove him out of a barge 'wher I supposyd to haue myscheuyd' (163). He was relieved from his plight thanks to a ring with which he had touched the foot of St Margaret back in England. This saint was very popular for being able to save anyone invoking her in distress, but she had a further special grace for those who wrote or read or thought on her life, for in her prayer before being martyred she made this request:

> More-ouyr, lord, lowly I the beseche
> For them specyally that my passyoun
> Othyr rede, or wryte, or other do teche,
>   . . . lord, for thy gret grace,
> Hem repentaunce graunte er they hens pace. (834–40)

These words really do initiate an originary authority. The very textual transmission of her Life forms a key part of the *sentence* of that Life, and in its own right constitutes a means to salvation for those who read, write or think on it. Margaret's (inextricably textual) puissance, and the self-same Life/text Osbern writes and others read is accorded an immanent property to save, a textual power inconceivable to subsequent literary periods. This textual power, spanning heaven and earth, has a long-sanctioned tradition in Middle English hagiography. Take, for example, the words of the saint in the early-thirteenth-century Life of St Margaret in the Katherine Group:

> Ich bidde ant biseche þe, þet art mi weole ant wunne, þet hwa se eauer boc writ of mi liflade, oðer biȝet hit iwriten, oðer halt hit ant haueð oftest on honde, oðer hwa se hit eauer redeð oðer þene redere liðeliche lusteð, wealdent of heouene, wurðe ham alle sone hare sunnen forȝeuene . . . Ant hwa se eauer mi nome munegeð wið muðe, luueliche Lauerd, et te leaste dom ales him from deaðe.[16]

Lydgate, in his *Legend of Seynt Margarete*, was later to versify the same address to the Almighty after his own fashion.[17] In Bokenham's *Legendys*, St Katherine's last prayer is like that of Margaret (7302–10). The request is immediately granted by God (7319–34), with considerable implications for the power and authority of her *vita*. John Capgrave's slightly earlier Life of the same saint, known to Bokenham, contains the same scene.[18] Such a prayer instantly sanctions and sanctifies the commemorative texts in which it appears, whose existence it overtly fosters, and which it empowers. Such a phenomenon might be regarded as a type of *signum efficiens*, a sign that brings into being that which it signifies. It also automatically confers succour on those who read and remember it. So, to translate or compile such hagiography is not only to serve a saint, it is also to enact (not just report) the primary *sentence* of the text/Life itself, to tap celestial power and to occasion the authority of the saint.

2. *(Un)caging Katharine: Arrek, Capgrave and the Reviser of the Life of St Katharine of Alexandria*

So far we have looked at manifestations of the one-to-one relationship between translator and saint as efficent cause. But how should a male writer negotiate *auctricitas* when he has to relate his saint to a complex process of textual transmission involving various antecedent human agencies? In completing and modernizing the earlier version of one Arrek in an attempt to enhance the cult of St Katharine in England, Capgrave asks for the saint's help:

---

[16] See *Seinte Margarete*, in *Medieval English Prose for Women: Selections from the Katherine Group and Ancrene Wisse*, ed. Bella Millett and Jocelyn Wogan-Browne (Oxford: Clarendon, 1992), 44–85, 78.

[17] John Lydgate, *The Minor Poems of John Lydgate: Part I*, ed. Henry Noble MacCracken (London: EETS, ES 107, 1911), 449–62.

[18] John Capgrave, *The Life of St Katharine of Alexandria*, ed. Carl Horstmann (London: EETS, OS 100, 1893), V. 1826–34.

Now wyl I, lady, mor openly mak þi lyffe
Owt of hys werk, if þou wylt help þer-too;
It schall be know of man, mayde & of wyffe
What þou has suffrede & eke qwat þou hast doo.
Pray godd, our lorde, he wyll þe dor on-doo,
Enspire our wyttys wyth hys priuy grace,
To preyse hyme & þe þat we may haue space! (Prol., 64–70)

Not that the old version was unworthy; on the contrary it was inspired by the saint herself, who appeared to its maker at his death and rewarded him richly for 'hys seruyce' (Prol., 221–4). But however meritorious the earlier version may have been, for Capgrave and his contemporaries its 'derk langage' (I. Prol., 209) now needs opening up anew, the later translator being intent on overtaking his meritorious predecessor with the help of the saint:

Neuyrthelasse he dyd mych thyng þer-too,
þis noble preste, þis very good man:
he hath led vs þe wey & þe door on-doo,
þat mech þe bettyr we may & we can
ffolow hys steppes. for thowte he sor rane,
We may hym ouyr-take, wyth help & wyth grace
Qwech þat þis lady schall vs purchasse. (Prol., 211–17)

It is not just a matter of merely displacing the old work, for, inasmuch as hardly anyone was using it, it had no significant cultural site from which to be dislodged. The usability of a text was regarded by medieval translators as a key determinant of further reworking. Tellingly, Capgrave's translation, in at least one important instance, missed out on being used when otherwise it might have been. For though Osbern Bokenham read and liked Capgrave's *Katharine*, he felt impelled to make his own Life of the saint afresh, simply because Capgrave's version was not at all easy to lay hands on (6354–64). This new version does not dislodge another version, even though it is in effect a substitute for it, or, rather, an understudy. Nevertheless, to return to Capgrave, it was his intention to carry on Arrek's good work, outdoing it by fulfilling it and bringing its intention to modern fruition. It is fitting that he should ask that his deceased precursor 'be a mene to kateryne for vs,/ And sche for vs alle on-to our lorde ihesus' (Prol., 230–1), because Arrek's version has been a *mene* already in the production of the new English version. Textual tradition traces the line of transmission of salvific grace and efficient causality.

As Katharine was one of the most academic of saints it is particularly fitting that she should help clerks, especially those compiling her *Vita*:

I dresse me now streyt on-to þis werk.
Thow blyssyd may, comfort þou me in þis!
Be-cause þou wer so lerned & swech a clerk,

Clerkes must loue þe, reson for-sothe it is!
Who wyll oute lerne, trost to me, I-wys,
He dothe mech þe bettyr if he trost in þis may.
Þus I be-leue, & haue do many a day. (III., 36–42)

This same grace will presumably help readers appreciate the *sentence* of
her Life. They are invited merely to 'trost to' Capgrave, but to 'trost in'
Katharine. In telling honestly of Katharine's trustworthiness, Capgrave's
'trost' is testamentary, whereas hers is originary. He sees himself as a mere
mean and an ultimately removable link in the chain of authority running
from saint to vernacular audience. As the post-textual devotional relationship between saint and audience is established, Capgrave is happy to be
effaced as intermediary, having gained through his literary service spiritual benefits.

Capgrave presents a clear conception of the immanent power of her
Life, the ultimate motivity and authority for which remain in heaven with
the saint and, ultimately, with God. The power and sanctity of the *vita* is
proved by the miracle that governs its transmission-history. In a somewhat
grotesque holy vision in which *ruminatio* becomes a sort of surrealistic
force-feeding, Arrek was made to eat a book, boards and all, after which
he found the hidden and buried codex containing her Life. He released it
from the ground, and by translating it, released it into English culture.
However, its circulation remained unsatisfactorily restricted right up until
Capgrave's day, and even when it was available it could only be read with
difficulty because of its 'derk' language:

It cam but seldom on-to any mannes honde;
Eke qwan it cam, it was noght vndyrstonde,
Be-cause, as i seyd, ryght for þe derk langage.
Þus was þi lyffe, lady, kept all in cage. (Prol., 207–10)

So, full textual power was still captive until Capgrave opened the cage and
let it walk wide in vernacular culture. In the prologue to Book III, repeating his cage image, he advertises that, through his Englishing, Katharine's
Life is now freed and at large:

Euene so was þis lyffe, as I seyd in þe prologe be-for,
Kept all in cage, aboute it was not bore.

Now schall it walk wyder þan euyr it dede,
In preysyng & honour of þis martir Katerine. (III., 27–30)

By letting the saint's Life out of the cage, this compiler claims to have
done no more than mechanically and obediently uncover it and unlock its
pre-existing ingenerate power. Thus he speaks of himself in the prologue
to Book I as doing no more than the worthy translator's task of making her
life (like the cage) more 'open' (see above, 192). His cage image evidently

appealed to the fancy of one 'spurious' reviser, for in MS Arundel 20, the last lines of the whole work, 1954–1981, which discuss some of the miracles at Katharine's tomb, are replaced with two stanzas. These lines culminate in a further reworking of the cage metaphor, in which Katharine is behind bars again, albeit in heaven:

> He þat thys lyue wryȝtis, redis or else cvthe here,
> Cryste, kyng off glorye, graunt þem þat grace
> Off alle þeir synnes mercy to purchace. . . .
>
> Now, gloryous Kateryne, be to vs ane eyde
> And specyalle succur yne þis perlous pylgrymmage,
> Þat after þis lyue we mey cum to thy cage.
> Amen.   (450)

This would seem to be a rather bizarre recycling of Capgrave's original image, which was predicated on the notion that a caged *vita* is an uncommunicated *vita*. Perhaps the reviser conceived of the heavenly lady as some kind of celestial anchoress tipping succour down onto earthly souls through her bars, and waiting for the saved to come to her in heaven, just as on earth the local enclosed woman might receive pilgrims at her cell.

3. *The Woman Saint as* Auctrix *of her Earthly Life*

Saintly *auctrices* were more than causes aiding the pen of the vernacular compiler, and more than heavenly dispensers of pardon and intercession for those who write and read their Lives. They authored the temporal events which originally earned them their canonisation. Significantly, they are recognised by their hagiographers as still in possession of their Lives (e.g., *thy legend/thy lyf* in Capgrave, Prol., 210; Bokenham, 336, 8276; Lydgate, *Margarete*, 55). At once actants and *auctrices* of narratable action, they are more than just items of textual signification, more than just prurient examples of lurid formulaic male violence against women, because with Christian free will they make their own 'auto-hagiography' according to the conventions they want to live up to, doing so in despite of the patriarchal order contemporary to them, by rejecting suitors, disobeying fathers, spurning marriage, and exemplifying colossal strength, articulation, endurance and intellectual superiority as they inexorably and knowingly manipulate events towards self-scripted martyrdom and ultimate sanctity. It would have been possible for late-medieval readers to indulge in the narrative as a fantasy of resisting the patriarchy of their own experience. Though it would be tempting (and misleading) to see these women as primarily anti-phallocratic role-models, it is nevertheless worth pointing out that it is possible to see the enclosed/religious life which these women saints represent as a form of evasion of patriarchal norms; for marriage was frequently worth rejecting, along with the ordeals of childbirth, marital rape, domestic violence, commoditisation, and so on. The religious life did offer some escape from these, giving a limited chance for mental and spiritual fulfilment. But such hagiographical texts also give out the opposite message: that Christian women should be obedient to the all-too-patriarchal requirements of the Church. Complex and contradictory response is endemic to such texts, a feature further intensified by the varying predispositions of readers.

Whatever their status as role-models, women saints get their own pious and gloriously 'difficult' way, frustrate all attempts to break them, and even use taunts and humour as they go. Bokenham's Christine reproaches her father, who is treated with consummate disrespect as a deceitful dunce for stupidly expecting her to worship false gods rather than the Trinity (2263–80). She smashes up his idols and hurls the gold and silver fragments out of the window for the poor in the street below (2339–46). She subsequently mocks the Prefect who orders her beating, reckoning little of any suffering he can inflict on her, capping it all, when her tongue is cut out, by spitting it into his eye, blinding the wretch, and uttering suitably contemptuous words from what speech organs remain. Bokenham's Cycyle delivers a learned disquisition on the Trinity. St Katharine, both for Bokenham and Capgrave, is fearsomely intellectual, an insuperable dialectician in command of the Liberal Arts who trounces rhetoricians and philosophers, converting them for martyrdom (Bokenham, 6664–6828; Capgrave, I. 365–434; IV. 799–V.329). Osbern's Mary Magdalen, though of the wrong sex to occupy the office, is a great and eloquent preacher (5780–5800). Lydgate's St Margaret seizes Satan by the head and treads him underfoot, taunting him that he has been overcome 'by powere femynyne' (295–329). These women are not just *materia* or actants; they have to be seen as historical, self-aware and self-fashioning *auctrices* of events and also as celestial *auctrices* helping their hagiographers. They dictate their narratives behaviourally during their lives and then again through textual grace after their deaths, at all times possessing immense individuality as both objects and directors of their own cults. Psychologically two-dimensional rhetorical constructs they may be, but according to late-medieval orthodoxy they had free will and living reality as special, transcendent, fully sentient, active personalities overlooking and intervening in the human domain.

Epilogue: *Inventio *Auctricitatis?*

Auctricitas, according to the *mentalité* of the day, could only be taken so far. It could only ever have been an intermittent gendered performance or translation of *auctoritas,* hardly constituting a challenge, re-inscription or subversion of it, but within its various bounds it had a distinctive puissance, albeit bracketed by the patriarchal order.

The authority involved in the above cases is not exactly the 'normal' authority of masculine textual culture, though it is subject to it. The linguistic putativeness of the term *auctricitas*, indicated by its asterisk, befits the qualified conditionality of female authority. The *auctrix* operated from behind texts, whose authority was already established anyway, as a putatively authentic but supplementary source (Mary), as a visionary (Bridget, Catherine of Siena, Julian or Margery), or in a gracious efficient causality aiding writers like Bokenham and Capgrave (as did many dead women saints). These three types of *auctrix* are disparate and marginal, but their very disparateness and marginality are what they share and what substantially forms them. *Auctricitas* inevitably involves supplementary special cases, marginal characters and, paradoxically, powerful archetypes.

Auctrices did not, as a rule, put pen to paper themselves. It was not easy for women so to do. As Gilbert and Gubar familiarly assert:

> Since both patriarchy and its texts subordinate and imprison women, before women can even attempt that pen which is so rigorously kept from them they must escape just those male texts which, defining them as 'Cyphers', deny them the autonomy to formulate alternatives to the authority that has imprisoned them and kept them from attempting the pen.[19]

Ciphers are supplements which/who adorn and confirm the prevailing order. According to Thomas Usk, 'although a sypher . . . have no might in significacion of it-selve, yet he yeveth power in significacion to other'.[20] Indeed, such women were of great utility in conserving the *status quo*. However, though *auctrices* do supplement the order, they also have a limited autonomy and agency.

This study has inquired into the feasibility of a version of medieval female authority, articulated from *within* general/male culture, an odd sort of authority where pen barely met paper because women were outside the normal agencies of authoritative discourse. Sometimes, as with the revelations of a Catherine of Siena or a St Bridget, the authority of women's works might be given vernacular authentication by being inscribed in prestige literary forms, as in *The Orcherd of Syon* and the *Speculum Devotorum*. Women saints were also excluded from normal discourse (by death) but had the power to speak, to obligate and to aid textual production. *Auctrices*, the female exceptions that prove the masculinist rule, are licensed to speak, generally through male scribes according to male permission. These holy women scarcely resisted male authority: they were no

---

[19] Cited in Toril Moi, *Sexual/Textual Politics: Feminist Literary Theory* (London: Routledge, 1991), 57.

[20] Thomas Usk, *Testament of Love*, in *The Works of Geoffrey Chaucer: Chaucerian and Other Pieces*, ed. W.W. Skeat (Oxford: OUP, 1897), vol. 7, 1–145, 72.

shrews.[21] They and their gender fictions exercised considerable power and even dignity, and imitated, reperformed, supplemented, complied with and believed in general/masculine authority, according to common contemporary understanding. To misquote: *Auctricitas est digna imitatione auctoritatis.*[22]

Acknowledgements

I am grateful to Alastair Minnis, Michael Alexander, Chris Smith and Rosalynn Voaden for helpful comments whilst I was drafting this article. I am also grateful for the comments of colleagues at the Scottish Universities Medieval Group Conference on Gender and Sexuality in the Middle Ages, held at Stirling University, September 26, 1992, where an earlier version of some of this material was presented.

[21] For discussion of female inauthority and rebellious stereotypes in a contemporary text consisting of ciphers, see Ian Johnson, 'Χρμbn: the Gendered Ciphers of the *Book of Brome*' (forthcoming).

[22] This is a reworking of Hugutio of Pisa's definition of an *auctoritas* as *a sententia digna imitatione*, a statement/teaching worthy of imitation. See Minnis, *Medieval Theory*, 10.